Strategic Project Management

Creating Organizational Breakthroughs

£19.99

D0230216

Strategic Project Management

Creating Organizational Breakthroughs

Tony Grundy & Laura Brown

THOMSON
LEARNING™

Australia • Canada • Mexico • Singapore • Spain • United Kingdom • United States

THOMSON

LEARNING

Strategic Management: Project Managing Your Business Strategy

For more information, contact Thomson Learning, Berkshire House, 168–173 High Holborn, London, WC1V 7AA or visit us on the World Wide Web at: http://www.thomsonlearning.co.uk

British Library Cataloguing-in-Publication Data
A catalogue record for this book is available from the British Library

ISBN 1-86152-979-1

First edition published 2002 by Thomson Learning

Typeset by Dexter Haven Associates, London

Printed in the UK by TJ International, Padstow, Cornwall

Contents

List of tables and figures

Preface

Origins of strategic project management

When one of the authors, Tony Grundy, studied for his MBA in the 1980s at City University Business School, he first encountered a subject called project management.

Of all the subjects studied in those murky evenings in the Barbican, somewhere near Moorgate, London, project management stood out perhaps the least. Even now, it conjures up memories of Gantt charts, network analysis and critical path analysis. These techniques seemed at the time to be solutions chasing problems. Unless one was destined to erect a new platform in the depths of the North Sea, what had one really to learn from project management?

But over the 13 years following his MBA, as a management consultant Grundy was destined to be involved in an amazing array of projects, including acquisitions, business process re-engineering (BPR), business development, cost management, culture change, disposals, and IT strategy. This was until the increasing threat of generic drugs and the wave of mergers in the mid-to-late 1990s and early 2000s.

Increases in competitive change led to intensified internal pressure to deliver much faster and to reduce time to market. The pharmaceutical industry increasingly looked to project management to accelerate drug development and clinical testing. Unfortunately, industry tended to see projects as standardized and as relatively uniform, which in reality they were not. As Laura Brown reflects:

> Each clinical trial project is different from the rest. For example, you have a different population to trial the drug out on, a drug with different characteristics of disease, and a different project team. There will also be a different set of regulatory stakeholders to manage. Above all, the organizational

timing and context will be unique. As a result, a project team, relying primarily on activity analysis and computer software, critical path and resource planning, will get bogged down with internal politics, often inadequate resources, inadequate project training and project team development. And this is before having to deal with endemic difficulties of seeing patients on a just-in-time basis – and likewise clearing regulatory hurdles.

This example demonstrates that even with a more *technical* project environment we see projects as beset with environmental uncertainty, interdependencies, struggles to allocate resources strategically, and a complex organizational environment.

What is 'strategic project management'?

Following from the above, traditional project management is not up to this challenge, and needs to be augmented by other perspectives.

By integrating the more strategic perspectives into traditional project management, something more powerful and effective emerges – a new process called strategic project management.

Strategic project management (SPM) can now be defined as:

> The process of managing complex projects by combining business strategy and project management techniques in order to implement the business strategy and to deliver organizational breakthroughs.

These business analysis techniques include strategic, operational, organizational and financial analysis.

To get a clearer understanding of the distinctive contribution of SPM to the management process, let us go back to three key reasons why strategic management itself is frequently disappointing:

- Strategic management appears to be at best only partially successful in helping organizations to think strategically and to implement strategies effectively. Many strategic decisions are made in a highly incremental and fragmented way, rather than according to an overall design or 'deliberate strategy' (Mintzberg, 1994). Because of this, the *business strategy itself* may not in many ways be the most appropriate level at which to conduct detailed strategic thinking. A better approach, frequently, is to conduct much (but not all) of this thinking at the level of the strategic project or a group of those projects, the strategic programme, sometimes known as a strategic breakthrough (Grundy, 1995).

- The implementation of strategy is often much more complex and difficult than its formulation – either at the business or the corporate level. So, instead of spending 80 per cent of the time in strategic planning and 20 per cent in implementation development, arguably this should be 20 per cent in planning and 80 per cent in implementation. Project management must therefore be capable of dealing with more complex, ambiguous and political issues than its traditional focus.
- Besides the above two problems in strategic management there is a further, significant problem in injecting strategic thinking into more micro project management. Business strategy projects themselves are sometimes managed by relatively narrowly based, mechanistic project management techniques. Activity analysis, Gantt charts and critical path analysis are all well and good, but managers frequently end up programming the wrong project, having not thought sufficiently about project options, project strategy, and the link back up to the business strategy.

These three deficiencies in both strategic management and project management gave birth to strategic project management. The SPM process developed over many years as a response to the increasing number and diversity of business projects that managers were facing. Initially the focus was on looking at how managers could link business projects back to the strategic goals of their business. Drawing on the PhD research of one of the authors into strategic and financial project appraisal, it became possible to bring in techniques of assessing how projects add to, dilute or even destroy shareholder value. This helped to integrate project management with both strategic and financial analysis.

Next, were added approaches to assessing implementation difficulty drawn originally from organizational theory – particularly in applying force-field analysis. Around ten years ago, the project management literature was almost totally devoid of any mention of force-field analysis. This approach was then further enriched by bringing in stakeholder analysis techniques found in the strategy literature and now developed further in this book.

Operational analysis was also helpful in extending and enriching traditional project management. For instance, as managers appeared to lack adequate problem-solving methods in the definition of many projects, the authors were drawn to the diagnosis technique of fishbone analysis normally associated with total quality management (TQM). Moving on to the imperative to prioritize projects more effectively, they brought in attractiveness implementation difficulty (AID) analysis, which had been discovered through managing cost breakthroughs when working with Amersham-Nycomed some years ago.

Project uncertainty was clearly one of the main reasons why traditional project management techniques ended up by producing spuriously accurate but unrealistic project plans. This led back to strategic management once again, and to scenario analysis in particular. The uncertainty grid was incorporated, to help bring to the surface and evaluate key project assumptions. Later this was expanded to incorporate scenario-generating and story-telling techniques to help flesh out and explore the possible trajectories that each project might take.

Finally, in the late 1990s, Grundy undertook some fascinating research into senior managers' behaviour when engaged in managing strategic projects (Grundy, 1998). This study focused on a small but influential team at BT engaged in project managing the analysis of BT's global technical strategy. Besides discovering much about how and why teams tend to get so bogged down in seeking to manage complex projects, some very practical techniques for monitoring and managing both the dynamics of projects – and of the somewhat turbulent behaviours associated with them – were drawn out.

So, SPM is very much an eclectic approach to managing projects as part of overall programmes in order to implement the business strategy and organizational breakthroughs.

Many companies have now benefited from some or all of the techniques contained in this book. These include BT, Hewlett Packard, Nokia, Prudential, Tesco and Yorkshire Electricity. Hopefully, over time, these techniques will be taken up by your own company.

This book will help a number of groups, particularly:

- senior managers engaged in turning business strategies into implementations through project management;
- practising middle and senior managers working on internal, cross-functional or within-functional projects at a strategic level;
- MBA students studying project management (essential reading) or as ancillary reading for strategic management courses;
- students studying for the increasing number of MSc courses in project management;
- other students engaged in management studies entailing a knowledge of project management, including accountancy and marketing courses, diplomas in management and undergraduate management degrees.

The structure and content of this book

Chapter 1 looks at how projects need to be managed strategically. Chapter 2 turns to the key links of projects with business strategy. Chapter 3 discusses the SPM project itself, and considers the first two phases of strategic project definition (and diagnosis), Chapter 4 phases two and three of SPM, by considering project strategy and plans together. Chapter 5 explores the intricacies of strategic project evaluation, and in particular grapples with the difficulties of putting a realistic financial value on a project. Many project management books either refer to texts on financial project appraisal or tend to regard this area as a question purely of discounted cash flow (DCF). We take the view that prior to the deployment of DCF techniques an analysis of key value and cost drivers is needed, and (potentially) a description of some key project scenarios.

Chapter 6 focuses on the practicalities of making projects happen, including project mobilization, control and learning, drawing from techniques of organizational analysis, including force-field analysis and stakeholder analysis. Chapter 7 examines the more purely behavioural dimension of SPM, Chapter 8 a number of generic types of strategic projects, explaining tailored checklists for applying SPM to them. This includes (organic) business development projects, acquisition projects, alliance and joint venture projects, operational improvement projects, and organizational change projects. Chapter 9 shows how these techniques can be deployed both to micro-issues within your role and also outside the sphere of business altogether – to everyday, personal life. It also finally draws together the key lessons on SPM, focusing especially on how to implement the techniques.

In conclusion, SPM has developed from many sources, all of which are essential in order to turn business strategy and organizational change into reality – and ultimately into shareholder value too. Now that SPM exists, people will no doubt wonder how we managed before it. Key to this is to read, digest and apply this book.

References

Grundy, A.N. (1995) *Breakthrough Strategies for Growth*, FT Pitman Publishing
Grundy. A.N. (1998) *Strategic Behaviour*, FT Pitman Publishing
Mintzberg, H. (1994) *The Rise and Fall of Strategic Planning*, Prentice Hall

CHAPTER ONE

Managing projects strategically

Introduction

In this chapter we first take a further look at the deficiencies of conventional project management. Then we explore the need for strategic thinking in managing projects. We then illustrate this with a case study drawn from one of the author's experiences of project managing strategic projects at ICI. Finally, we introduce the five key steps of SPM: defining the project, creating the project strategy, detailed project planning, implementation and control, review and learning.

Throughout the book you will be invited to invest some time in working through exercises on your own projects so that you can extract maximum learning. Whilst some readers may be tempted to skim these, they really will enhance your retention and incorporation of the tools and techniques by the order of at least 100 per cent. Please do not be tempted just to browse the book.

Deficiencies in conventional project management

Conventional project management is very much the offspring of Taylorian Scientific Management. Although the idea that management is a science, and should be managed as such, is no longer much in vogue – the rationalist assumptions embedded in project management carry on.

Not that there is anything wrong with the idea that business projects can and should be managed on a rational basis in principle. Indeed, this book very much springs from that premise, however much modified its approach is, to deal with the messier aspects of projects. Nevertheless, we believe it is important to avoid the naivety of assuming that rational analysis is the prime mover in project management. Chapter 7 in particular highlights the role of people and behaviour in the project management process. Rather than being a little extra, a tack-on to the more rational techniques of project management, the softer, behaviour-related aspects are fundamental.

Whilst all books on project management contain something on the behavioural side, one's impression is very much that this is about 'by the way, whilst you are at it, remember that people need to be managed alongside the projects'. The very heart of conventional project management texts is centred invariably on activity management – the targeting, scheduling, measuring and controlling of tangible activities through time.

Outside the land of major construction projects the real issue is far less the management of interlocking detail. Instead, it is about making sure that managers do not lose sight of the really big picture. 'Why are managers even doing this project and not another one?' is a very real question to ask often. Where projects are riddled with uncertainty the relatively precise definition of activity durations becomes first an academic irrelevancy. Worse, as business projects are particularly vulnerable to knock-on effects, the most important critical success factor seems to be to identify how projects can be made more resilient generally rather than worrying about whether a particular activity might overrun by 10 per cent or so.

EXERCISE: REVIEWING PROJECT OBJECTIVES

Choose one project which you have undertaken in the past, for example a job move, a house move, getting married, a holiday.

1   Why did you embark on this project?
2   If you cannot easily say why, looking back, what should have been your objectives?
3   Where the project ran into difficulties, to what extent were these due to: traditional deficiencies in project management (e.g., estimating the time, resource management and monitoring)? Less tangible deficiencies (e.g., politics, stakeholder agendas, ownership of goals, interdependencies, uncertainties, etc)?

In today's organizational climate it becomes the kiss of death to organizational speed to place burdensome demands of form-filling for projects. The advent of personal computers has not necessarily helped either. Whilst fulfilling a useful role in helping project managers capture key data for projects, there can be a tendency to collect information so that it can just go on the computer. In fact we have heard it said by a number of project management practitioners that the last thing one should do is to put project details onto project management software. In their view it is essential to make sure that a company has become familiar with project management routines first. Looking back to your exercise (above), were not the most difficult issues of your project of a less tangible nature?

We are not, of course, suggesting for a moment that one should not perform activity analyses, and sometimes in considerable detail. We are merely highlighting that one must keep a very strong sense of proportion when doing so, especially to avoid making it look like rocket science. If one does, then one will surely miss the other and frequently more crucial issues which surround why we are doing the project, what value do we hope to get out of it, and how can we avoid the greatest sources of difficulty.

Table 1.1 demonstrates the contrast between conventional and strategic project management.

EXERCISE: REFLECTING ON A PAST STRATEGIC PROJECT

Thinking back to a strategic business project which you have been involved in, to what extent should its critical success factors be addressed by conventional project management approaches or by strategic project management approaches? To what extent were these addressed?

TABLE 1.1: Conventional project management vs SPM

	Conventional project management	Strategic project management
Link with business strategy Project Definition	direct and explicit usually portrayed as a 'given'	vague and distant highly flexible, creative, depending on options
Project planning	follows on directly from project definition	only done once a project strategy is set
Attitude to detail	absolutely central – it is all about control	important but only in context – tries always to see the big ('helicopter') picture
Importance of stakeholders	emphasis on formal structures: project manager, team sponsor	Far-reaching stakeholder analysis – requires continual scanning
The importance of uncertainty	coped with through critical path analysis (after activity planning)	uncertainty analysis done first, then activities planned

The relevance of strategic thinking to project management

Strategic thinking is relevant to project management at a number of levels. First of all, business projects often materialize as a result of formal or informal strategy development. For instance, in the ICI Bioventure case study (coming later in this chapter), the ambitious growth plans ICI had for its Bioventure Division spawned a number of acquisitions which were not only projects in their own right but also subsequent integration and business performance issues.

Besides projects which are thus of a corporate development and external nature, there are frequently internal projects which are aimed at reaping major organizational change, for example BP's Culture Change project or SmithKline Beecham's 'Simply-Better-Way' project.

A second level where strategy comes in is the individual business project which has materialized on a 'bottom-up' basis. Each project of that kind then needs to be linked back up to the business strategy. This should be accomplished by teasing out the strategic objectives of each and every major project.

The third level for strategy input is within the project itself. Each and every project has both an internal environment and, hopefully, also some strategy for achieving its own, inherent advantage.

It is only over a very small number of years that the imperative of generating a strategy for the project itself (over and above the corporate or business strategy) has been really appreciated. One of the main reasons why this has not been the case is that strategic thinking is typically associated with 'very big picture' thinking. But in reality there is just the same need for more localized strategic thinking for specific projects as there is at that much higher level. Also, as we have already mentioned, the more narrow, operational focus of projects does tend to lead people to ask the question, 'Why do I need a strategy for that project?'

So what does strategic thinking mean more generally? 'Strategic thinking' can be defined as the creative and relentless process of teasing out options for action which offer maximum advantage to arrive at an implementable, cunning plan.

Strategic thinking thus contains a number of key elements:

- creative: strategic thinking requires thinking outside the box;
- relentless: it is not something just purely intuitive, but typically requires analysis techniques;
- options: invariably there are many options, not merely for what you could do, but also for how you might do it;

- action: strategic thinking does mean thinking in concrete terms of the actions that will be needed by whom and by when;
- advantage: it also is continually focused on getting a lot out of the minimum;
- implementable: it must help turn the very difficult into the easier and into the feasible;
- cunning plan: the hallmark that strategic thinking has happened is that it is manifest in the tangible 'cunning plan' (taken from the TV series *Blackadder*).

Strategic thinking is often depicted as helicopter thinking. This is now immortalized in the strategic thinking guides of diverse companies including Domino Printing Sciences, Lex, Nokia, Storehouse, Tesco and Yorkshire Electricity – as wide a range of companies as one could possibly hope for.

Figure 1.1 depicts a helicopter flying over rough, hostile terrain. Walking, the alternative to the helicopter, only obscures vision – notice how the competitor's gun is concealed from vision – and the customer. Also, if walking on foot, there is every tendency to go down the rabbit holes, which are inordinately interesting.

Having made extensive use of this picture over the past five years, we have coined the phrase 'rabbit-hole management' to capture the fact that going down the rabbit hole can become too much of a habit. Figure 1.1 should be used during every project management meeting in order to

FIGURE 1.1: Strategic thinking – as helicopter thinking

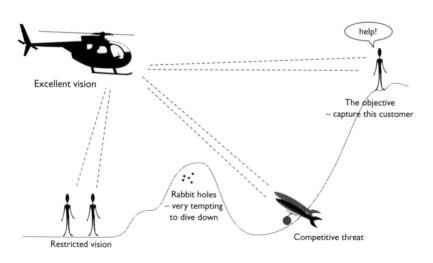

avoid too much preoccupation with the wrong level of detail. It is particularly useful for helping managers to avoid getting bogged down in petty or narrow, personal agendas.

In summary, strategic (or helicopter) thinking is useful for:

- checking whether a particular project is the appropriate vehicle for the strategy in any event;
- generating other options for implementing the project;
- understanding key opportunities and threats that the project faces in its environment and its internal strengths and weaknesses;
- interrelating the project with others in order to understand its total rationale and value.

CASE STUDY: ICI BIOVENTURE

Although the events of this story occurred some years ago, the experiences are as vivid as if they had happened yesterday, and the learnings are equally valid. In the late 1980s, author Tony Grundy was seconded from a large consulting group to become head of Finance, Planning and Acquisitions, a division of ICI. This business no longer operates in the same or even similar form to how it did then. We will call the division ICI Bioventure.

ICI Bioventure was then a £100-million turnover mini-group of companies with operations in three global regions:

- UK: a research centre and some minor product processing activities;
- US: a significant bioventure business with both seed development activities and seed processing which had been acquired in the last two years;
- Europe: a very recently acquired business in continental Europe which was a major and successful product processing operation. By recently, I mean one week before I arrived on the scene.

ICI Bioventure's headquarters was located in a beautiful, woodland, rural setting. It shared a common site with a large part of ICI, which we will call ICI Global Technology. I was to have a joint reporting relationship to the European general manager (who in turn reported to the managing director of the International Bioventure Division) and also to the divisional financial controller of ICI Global Technology.

Following ICI's recent acquisition of its European seeds operation and the appointment of the former head of Finance, Planning and Acquisitions as its finance director, I was identified by my consulting company as being the 'ideal candidate' to be seconded for 'between three to six months' to fill this role.

Meanwhile, I had made the mistake of taking two weeks' holiday in North Yorkshire. While I was combating the coastal sea mist, my superiors were busy plotting my next six months' work.

I returned to my desk on Monday morning expecting to have a relaxed week. Instead, I found at note which read:

> Dear Tony,
>
> I expect you have had a most restful two weeks. I know how pleased you will be that we have found you another project to keep out of the office. From 9 am tomorrow you will be (until further notice) the head of Finance, Planning and Acquisitions for the fast-growing, £100m turnover of ICI Bioventure.
>
> We know a bit about the assignment which I can share with you. However, their finance people have offered to tell you more about it, so I guess a quick session with myself and the client partner will help you gain a good overview.
>
> Oh, you may need to pack, as it is over 100 miles from Cambridge. I am sure you will be able to negotiate adequate living costs from your new client.
>
> Best of luck, your consulting partner

This perhaps highlights our No 1 learning lesson in SPM: unless you attempt to get the ownership of someone to the project that they are being asked to manage, it might just undermine their commitment!

Thinking back, it looks less than an accident that I was given so little thinking time to assimilate my latest mission. Senior people, I suspect, often relish the task of choosing someone for a project – without any prior consent on their part. It is part of the inevitable power-play of organizations, but it can be highly undermining to eventual delivery. Managing difficult business projects successfully requires a tremendous tenacity and single-mindedness that does not mix well with any sense of being made a victim.

The major acquisition in Europe obviously raised integration issues which need to be project-managed. Worse, the US sub-sidiary had posted some disappointing – to put it kindly – results. It was a very urgent and important diagnosis project to ascertain why this had happened, what measures could be taken to ameliorate this situation, and to find out what lessons could be learned generally.

Another (certain-to-become) project was the need to deliver a three-year divisional plan over the following three and a half months. This project would naturally be influenced by the out-come of integration work on both the US and the more recent European acquisition.

The division was also contemplating another major acquisition in the UK. Fortunately, ICI's bid was unsuccessful, which meant that I was not engulfed in post-integration work from that parti-cular direction (the good news). The bad news was that no soon had we dried the tears from our eyes, when immediately one manager spotted a smaller UK acquisition and another manager identified an additional acquisition target in Scandinavia.

With new projects coming thick and fast I was beginning to wonder whether I would ever escape even when my successor, a senior finance manager from elsewhere in the group, was due to arrive in four to six months' time.

My own team of three qualified accountants were also in some-thing of a state on my arrival. Two of them been working around the clock on the abortive UK acquisition immediately before my arrival, and their morale seemed at an all-time low. This acqui-sition had generated some interesting differences of opinion which had left them feeling somewhat bruised. And now they had some smart management consultant telling them what to do.

So, by this stage, not only was there a potentially much greater project workload than could possibly be handled with the existing resource, but it threatened to get even worse. What other emergent projects could come out of the woodwork?

Now it is apparent from this situation that a) I faced a large number of projects; b) that most of these were ill-defined in terms of timescales, outputs, inputs, value and difficulty; c) there were significant interdependencies between these projects; d) the existing workload could be magnified by additional, emergent projects including further acquisitions, post-acquisition work, other business development projects, and also in setting up the necessary infra-structure to cope more effectively with high growth.

On top of these projects I had three additional projects to manage:

- I had been thinking about moving consulting firms for some time, and the letter on my desk on my return from Yorkshire was the final straw. I needed, in the same period of time, to find a job in another consulting firm and to achieve this without detriment to the ICI secondment – that might otherwise have tarnished my reputation, which I sought to retain intact.
- As the secondment ran through the summer months, I wanted to move my family down to ICI from 120 miles away so that

they were not bored silly over the summer months, and I would also be able to see them.

- I had also planned to have a minor but important operation during that period.

So, remembering what I had learnt about project management, I sought to apply it to the situation with gusto.

First, I identified the overall goals of the total project. These were:
- to deal with all the management issues thrown at me by the ICI situation without letting any balls drop;
- to achieve the handover smoothly and, if possible, to move on in four to five months rather than in six. And especially, to avoid the project lasting longer than six months;
- to learn a lot in the process, and to add to my CV that I had been a senior line manager at ICI;
- to find a job in a different consulting firm in the process;
- to avoid undue disruption to my family;
- to avoid disrupting my final MBA exams, which I took five weeks into the secondment.

I had taken the important project management principle on board: manage backwards from the project objectives.

My second step was to do a thorough diagnosis of the current situation. This in itself was reasonably complex and required a mini-project in its own right. This was completed by the end of the first week. An associated, soft mini-project was to establish credibility with my own team – who admitted some weeks later in the pub that they had been waiting for me to fall over.

At this juncture I reasoned that besides establishing a project plan overall for the next four to five months, the main priority was to improve the morale of my team. I felt that unless I did this then I would not have sufficient resources to be able to address the mountain of work associated with both acquisitions and with the ICI three-year plan.

Intuitively, I had therefore identified the soft critical path of activities which I would need to manage for a good chance of success.

Although my team did not feel concerned about the three-year plan at that point, I decided we needed to create a project plan for that process in detail, with key activities, outputs and milestones. My staff were a little surprised at my insistence on this point at first, until they reflected that the previous year the planning inputs had been late and needed rework, causing a last-minute panic of considerable magnitude.

I needed that like a hole in the head – just at the time when the acquisitions-hungry management team went in search of prey in September, following the summer holidays.

I was also wary of the near-certainty of making another acquisition during the summer months, as I knew this would generate significant integration work into early autumn. And, in addition to this, I had a slightly uncomfortable feeling about some transfer pricing issues which were beginning to bubble up in the UK. I had had some (limited) experience of transfer pricing disputes from the past when I worked in a French company. I felt that the people at ICI were likely to be much nicer about sorting this (a key project assumption) but human beings are fickle, and I was liable to be disappointed.

After the first four weeks, we had successfully put in train:

- a project plan to cover the next four months of activity;
- a detailed plan for the three-year plan, which was now being implemented;
- the morale of my team was very good and there was a definite sense of purpose and confidence;
- the UK acquisition had fallen by the board but was now replaced by the smaller acquisition target. This had begun my new project No 1;
- the first quarter's management reporting (a mini-project) had highlighted that US operations had major performance problems. New project No 2 was to investigate this situation;
- I had visited the new acquisition in Europe and highlighted the action areas in management reporting and planning;
- a possible new project for the Scandinavian acquisition target had appeared. I talked our top management out of proceeding with this on the grounds that a) was it really attractive/did it fit our strategy? b) would we be able to do it and integrate it effectively? c) would it be credible to put a business case for this acquisition to group head office at a time when our credibility had taken something of a hammering? This new project was put on ice;
- new project No 3 was to sort out the transfer pricing problem;
- new project No 4 was to deal with integration issues around the now-consummated, small UK acquisition.

In addition to these projects, I did move my family down to the ICI locality at least over the summer holidays, and I had the planned operation. Interestingly, I had not been informed by my doctor that it would take me a week to recover fully from the operation. During meetings to discuss the potential Scandinavian acquisition, I felt myself slumping under the table with pain. It is just possible that this helped me be even more challenging than normal in questioning that project, helping me to avoid a weekend in Denmark which I fancied a lot less than other members of the management team.

But as we shall see later on, personal agendas can and do play an enormous, if unspoken, role in dictating the direction and outcome of business projects.

I also had to plan for acts of God. I left a week's float time to accommodate unseen eventualities during the three-year plan process. By coincidence, just before the time we submitted our plan, we experienced a hurricane. I awoke one morning to find trees blown over everywhere. Power was down for ten days. Pubs ran out of food, computers did not work, spreadsheets did not happen. Nevertheless, we made the deadline whilst ICI Global Technology did not (I confess that we had a back-up power supply, whilst they did not).

Despite the flurry of work through which project management became a steadier and well directed process, I was also able to find another job as a consultant. ICI immediately offered me my next project there as a take-away. I declined.

Besides the foreseeable and the emergent projects I also undertook a final one – new project No 5 became one to set up acquisition process (pre-, mid- and post-deal).

I now look back on that six-month period not only with fondness but also with much gratitude for the learning which I took away from it. More specifically, we can distil ten key learning lessons for SPM from it:

- Diagnose the project sufficiently, especially the reasons why there are problems. What are you looking to get out of it, what are the overall deliverables?
- What options are available to create these deliverables?
- What further projects (or mini-projects) will also be required to reach these deliverables?
- What key, taken-for-granted assumptions have you made, and what could go wrong, when and how, if these are not fulfilled?
- Be prepared to say no to projects or subprojects which are either not fundamentally attractive or are too difficult – given your resources or other reasons, or both.
- Do not skimp on mini-projects (such as improving team morale) that are on the 'soft' critical path.
- Recognize new projects for what they are, for example, transfer pricing was sufficiently complex enough to be called a project.

- For each and every project, anticipate ahead of the activity the likely value that it will create.
- Position each part of the project effectively within the organization so that it gets the attention it deserves.
- Recognize that the personal agendas of both yourself and of others have to be identified and managed too.

My experience at ICI highlights the fluidity, open-endedness and apparent unpredictability of business projects. Not only do they expand or contract in scope, but they also can appear to veer off in new directions or at tangents.

Their critical paths are also not at all obvious as there are many choices in the order in which one conducts activities. This order is not merely determined by what has to be done purely in operational sequence, but there are also political priorities to be sorted. Observing and working with practising managers might suggest that political sequencing is the most important way of organizing project activities.

This experience at ICI therefore demonstrates the utility of a number of project management techniques. These include:

- defining the project(s),
- defining project scope and interdependencies,
- targeting the deliverables or, in more traditional language, the results,
- identifying the key activities or subprojects,
- planning and managing timescales,
- mobilizing resources.

But in addition to these more traditional aspects of project management, we also see:

- problem diagnosis,
- looking at options – not only for which projects to do but how to do them, especially acquisitions,
- managing stakeholders – those individuals with an interest in the project,
- dealing with uncertainty,
- trading-off not merely tangible but also less tangible value,
- creating a strategic vision for the project (i.e., to complete the ICI project without annoying my family and whilst still finding a job elsewhere),
- identifying key implementation difficulties.

The above areas reach beyond the domain of traditional project management, carrying us explicitly into the land of strategy, finance and organizational analysis, and into what was to become SPM.

EXERCISE: MANAGING A MISSION IMPOSSIBLE PROJECT IN THE PAST

Choose one project which you were involved with in the past, which appeared (with perhaps the benefit of hindsight) to be a Mission Impossible project.
1   Was this imposed upon you, or did you actively allow yourself to get involved in it?
2   Did you sense this as a Mission Impossible project at an early stage? What signals gave you the clue?
3   Did you actively consider radical options for the project's strategy before the difficulties began to become insuperable (e.g., to do it very differently, or even to not do it at all)?
4   Did you call for help, or did you try to brave it on your own?
5   Overall, what were the key learnings from this project? Consider things which you would do differently, again, or not do at all.

Strategic project management process

The SPM process contains five key stages (see Figure 1.2):

- defining the project,
- creating the project strategy,
- detailed project planning,
- implementation and control,
- review and learning.

Figure 1.2 emphasizes that project management may require the project to be redefined or the project strategy to be revisited. It also highlights the

FIGURE 1.2: SPM: The process

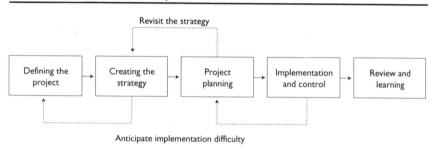

Revisit the strategy

Defining the project → Creating the strategy → Project planning → Implementation and control → Review and learning

Anticipate implementation difficulty

need to anticipate the project's implementation difficulty – at the planning stage and even earlier.

Defining the project involves:

- diagnosing any key problems which gave rise to the project in the first place,
- defining the project's scope and main focus,
- clarifying any key interdependencies,
- creating an overall vision for the project at a very high level, and its key objectives,
- thinking through, at least initially, who the stakeholders might be.

The above reveals that defining the project is not something which is done in five minutes, nor is it self-evident. Project definition involves a good deal of reflection about the purpose and context of the projects.

Creating the project strategy entails:

- exploring the external and internal environment for the project at greater length;
- defining more specifically the key strategic goals of the project;
- examining strategic options for what to do and how to do it, including push vs pull strategies – a push strategy is one where little discretion is allowed to those stakeholders impacted on by the project, while a pull strategy is one where the degree of discretion is higher, either over the project's goals or the project's process, or both;
- a preliminary appraisal of the project's overall attractiveness and implementation difficulty;
- further thinking about the positioning of key stakeholders, and how these might be influenced.

Project strategy demands even more thought than project definition, as there may be many ways of implementing the project.

Detailed project planning requires:

- a detailed analysis of the key activities and/or subprojects which the overall project strategy requires
- an analysis of how these activities are networked in a sequence, given their interdependencies and also an analysis of their critical paths (see our subsequent chapter on project planning);
- an appraisal of key uncertainties along with contingency plans and impact analysis;
- a financial appraisal of the project's value and cost drivers, along with an overview of the financials.

Whilst this is the core of traditional project management, project plans will only ever be as good as the project strategies they are based upon.

Implementation and control necessitates:

- definition of project milestones and responsibilities,
- key implementation difficulties highlighted and countermeasures built-in to resource, action plans,
- some preview of likely project dynamics.

Implementation and control requires continual checking back to the project's strategy and vision to ensure that apparent delivery of milestones is actually fulfilling the original purpose of the project.

Review and learning involves:

- revisiting the project to assess whether the targeted deliverables were achieved, whether the implementation process went smoothly or not, how effectively was the project positioned politically, and other behavioural lessons;
- asking how the strategic project management process could itself be improved.

Review and learning is thus not merely a peripheral part of the process but the driver of continuous improvement in the project process. Generally speaking, review and learning is frequently the weakest link in the strategic project management chain. For example, in the pharmaceutical industry relatively few clinical research projects are subjected to a formal learning review. This is even though they are frequently not completed on time, and this may result in delays costing millions of dollars of revenue.

EXERCISE: DIAGNOSING STRENGTHS AND WEAKNESSES OF YOUR PAST PROJECT PROCESS

Choose one project which you have been involved in, in the past.

1   How well were the following aspects of the process managed? Rate the following categories where 1 = Very Weak, 2 = Weak, 3 = Satisfactorily, 4 = Very Well, 5 = Very Well Indeed:

- Defining the project
- Creating the project strategy
- Detailed project planning
- Implementation and control
- Review and learning

2   What was your overall score for the project?
3   How well did you judge that it went overall?
4   To what extent did earlier stage deficiencies (e.g., defining the project or creating the project strategy) detract from later stages such as implementation and control?

Conclusion

Managing strategic projects demands far more than merely traditional project management techniques. In addition, such complex projects demand a considerable skill in strategic thinking. This strategic thinking is required at all stages of the project but particularly in the first two stages of strategic project management:

- defining the project,
- creating the project strategy,
- review and learning.

In the next chapter we will take this theme further by investigating the key links between projects and business strategy.

But, before we move on, check that you have actually devoted sufficient time to doing the exercises in this first chapter. This will help you to get full value from the book as it proceeds and will also establish a good learning process for the rest of your reading. If you did not work on the exercises as you were reading, then just spend 20–25 minutes doing this now.

CHAPTER TWO

Linking projects with business strategy

Introduction

In many organizations business projects are only loosely connected to the bigger picture of the business strategy. This may be due to a variety of reasons. First, those at the project level may not be fully aware of the business strategy itself except in the most general way. Top management might be reluctant to share this picture out of concern for commercial sensitivity, especially in terms of future direction. Or, they may wish to reserve power centrally or for political reasons. Finally, the project managers themselves may not see it as so important that they are aware of the detailed and specific content of the business strategy.

Second, the strategy itself may not be clear and worked out in detail. Whilst it may contain some strategic thinking, these ideas may not be fully integrated, mutually consistent or worked through. Sadly, it is rather hard to link one thing (a project) to another thing (a business strategy) if the second thing only half exists.

Not only might the content of the strategy be unclear but the very meaning of 'strategy' may itself be ambiguous. 'Business strategy' is a much-used but also much-abused term. For instance, in one major multinational telecommunications company, literally hundreds of managers had the word 'strategy' in their job titles. But no-one had actually even defined what the word meant.

A conventional definition (definition A) of the word 'strategy' is the means of getting from where you are now to where you want to be – and with competitive advantage.

This definition is useful in that it emphasizes the need to know who you are – and to know this intimately first – before deciding both where you want to be and how to get there with competitive advantage.

This definition is very much one of a 'deliberate strategy', that is, one based on a well-articulated design to match the organization and its aspirations with its present and future environment (Mintzberg 1994).

A more stretching, and in some ways superior, definition (definition B) of strategy is the intuitive sense, not of where the business actually is but where it ought to be, and of what needs to happen to bring about this ideal state.

Increasingly, we prefer definition B to definition A as it justly emphasizes the more creative and imaginative role of strategy. In Mintzberg's terms it is more of a 'visionary strategy'. For example, when James Dyson in the UK invented the vacuum cleaner without a bag back in the 1990s, he worked backwards from what he wanted to achieve to create his business strategy, otherwise he might simply have replicated a slightly modified Hoover or Electrolux strategy.

One way of remembering that strategy is about the 'ought' rather than merely about the 'is', is to think of it in a way reminiscent of the worldwide successful Spice Girls pop group who coined the slogan 'what do I really, really, really want'.

So, according to the Spice Girl approach, we arrive at definition C: strategy is what we really, really, really want.

EXERCISE: THE VISIONARY STRATEGIC PROJECT

Think of a present project in which you are involved, either in business or in your personal life.

1   As currently formulated, does the project give you an average result, aimed at merely removing some worst aspects of a problem?
2   Does it receive its inspiration from what you really, really want?
3   If the latter, how does this inspiration drive all of your thinking about the project strategy and its resource plans?

Our final definition of strategy is again a humorous one. Definition D is quite simple: strategy is the cunning plan.

The idea of the cunning plan comes from the television comedy series *Blackadder*. The character Baldrick always reminds us of the need to think up the cunning plan when the characters get themselves into situations of insuperable difficulty.

In many respects, the second and third definitions of strategy are the most helpful ones to managers. Whilst not claiming to be a high concept, the Spice Girl and the cunning plan approaches to strategy are ones that can be remembered more easily and also applied on an everyday basis.

The variety of strategies exist for two main reasons. First, this high-lights the diverse nature of business strategy, for if projects are to be linked successfully to business strategies then this must surely make ample recognition of the very nature of those business strategies first. This happens by examining the strategy mix and its impact on the strategy, on its implementation and at the project level.

Next, the impact of incrementalism on projects, how this can create a less favourable environment for the project, and how this can be diagnosed is examined.

Then, the role that SPM can play in supporting breakthrough thinking and advantage is discussed.

Finally, business strategy will be looked at more dynamically as a stream of projects. Whilst strategy is, in practice, often made incrementally, rather than seeing this a threat to strategic planning as Mintzberg does (1994), we can now see the project as being an important unit of strategic analysis. SPM thus becomes a way of emergent strategy becoming deliberate.

The strategy mix

To fully explore the literature on different forms of strategy and the role of incrementalism in strategy could easily take a thousand pages. But perhaps most readers would like to be spared this academic ordeal, so the substance of such a treatise is achieved in a few pages in order to concentrate on the key insights for both strategic project management and strategic management generally.

Earlier literature on corporate planning, particularly in the 1960s and 1970s, was often intoxicated with the notion that a number of guiding principles could be laid down in order to steer corporations, their divisions and ultimately their strategic business units (SBU's) to success (Ansoff 1965). Apart from increasing uncertainty in the external environment, the main factor impeding these impulses was the day-to-day behaviour of managers, which did not seem up to this rationalist challenge.

Rationalist strategic thinkers became more advanced in pre-scribing conceptual frameworks – culminating in Michael Porter's two seminal works in the 1980s while at Harvard, *Competitive Strategy* (1980) and *Competitive Advantage* (1985) – managers themselves seemed to be stuck in a kind of a strategic Stone Age. Dubbed the Design School by Henry Mintzberg (a term propagated in his aptly-titled book *The Rise and Fall of Strategic Planning*), by the mid-1990s rationalist thinking seemed to have reached the summit of its development with nowhere else to go.

Mintzberg's critique of the Design School rested upon his characterization of how strategy actually appears to happen. Mintzberg suggested that most of the manifestations of strategy are very much implicit, fragmented and fluid. Whilst formal strategic plans sometimes exist, they were infrequently acted upon and most strategic action manifested itself in a more haphazard behaviour. Usually the only real way of defining a strategy for Mintzberg was to look at strategic actions after the event, and then to try to discern if there was any pattern. Mintzberg's definition of strategy was one of a pattern in a stream of decisions or actions.

Let us now therefore go one stage further, paraphrasing Mintzberg as: strategy is a pattern in a stream of explicit and implicit strategic projects designed to create a specific competitive positioning.

Whilst many decisions or actions may not be identified as projects, certainly if they are truly strategic then they ought to be projects, whether this is made explicit or implicit. For if we go back to the classic definition of a project – a complex set of activities with a predefined result which is targeted over a particular time and to a specific cost – then strategic decisions or actions are necessarily projects.

This point that business strategy is effectively a collection of mutually aligned projects designed to create a specific competitive positioning is a most important and helpful one. It is important because it shifts much of our frame of reference in strategic management from the very big picture, indeed, to the more tangible and management level. In effect, this recognizes that most strategic thinking should be done at a smaller scale level than is typically appreciated. We call this level that of the mini-strategy. This approach is helpful because it enables management (at all levels) to get a better grip on business strategy, especially so that they actually get on and implement it.

Mintzberg cleverly called strategies which are not obvious until they have actually happened emergent strategies. Behaviourally, this proved to be an attractive notion to many managers as it helped to excuse strategies for being partial and complete, and managers themselves from having to take onerous responsibility for their deliberate strategies. It is not being suggested that this was what Mintzberg intended, but this is what actually emerged in organizational reality.

Stepping back from Mintzberg's debate (which, as it turns out, was mainly aimed at Igor Ansoff's very rational and logical Design School of strategy), let us briefly review the relative advantages and disadvantages claimed by the school of design, or deliberate, strategies and the emergent strategy school. We will soon then see how important and relevant the mix of deliberate, emergent and other strategies is for SPM.

Whilst Mintzberg's extension of the types of strategy from one to two (deliberate and now emergent) is laudable, these two forms simply do not go far enough. We have therefore added three additional forms: the submergent, the emergency and the detergent, giving:

- deliberate,
- emergent,
- submergent,
- emergency,
- detergent.

These forms of strategy are depicted in Figure 2.1 which shows a deliberate strategy at the start, often moving into an emergent phase. Unless its duration and implementation is steered, it may drift into submergent or emergency phases, or even detergent (where it is tidied up).

A submergent strategy is a deliberate or an emergent strategy which has ceased to work. In this phase managers often redouble their efforts, putting in more time and resource without questioning the original scope of the project, and the basis of the project strategy. Examples of submergent strategies in military history are the Cuban Missile Crisis in the 1960s, the Vietnam War and, more recently, the war in Kosovo.

An emergency strategy is one where there is so little coherence to action that there is no real sense of direction at all.

Finally, a detergent strategy is one where a strategy which has not worked in the past is now being rethought, and its various parts which did not work in the past are being discarded, or changed (Grundy 1995).

FIGURE 2.1: The strategy mix

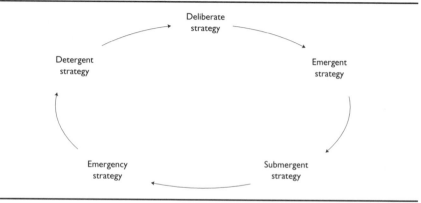

Any strategy can be analysed to discern which stage of its evolution it is presently at. A strategy which is in two or more of the above phases simultaneously is said to have a strategy mix.

Besides asking oneself where the business strategy and the project strategy is, *vis-à-vis* the strategy mix, it is also imperative to examine the strategy mix as it changes over time. Taking a typical project, initially there may be an intensive phase of deliberate strategy but quite quickly this opens out into a number of emergent strategies. Some of these strategies fan out, losing their sense of direction and thus becoming submergent or even emergency strategies.

Opening it out just a little bit more, let us imagine the patchwork of strategy existing in an organization. At any one time there could be a very clear, deliberate strategy in some business units, whilst others are far more emergent, some submergent/emergency, and one or two are actually detergent. At the corporate level there could be a largely detergent strategy. Then there might be some key organizational projects going on either within or across business units. Some of these may be start-up, deliberate projects. Others might be mature but still deliberate projects. There might also be some highly emergent projects and some (sadly) submergent projects. The result is therefore one of a confusing patchwork of strategy – giving rise to inevitable cynicism.

Does this sound like your corporation? Possibly. The cost of this patchwork could be very significant in terms of a lack of focus for resource allocation and for project prioritization, and a blunting of organizational energy and enthusiasm.

The strategy mix is thus a helpful way of visualizing more about how a project may evolve over time within its changing environment.

The strategy mix can be used for diagnosis at a number of levels, for example for projects at:

- a corporate strategy level,
- a business strategy level,
- a breakthrough programme level (i.e., involving a number of interdependent projects which will combine to support the business strategy),
- the project level itself.

Due to the importance of the various forms of strategy, it is worthwhile fleshing each strategy type out further, as follows.

Deliberate strategy

A deliberate strategy is one which has a very clearly formulated idea of how to get from A to B. Deliberate strategies, if innovative and skilfully crafted, can offer a more direct route to your strategic objective for growth. The proviso here is that any deliberate strategy needs to anticipate both pending external change and complexities of implementation.

Deliberate strategies vary considerably, however, in the extent to which:

- A is actually where you are now;
- whether B is worth going to and thus whether shareholder value will be generated;
- whether the strategy actually exploits your competitive advantage;
- whether the implementation issues are sufficiently thought through;
- whether your commitment to a particular strategic route is sufficient to withstand setbacks;
- whether the strategy has sufficient flexibility to respond to change or not.

An example of a deliberate strategy is for a grocery supermarket to diversify into non-food activities like fashion clothing, CDs, electrical goods, etc.

Emergent strategy

An emergent strategy (as we have already mentioned) is one which is hard to detect as an explicit strategy at the time. Emergent strategies are more commonly ones whose pattern can only be detected virtually after the event, once the pattern has been knitted together. Emergent strategies vary in terms of how coherent this pattern is after the event and whether they exploit opportunities in different strategic directions thus, in effect, partly cancelling each other out. In the former case emergent strategies are helpful, whilst in the latter case they are positively unhelpful. Emergent strategies can help achieve strategic breakthroughs by exposing unlikely opportunities.

An example of an emergent strategy is for an existing service company setting up an e-commerce business as a response to attack by new e-commerce rivals.

Submergent strategy

A submergent strategy is one which was either originally a deliberate strategy which has gone wrong or an emergent strategy which has got itself into real trouble. The submergent strategy is an unrealized strategy which has led to damaging results.

One manager described submergent strategy at a major insurance company as being as follows:

I don't think we really monitored where we were against the plan. We discovered this too late... It was as if we were on the Titanic, with water levels slapping onto the deck, and you suddenly realize, 'My God, we are sinking,' and to put it bluntly we need to understand that we are shipping water, and it is self-evident that we are slipping beneath the waves... '

An example of submergent strategy is that of Marks & Spencer's attempts in 1998 to turn its business around under the existing management team.

Emergency strategy

Emergency strategies are characterized by very little longer-term pattern in strategies with these being mainly reactions to short-term pressures or temptations. Emergency strategies are 'off the highway' of achieving longer-term strategic direction. An emergency strategy would hardly count as a strategy at all unless it was so prevalent as it is in everyday reality.

A controversial example of an emergency strategy is Marks & Spencer's attempts in 2000 to rejuvenate its clothing strategy by launching designer sub-brands without attributing them to named designers in an effort to make up for Marks & Spencer not being seen as a trendy brand.

Detergent strategy

A detergent strategy is often called refocusing strategy. The idea of detergent strategy is perhaps more powerful as it links directly to cleaning up a mess left by an emergent, submergent or emergency strategy. A detergent strategy can be found either as part of a major and dramatic turnaround or as a more localized attempt to prepare a more solid basis for new deliberate strategies. An example of a detergent strategy is that of IBM's rationalization of its hardware businesses which entered the 1990s as overmanned, unwieldy operations and entered the millennium as a much leaner operation.

A key conclusion from the notion of the strategy mix is that no single form of strategy is therefore appropriate to managing strategies in different contexts. Deliberate, emergent and even detergent strategies need to be managed together in a deliberate juggling act.

The above forms of strategy are all extremely important to business projects for two reasons. Firstly, the strategy mix may be predominately of an emergent, submergent or emergency nature, meaning that it is very difficult, if not impossible, to make linkages between the project and its higher level business strategy. Secondly, the project itself may be in a more emergent, submergent or emergency state. Although this is clearly undesirable, it is by no means an inconceivable state. Many projects lack sufficient clarity of purpose and inherent advantage to actually succeed.

Where the business strategy is very fluid it is that much harder to engender a logic and clarity at the project level. Equally, where key business projects have the habit of not being terribly well thought through, then there is perhaps an even greater tendency for the business strategy to become fuzzy and shortsighted.

Before we leave the strategy mix for a while, let us do a brief recap.

First, the various levels of strategy are often loosely interconnected, meaning that it is not often straightforward to link projects with business strategy. Second, the business strategy itself might be fluid and ambiguous. Third, the business strategy might be at a lower point in the strategy mix cycle (a blend of submergent, emergency or detergent strategies) and here there will be very little to link projects back to. Fourth, different projects themselves might be at a different phase of their own strategy mix: some may be mainly deliberate or emergent, or perhaps mainly at the submergent/emergency phases, or maybe mainly detergent.

To make life slightly more complex, strategies can be developed primarily for external, strategic positioning (for example product/market development or acquisitions and alliances), or they may be mainly concerned with implementation. This raises the possibility of strategies being deliberate in terms of strategic positioning but emergent in terms of implementation planning (the internal how of the strategy). Equally, strategies might be emergent in terms of strategic positioning but deliberate in terms of implementation planning, although this is less likely.

This invites us to explore a number of combinations of deliberate and emergent strategy, as follows.

Blending deliberate and emergent strategies: strategic positioning vs implementation

Strategies can be characterized as a simple matrix of deliberate vs emergent and strategic positioning vs implementation strategy.

In Figure 2.2 it is quite plausible to have a deliberate strategy for both strategic positioning and for implementation strategy. Assuming that these deliberate strategies are both appropriate to the situation – and cunning – would be wonderful.

Or, it is possible to have a deliberate strategy for strategic positioning but an emergent implementation strategy. This combination of

FIGURE 2.2: Blending deliberate and emergent strategies

	Deliberate strategy	Emergent strategy
Strategic positioning		
Implementation strategy		

strategic forms would probably coincide with an unrealized strategy. And another possible scenario is for both strategic positioning and implementation strategy to be emergent. With this combination a company would be very lucky indeed to achieve its strategic goals. Here not only is it unclear why it is pursuing strategies in terms of competitive logic, but it also lacks a clear implementation plan to achieve these goals.

But a surprising combination is that of having an emergent strategic positioning but a deliberate implementation strategy. I would argue that probably many companies are likely to follow this model. These companies are often not so much successful for their initial clarity of strategic thinking but for their implementation skills. Such a combination might work well as long as the intuitive direction for its competitive strategy is appropriate. Where there are major shifts in the external environment and the internal organization is less than fully responsive to these changes, this can result in corporate crisis. A notable case of this was Marks & Spencer in 1998–99.

Emergent strategy does not necessarily mean 'directionless' at all – a strategy can be experimental and only at a later point, once successfully implemented, might the strategic positioning become clearer.

The role of incrementalism

There has been a long tradition of both strategic management and organizational theorists who have drawn our attention to the messier characteristics of the strategic decision process, of which business projects are a key part. Braybrook and Lindblom (1963), for instance, described strategic decision-making as disjointed incrementalism to success in such that decisions are taken in semi-isolation from each other, producing a disjointed pattern of strategic thinking and action. March and Simon (1958) more crudely called this syndrome 'the garbage-can model of decision-making' to exaggerate its apparent randomness. Quinn (1980) more kindly described it as 'logical incrementalism' to reflect the fact that new decisions (and equally, therefore, strategic business projects) get overlaid in as logical a way as possible to the existing mess.

Again, many managers will respond with an intuitive 'aha!' to these descriptions, especially that of Quinn, who gave ample recognition to the limited rationality which nevertheless occurs in management. But even where there is a predominance of incrementalism, this does not mean that it has to be that haphazard. For illustration, just as when James, son of one of the authors, plays with his Lego freestyle, although he adds individual pieces of Lego in an incremental fashion, he is still doing it in order to work towards, for example, a rocket station, a pirate ship or a football stadium. But when managers play the equivalent of 'business project Legos', we might sometimes see things emerging like a rocket-pirate-ship-football stadium or some equally impossible mess. Here, the manager might have started off with a rocket station but another manager then shifts the focus to a pirate ship, and yet another gets the football stadium angle in.

In the above example the mess only appears after the event. Turning Mintzberg on his head, we can now define a disjointed strategy as a mess in a stream of decision or actions.

We can therefore distinguish between haphazard incrementalism (as per the incrementalist school of decision-making) and a more visionary version of enlightened incrementalism. In enlightened incrementalism managers do try to work to an overall vision for not only individual projects but also for strategic breakthrough programmes and for the business strategy itself. But, at the same time, they are equally mindful not only of the specifics of the current project opportunity but also of their project's legacy, based on other projects or initiatives in the organization, both past and present. This historical legacy is almost inevitably going to be a result of post-incrementalism. Whilst taking this inevitability on board, project managers do need to continually go back to the Spice Girls approach – what do we really, really, want?

To get a better handle on the causes of incrementalism, let us examine next how the internal competitive environment of the project impacts on its development and positioning.

Understanding the internal competitive environment

The causes of incrementalism can be understood better by using a picture adapted from Michael Porter's five forces competitive model for competitive environments – see Figure 2.3. To the very left of the picture we see the legacy from past projects. To the centre we see competitive rivalry with existing projects. To the right we see future projects – which might either be supported by this project or potentially might need to be forgone if we do this particular project.

To the top of the picture we see projects which are interdependent with this one – and which are likely to suffer if this one does not go ahead. And to the very bottom we see substitute projects.

Not only does this model explain the potentially negative impact of incrementalism, but it also helps diagnose the project's organizational environment.

For instance, a project which scores highly with the following five forces criteria is going to have a particularly favourable project environment:

- high fit with future projects,
- high synergies with interdependent projects,
- low rivalry with other projects,
- low threat with substitute projects (other ways of doing the same thing),
- a lack of legacy of past projects.

FIGURE 2.3: Project forces analysis

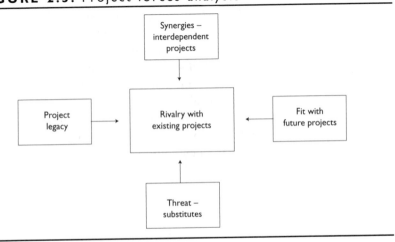

Conversely, one which scores poorly on these five forces criteria is likely to have a very rough ride.

One of the authors when writing this particular book had a helpful legacy from past projects – he had already had seven books published and had strong links with his publishers. He also had interdependent projects as he was running an increasing number of SPM courses and also consulted in that area.

There was, however, high rivalry from other projects, namely in the guise of:

- his consulting work generally, which pushes writing this book into long-range travel time and/or overtime),
- helping his fiancée through her MBA,
- another book he was writing in parallel.

This would give the project a low score.

This book will no doubt support further consulting work/training work in the future but slowed down his plans for a book on 'demystifying strategy and avoiding strategy consultants', which has now been scheduled.

Overall, the score for the project of writing this book was not bad. But even these few negative factors had been sufficient to slow the momentum of this strategic project.

Project programmes, interdependencies and strategic breakthroughs

A key lesson from our section on incrementalism is that it is likely to be extremely difficult to manage every issue worthwhile being called 'strategic' within a single process – whether this is called the 'strategic plan' or 'value-based management' or whatever.

However, by forcing the organization to be more selective in its focus of attention, there is greater likelihood of being able to turn strategic issues and thoughts into real action.

To achieve this, breakthrough management now comes to our rescue.

Business projects are often seen by managers as relatively separate activities, unlinked to one another, but in reality many business projects form part of bigger programmes which in turn form a central part of the business strategy. These linkages between projects will be much stronger where there is a relatively clear and primarily deliberate business strategy. Very substantial and important projects (or clusters of projects) can thus aptly be called 'breakthrough projects'. A breakthrough project is defined as a project which will have a material impact on either the business's external competitive edge, its internal capabilities or its financial performance, or all three. The idea of breakthrough comes from the Japanese philosophy of *hoshin*, or breakthrough management, which is an increasingly well-recognized management technique. Companies who have exploited *hoshin* include Texas Instruments, Hewlett Packard and SmithKline Beecham (see Figure 2.4).

Hoshin has a particularly great appeal in high technology markets principally, because it helps companies to prioritize. *Hoshin* actually prescribes that only a really small number of breakthrough projects or programmes should be attempted at any one time in a particular business area. The absolute maximum of these projects is three, and the minimum is one.

By restricting the number of breakthrough projects to a minimum, the following advantages are likely to accrue:

- critical mass of resources is more likely to be achieved;
- marginal projects will not be undertaken;
- organizational attention and communication will be focused on a much smaller number of things at any one time;
- the organization is less likely to wear itself out on many very difficult projects.

FIGURE 2.4: Business strategy as a stream of projects

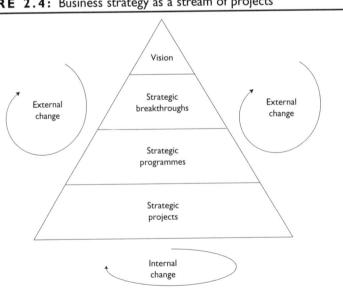

The advantages of having a very tight number of Breakthrough Projects significantly outweighs the perceived drawbacks of concerns that three major areas are not very much then. Further, if it were possible to launch and get reasonably well developed projects within, say, a six-month period, then this would permit as many as nine over an 18-month period (or three projects within each six months).

Whilst *hoshin* is found practised more in technology businesses, service industries can find this approach equally beneficial. For example, when Tesco plc, over the crucial four-year period of 1995–98, overtook Sainsbury, it successfully implemented a number of what one might call breakthrough projects, especially: Tesco's Loyalty Card; its acquisition of the supermarket chain William Low in Scotland; the integration of that acquisition; its customer-first philosophy; expansion into non-food (e.g., fashion, CDs, etc.); its entry into financial services; product quality enhancement; home shopping; new formats and head office simplification. This rate of breakthrough programmes averaged at two-and-a-half per annum (or ten over the four years).

Each of these breakthrough projects could be clustered alongside others with which it has the closest similarity to, and interdependence with, as follows:

- expansion: the acquisition of William Low, product enhancement, home shopping, new formats;
- related diversification: non-food, Tesco Personal Financial Services;
- infrastructure: customer first policy, head office simplification.

Reverting to our earlier jigsaw puzzle of enlightened incrementalism, we can now view any new projects against that backdrop. For instance, if following its very successful growth in the 1990s Tesco wanted to make sure that it was managing its (by now) more complex activities for shareholder value, the corporate centre might hypothetically consider launching a project on managing for shareholder value (as have BP, Boots and Diageo in the past).

Such a project would help to reinforce Tesco's strategic vision and would fit reasonably well with the organizational and project legacies. The project specifics might be not quite so easy to implement within Tesco as it would require a considerable deepening of understanding of value creation within Tesco's business. This would not be easy to achieve in the very fast-moving environment of retail, which does not easily support any elaborate weighing of financial technicalities. It would also have to somehow fit with current projects underway or ones which are still being bedded in, such as Tesco's own version of the balanced scorecard.

So, apart from question marks over its fit to a retail culture generally, such a project looks like more enlightened than haphazard incrementalism.

Seeing business strategy as a stream of projects

In this section we examine how a business strategy can be seen as a stream of projects (Figure 2.4). This group of projects is not static but represents rather a flow of projects over time which collectively shifts or transforms the business. An important premise in this book is that strategic management should give its primary attention to managing strategic projects within an overall strategic vision of the business rather than to developing comprehensive, catch-all business strategies top-down.

To achieve this we focus on a substantial case study from the British football industry, based on Arsenal plc, a leading UK Premiership side. The novelty of this case study was firstly in its putting strategic projects at the very heart of strategic management. Secondly, it also focuses on a number of strategic decisions which are perhaps not normally thought of as being projects.

CASE STUDY: SPM IN THE FOOTBALL INDUSTRY

Introduction

The following case study focuses particularly upon Arsenal Football Club and especially on its achievements during the 1997–98 season. During that season, Arsenal won the Double, the Premier League and the FA Cup, in the same season.

Although perhaps at first sight an unlikely domain for SPM, we will soon see that strategic projects and their evaluation are most pertinent to the football industry. Regardless of whether you are a close follower of the sport, there are many lessons from this case for SPM. Indeed, it is hard to ignore developments in this industry given the media attention it attracts.

Industry overview

Football is a volatile and unpredictable sport where outcomes are determined by a combination of skills and by the interaction of both strategy and tactics – and luck. Some ten years ago, leading English clubs had predominantly English and frequently local players. Increasingly, football Premiership teams have adopted different kinds of strategies for sourcing and developing their players, and also varying styles of play. For instance, Chelsea is renowned for its deployment of Italian and French players; Manchester United has sought still to homegrow its players, topping up with stars from elsewhere for in-fill positions. Since the arrival of new manager Arsene Wenger from Monaco, Arsenal has introduced a number of French players to add to its Dutch collection and more recently from Africa and South America.

Since the start of the new Premiership League one particular team, Manchester United, has stood out as being dominant. Winning three out of four Premiership titles prior to the Arsenal Double and similar titles since then, Manchester United were also the most successful team off the pitch too. United exploited its brand aggressively, generating considerable merchandizing and media revenues as interrelated business streams.

In the latter part of the 1990s and early 2000, Manchester United has led the way in exploiting related (and sometimes less related) diversification with themed cafes, ideas for theme parks (with United as the theme) and their own satellite channel and website, each of which were strategic projects.

To understand more about how the football industry operates at a strategic level prior to exploring how strategic projects add value, let us first consider the industry's critical success factors, both for traditional and new areas of value creation. These include:

- consistently high performance in the Premier League, giving regular access to the European Cup tournaments;
- winning other UK trophies which give similar access to European tournaments;
- strong, positive cash flow based on high ground attendance and solid revenues from merchandizing, media coverage and from sponsorship;
- attracting, integrating, nurturing and developing excellent players;
- a surprising disposal of high-profile players at the peak of their performance, potentially as they are just about to decline or underperform;
- having a commercial strategy which gives a clear focus for revenue growth for merchandizing, media and for other activities.

Clubs that have consistently been able to fulfil these critical success factors in the mid to late 1990s include: Manchester United (a world-famous side), Chelsea and Arsenal. Clubs then aspiring to this strategic group include Liverpool, Newcastle, Aston Villa and Leeds.

Strategic projects in the football industry

The analysis of a football club as a series or stream of projects is not quite so obvious, but nevertheless very fruitful, as we see as follows (grouped by strategic programme).

A range of strategic projects are faced by the leading football clubs. These include:

Merchandizing
- The launch of each new season's merchandizing
- Setting up new distribution outlets and channels
- Overseas marketing strategies

Media
- Negotiations with media companies
- Setting up one's own satellite TV station, as Manchester United has done

Sponsorship
- Negotiating and renegotiating sponsorship deals

The ground
- Ground extensions
- Ground relocations
- Leisure facilities
- Giant TV screens

Players
- New player acquisition: scouting and negotiation – both separate projects
- New player integration
- Foreign player integration
- Player disposal (as a routine)
- Player disposal – for troublesome players, for example where they push the referee over, pretend to snort cocaine after scoring goals, disappear from matches before the game is finished, generally elbowing eyes badly, require intensive psychotherapy etc.
- Following on from the above, player counselling and support generally
- Acquisition of new feeder networks, from joint ventures or through satellite television, in the UK and abroad

Training and development
- New training programmes for the entire team
- Energy and morale-building programme
- Individual training development programmes
- Sorting out injuries and getting fitness back
- Developing new styles of play (e.g., forward, midfield, defence)
- General improvement of morale, which occurred for example when the sacked ex-Arsenal manager George Graham improved Leeds United and then resuscitated Spurs in 1998–99

Matches
- Each match is, in effect, a project
- Each competition and phase of it is a project
- Competitor analysis which, whilst ongoing, could be project-managed

Managers
- Hiring them
- Firing them

Financial
- Club flotations
- E-commerce possibilities

Each and every one of these 30 areas of activity are, in effect, strategic projects. Although some of the projects add value in their own right, in general they add value only through alignment with other areas of activity. Value is typically added through the projects being part of an overall set (called the 'strategic project set'), rather than independently. This concept is explored further in chapter 5.

Interestingly, out of these 30 project areas 18 were related to playing on the field. Whilst this is hardly surprising, considering the nature of the business, in reality a high proportion of long-term value creation in football comes from non-football-related activities.

Whilst Arsenal was, at that time, very successful on the pitch, the club notably lagged behind Manchester United in its commercial strategy. The lack of aggressive breakthrough projects in the latter area, save for sponsorship deals, undermined Arsenal's ability to keep up with United's cash generation potential.

There are clearly many interdependencies to be dealt with when putting an (approximate) value on projects. For example, buying a new, foreign forward may add value only when the following interdependencies are aligned:

TABLE 2.1: The strategic gap

	Manchester United	Arsenal	Gap (points)
August	2nd	4th	4
September	2nd	1st	1 Arsenal
October	1st	2nd	1
November	1st	5th	7
December	1st	6th	12
January	1st	5th	8
February	1st	2nd	12
March	1st	2nd	3
April	2nd	1st	4 Arsenal
May	2nd	1st	1

Key Manchester United injuries: September: Keane (out all season); March: Pallister and Giggs

- the club has not overpaid for the player;
- the player wants to come anyway (and does not get quickly homesick);
- the player gets used to the English game quickly;
- he doesn't get injured;
- he plays well with his co-striker;
- the club's midfield are able to play the right kind of balls through for this particular player;
- and so on.

Each one of the above interdependencies will vary in both its degree of importance and how much influence the club has over it. Whilst some of the above interdependencies look as if they are of low influence (e.g., he doesn't get injured) even here there is some degree of influence (e.g., substituting an injured player early on).

Selling players, too, can be an interesting experience. Whilst Nicholas Anelka, the Arsenal forward, was instrumental in Arsenal's 1997–98 Double, during the following season he became particularly restless. His brothers, acting as his agents, arranged in clandestine fashion for a sale to a foreign side. Ultimately, he was sold to Real Madrid for the princely sum of £23 million. During his first six months at Real Madrid he managed to score only one goal and ended up suspended for 45 days for bad behaviour, causing his new club Real Madrid a turnaround project.

As Arsenal bought Anelka for a mere £1 million, this must rank as about the best strategic project (from acquisition through to disposal) ever done by the club. The profit on the sale was around £900,000 a month over the period Anelka was at Arsenal.

No doubt Arsenal's mind-set is very different from Manchester United. Whilst Arsenal's concern not to overexploit football commercially is laudable, there does seem a strong case for rebalancing the focus of breakthrough projects at Arsenal. The issue remains a burning one for the club.

Now that we have examined both the football industry in a broader canvas and the range of strategic projects, let us now focus more specifically on the Arsenal Double in 1997–98 (all projects being italicized).

The Arsenal Double, 1997–98

The 1997–98 season began with Manchester United rapidly taking the lead. Arsenal were, however, in hot pursuit. This was only Wenger's second season at the club. Initially he had made few changes to his core team but gradually and incrementally he began to bring in new players from France and elsewhere. These acquisition projects would, it was hoped, in themselves bring forth a strategic breakthrough, but subsequently it transpired that a number of further innovations were needed.

Frequently, project management means letting go of things which have worked well in the past. Wenger's sacrifice was to make way for the new by losing some of the old (or *disposal projects*). England player Paul Merson was sold to Middlesbrough in the early 1997–98 season where he had an outstanding season albeit in the First Division. Welsh international forward Hartson was sold to local rivals West Ham, where he too had a prolific goal-scoring season, although his later experience at Wimbledon has been disappointing. Whilst Arsenal began the season well (see Table 2.1), by autumn the team's performance weakened. As the 1997–98 season wore on some commentators began to feel that perhaps the sale of Merson and Hartson had been premature. If the goal of the project was to raise cash for new and more exciting players without disappointing the fans, then Arsenal was failing at that stage. But strategic projects require patience and it was premature at that point to criticize Wenger's projects and programmes to compete on a parity with Manchester United. Arsenal faltered and then suffered significant defeats in the autumn and early winter months.

In December 1997, Arsenal suffered a telling defeat at home to Blackburn Rovers, losing 3–1. There were rumours of a divide between the old, mainly British and the newly arrived foreign players, requiring a fast integration and team morale-building project. A further issue was that the famed but no longer so youthful Arsenal back-four defenders seemed to be weakening. Would Wenger need to dismantle and discard the line that had been the backbone of Arsenal's strength for nearly ten years? At this time, Tony Adams, a lynch-pin defender, even thought of retiring from the game entirely because of exhaustion and deteriorating form due to injury. *Rejuvenating Tony Adams* was a short-term project which subsequently paid huge dividends for the rest of the team. Tony Adams was still, in 2000, a prominent Arsenal and England player.

The prospects for Arsenal winning the Premiership now looking now extremely bleak, Wenger faced a turnaround situation to get Arsenal into a European competition during the following 1998–99 season. Arsenal were knocked out of the UEFA Cup early on and then struggled against non-Premier League sides in the FA Cup through replays. Arsenal faced a very steep uphill task to secure a successful season.

By this point Manchester United looked set to make it four titles out of five. By December they were 12 points ahead of Arsenal (see Figure 1), making their position seem impregnable.

The Arsenal line up now ran like this: the Dutch international Bergkamp was paired up as Arsenal's strike force with Ian Wright, Arsenal's top goal scorer. Wright, however, suffered a series of injuries in the autumn which put him out for the rest of the season. Wright, a prolific goal scorer, now had stand-ins in Anelka and Wreh. In late 1997, neither of these new players looked confident in filling the gap left by Wright, who was a very hard act to follow and whose potential *disposal project* was not too popular with the fans. Overmars, a Dutch winger bought by Arsenal in the summer, seemed unsettled in adjusting to the English League (another *integration project* for Wenger). In acquisition terms, Arsenal seemed to be suffering significant integration difficulties. Ironically, by 2000, Overmars was sold for around £20 million in a package with Petit worth £30 million, showing the value of player integration and development.

In midfield, two new French players, Viera and Petit, had been introduced over the past and current season, but this partnership had yet to fulfil its potential.

In December 1997, Arsenal lost their third Premiership game – this time against Liverpool. A team integration project was to ensure that the midfield players and forwards worked harder, particularly to close down the opposition. According to commentators, the overseas players needed to understand the physical toughness of the League (a *playing-style project*) and be committed throughout all of the match (an *integration project* once again). Meanwhile, the English players needed to understand how best to exploit the flair of the overseas player (*playing-style project*).

Arsenal's playing strength improved dramatically in a number of key ways over the January–March period:

- Anelka improved his game and a new flow of goals emerged (*player improvement project*).
- Overmars, the winger, found his feet and became an unstoppable force against most defences, beginning another flow of goals. This breakthrough appeared to come by removing factors constraining his play, allowing him to achieve his full potential (*fitness improvement project*).
- The Viera-Petit axis in midfield became generally acknowledged to be the strongest midfield pairing in the league besides becoming active goal scorers (*new style of play project*).
- Parlour went from strength to strength in midfield, almost making it into England's World Cup Squad (*player improvement project*).
- The back four remained solid. Even Arsenal's defenders began to seek out goal-scoring opportunities, with England player Adams becoming a 'virtual centre forward' for corners (*new style of play project*).
- The team had *revitalized energy*. In late season they appeared to gain more energy the more they played (an *energy and morale project*). Although this breakthrough appeared simply to emerge, it was skilfully directed by Wenger's special training and player support measures (*training project*).

In terms of results, instead of the previous season where Arsenal lost games to the leaders Manchester United, in 1997–98 Arsenal won both games. The effect was a 12-point swing to Arsenal.

The above breakthrough projects were multiple, complementary and self-reinforcing. The overall pattern of Arsenal's play had changed – and as part of a deliberate strategy by Wenger.

In a game where results are settled by often fine differences, Arsenal's late season rejuvenation thus appears to have been inspired by a number of strategic projects both on and off the pitch.

These projects resulted in an interrelated number of deliberate and emergent breakthroughs which came to the fore just at a time when its main opposition, Manchester United, was weakening.

Seven key lessons for SPM

We can perhaps distil seven key lessons for Strategic Project Management from our analysis of Arsenal's unexpectedly out-standing 1997–98 season. These include:

- Managers should look hard for sources of cumulative competitive advantage in strategic projects – and then align these vigorously and obsessively. They should seek out virtuous cycles of success or feedback loops, for example football success builds your brand, facilitates merchandizing, pays for world-class players.
- Try to combine deliberate and emergent, or unexpected strategic projects simultaneously. Not all breakthroughs have to be highly designed or deliberate; they can be seized during the fluid competitive interplays of the moment. Strategic management (to borrow a footballing analogy) suffers sometimes from being just a little too 'set piece'.
- Seek out not just the tangible but also the behavioural strategic projects – especially teamwork and team spirit.
- Successful strategic projects demand continual injection and generation of much energy. Organizations should strive to avoid trapping strategic energy in projects not thought through, under-resourced, or not pursued with enough stamina.
- Also, strategic projects may require spontaneity and thus have a different feel to them than more set-piece, deliberate strategies. Arsenal's breakthrough momentum faltered perhaps in the 1998–99 season due to the very loss of this spontaneity.
- Managers should focus their breakthroughs within a manage-able domain – and not on too many fronts. Wenger once said that it was Arsenal's good fortune that it did not play in the tiring European Cup in 1997–98, unlike Manchester United who dissipated considerable energy on Europe.
- The most effective strategic projects appear to come more through natural strategies – that is, ones which are grounded in what is most naturally likely to work best, rather than by con-trived strategies. Many deliberate strategies appear to be doomed to failure from the start simply because they contain built-in flaws, contradictions and disadvantages.

The Arsenal case study underlines the need for a concentrated focus of attention on key strategic projects in order to give a business strategy more form, momentum and effective delivery.

To amplify the point about the importance of concentration of energy within a small number of strategic projects, let us end with a brief quotation from Sun Tzu, the Chinese writer on military strategy (1991):

> So when the front is prepared, the rear is lacking, and when the rear is prepared the front is lacking. Preparedness on the left means lack on the right, preparedness on the right means lack on the left. Preparedness everywhere means lack everywhere.

Conclusion

Strategies are not always very clear and deliberate. Instead they form a strategy mix which will shift over time, moving from deliberate to emergent and back again to deliberate – hopefully without going around the cycle of submergent, emergency and detergent strategies. Or, potentially, it may shift from emergent to submergent and then become an emergency strategy. Or, it could move through any of these modes and then to detergent, where it becomes sorted out.

The strategy mix partly accounts for why it may be difficult to link projects with strategy. Equally, each individual project may itself move through the strategy mix, starting off with clarity of scope, objectives and linkages (a deliberate strategy), and then slipping into the other phases of the strategy mix.

Turning to the dynamics of strategy, and of strategic projects, we saw that a typical flow of project decisions was highly incremental and fluid. This led to internal rivalry between projects and to somewhat chaotic influences on the trajectory of strategic projects. Whilst tolerating, to at least some degree, this ambiguity and uncertainty, we needed to establish greater clarity, priority and linkages between projects.

Rather than embracing a comprehensive framework of strategic planning – which would set out to cope with everything – we saw breakthrough management as helping gain a selective focus on the really key strategic projects or programmes. This involved selecting only a small number of big and difficult projects for attention at any one point in time, and also the management of key interdependencies between those projects.

Finally, we took a longitudinal look at business strategy as a stream of strategic projects using Arsenal plc as an example of how alignment – at least over a 12-month period – produced some real strategic breakthroughs.

References

Ansoff, I. (1965) *Corporate Strategy*, New York: McGraw-Hill.

Braybrook, D. and Lindblom, E. (1963) *A Strategy of Decision*, New York: The Free Press, Macmillan.

Grundy, A.N. (1995) *Breakthrough Strategies for Growth*, FT Pitman Publishing.

March, J.E. and Simon, H.A. (1958) *Organizations*, New York: John Wiley.

Mintzberg, H. (1994) *The Rise and Fall of Strategic Planning*, Prentice Hall.

Porter, E.M. (1980) *Competitive Strategy*, New York: The Free Press, Macmillan.

Porter, E.M. (1985) *Competitive Advantage*, New York: The Free Press, Macmillan.

Quinn, J.B. (1980) *Strategies for Change: Logical Incrementalism*, Homewood, Irwin.

Sun Tzu (1991) *The Art of War*, London and Boston: Shambhala.

CHAPTER THREE

Strategic project definition

Introduction

Defining the project is probably the most critical phase of strategic project management. Unless the problem or opportunity giving rise to the project is thoroughly diagnosed, then it is quite possible to end up with an inappropriate project strategy and even the wrong project entirely.

Recapping on strategic project management as a whole, we see the following stages in the process:

- Defining the project: what is the scope of the opportunity (or threat)? What are its objectives and possible benefits, costs and risks? What is its overall implementation difficulty and who are the key stakeholders?
- Creating the project strategy: what is the external and internal position and how are these likely to change? What options are available for implementation and how attractive are they vs difficult to implement? Which stakeholders now need to be mobilized to make it happen?
- Detailed project planning: is the timing good? What resources are needed specifically, and when are they needed to deliver a result effectively?
- Implementation and control: is implementation proving effective and if not, why not? What new implementation forces and stakeholders have come into play and how might these be handled? Do the original objectives need revisiting, and are these more easily met by other strategies for growth? If so, what are the costs of refocusing efforts? Is the strategic project on track in terms of its intended competitive, financial, operational and organizational results?
- Review and learning: were the goals achieved? If not, what were the factors which could have been controlled or been attempted to influence but weren't? Or, do the original competitive strategies or their

implementation plans need to be revisited and changed? Finally, were the implementation difficulties much greater than envisaged, and if so, why?

Typically, managers focus 80 per cent of their efforts on those areas of the implementation process which carry only 20 per cent of overall importance. Table 3.1 graphically illustrates this tendency:

Note the enormous difference in time between what, in an ideal world, it is felt that managers should spend on diagnosis and what they actually do spend. Also note the need to spend considerably more time on learning.

So what does diagnosis actually entail? Diagnosing a strategic project involves:

- scoping the project,
- defining the key issues,
- identifying the key project objectives,
- anticipating the project's key stakeholders and difficulty.

Scoping the project

One of the major pitfalls facing managers inexperienced in managing strategic projects is underestimating its scope. The scope of a project is very much driven by three major factors: size, duration, key interdependencies.

These three variables effectively form the strategic project scope – see Figure 3.1. The scope of the project can crudely be defined as: project size x duration x interdependencies.

TABLE 3.1: Time analysis

	Actual Time	Ideal Time
Definition and diagnosis	2 per cent	20 per cent
Strategy and planning	10 per cent	20 per cent
Implementation	80 per cent	40 per cent
Control and learning	8 per cent	20 per cent

Source: *Implementing Strategic Change,* A N Grundy, Kogan Page, 1993

CASE STUDY: BP CULTURE CHANGE – PROJECT 1990

Taking the example of BP's culture change, which began in 1990 with the goal of transforming its organization, our analysis exposes a rather large project.

Project Size
- All of BP's business units
- Every level of the organization, from chairman down to operator
- Worldwide
- Covering all key management and staff behaviours and underlying values

Project Duration
The initial phase was of one year, then follow-up and reinforcement took a further two years. Harvesting the benefits absorbed the next seven years; the total duration of the project was an entire decade or so.

Project Interdependencies
- Performance management
- Training and development
- Career-pathing
- Competencies
- Rewards and recognition
- Process reengineering – administrative
- Process reengineering – managerial
- Quality management
- Structure change / delayering
- Decentralization
- Strategy development (e.g., acquisitions and their integration, divestment)

FIGURE 3.1: Fishbone analysis

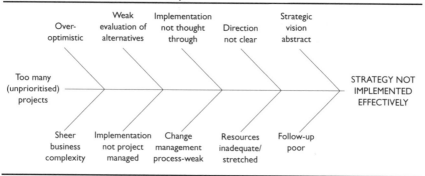

- Managing for shareholder value
- International management

The above list appears awesome – and these looks are not deceptive. Project 1990 was conceived by BP Chairman Sir Bob Horton as a deliberate and comprehensive intervention aimed at bringing BP's management from an imperial/bureaucratic culture set in the 1950s and 1960s into the year 2000 – in one leap.

Whilst cynics may criticize BP for the way it may have handled culture change (especially those who lost their jobs in the process), it is hardly deniable that the exercise helped position BP as a world-class oil company by the year 2000.

Whilst it could be argued that the giant task might have been split down further, this almost certainly would have resulted in considerable inefficiencies and inconsistencies across the group.

Coming back now to the reader's practical situation, you are invited to perform the following exercise.

EXERCISE – SCOPING A PROJECT

Choose a strategic project which you either have had an involvement in or perhaps are about to become involved in.

1   What are the dimensions of its size, especially
   - which parts of the organization does it impact upon?
   - how significant is this impact?
   - how different will this impact be in different years?
   - what is the potential scale of investment required?
2   What is its likely duration, including:
   - project feasibility study and business case?
   - piloting the project?
   - roll-out?
   - hand-over?
   - reinforcement of any intended changes (eg in behaviour)?
   - further development?
3   What are its key interdependencies:
   - internally, between its various activities?
   - externally, with other projects it supports?
   - externally, with other projects which it might compete with or cut across?

Defining the key issues

Our next major step is to diagnose the key issues within a project. This should be done preferably before drawing out the project's objectives as we need to explore much more about why we need to look at the project in the first place. This may require a harder look at why current problems exist (for example, with fishbone analysis) or by looking at what visionary strategy might be available by opening up one's imagination (using wishbone or from-to analysis).

Our key tools for diagnosing the key issues within strategic projects are fishbone analysis, performance drivers, wishbone analysis, gap analysis and from-to analysis. See Table 3.2 for the functions these five techniques serve.

Root-cause (fishbone) analysis

Root-cause analysis is an easy way of going behind the more immediate definition of the problem or opportunity. For instance, Figure 3.1 indicates how root-cause analysis can be used to identify why a major telecommunications company experienced difficulties in the implementation of its strategy.

In Figure 3.1 we see the major symptom of the problem drawn at the right-hand side of the page. This is to signify the present situation. We then work backwards to the root causes of the problem. This is exactly the same as cause-effect analysis, except that we are working backwards from a single effect to many causes.

Each and every one of the bones of the fishbone can ultimately be traced to its root cause or causes. In fact, Figure 3.1 does not fully trace

TABLE 3.2: Analysis function

Technique	Application	Benefits
Fishbone analysis	Problem diagnosis	Visual and diagnostic
Performance drivers	Diagnosing performance	Focuses the project on delivering business performance
Wishbone analysis	Opportunity creation	Visual and creative
Gap analysis	Targeting the project	Focuses managers' minds on the important
From-to analysis	Scoping the project	Scopes the depth and breadth of the project

back to these root causes as we are still left with some of the bones at the level of symptoms, for example 'lack of prioritization'. Clearly we could perform another fishbone to get to the root causes of why there was a lack of prioritization.

It is important to note that there is no particular order to the bones of the fishbone. Whilst one bone will probably link on to the next (in the ideas stream), it is likely to hold up the analysis if you try to sort them out as you go. If a group really wants to do this, then the bones could be created using Post-it notes which are subsequently re-sorted and repositioned once the first-draft fishbone is complete.

One thing to watch out for when using fishbone analysis is when several problems masquerade as a single problem. In this case, the symptoms may need to be split, creating a number of mini-fishbones.

Due to the frequency with which this occurs, we decided to create a new technique linked to fishbone. This involves drawing an array of smaller fishbones to represent almost a shoal of problems. As each problem can be quite difficult in its own right, we came to call this piranha analysis, after that deadly tropical fish which, when part of a large body of piranhas, can do serious damage to a human being in a remarkably short period of time.

Many organizational problems are of a very similar kind. Whilst individually they do not amount to all that much, combined or fused with one another they become intractable.

Figure 3.2 represents one such piranha-like problem, namely that of an insurance company which found difficulty in complying with Year 2000 computer-programming dilemma (Y2K). Whilst the existence of Y2K itself was one of the symptoms, two other equally important symptoms were 'IT projects are always late' and 'we are not very good at IT'.

FIGURE 3.2: Piranha analysis – the Y2K problem

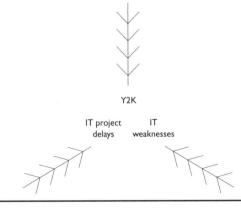

It is crucial to ensure that you have defined the symptoms of a problem (which is leading to a strategic project) fully, as otherwise you may end up diagnosing and dealing with it only very partially.

Whilst fishbone analysis is most commonly applied to dealing with existing problems, it can also be used in a number of other, and less obvious, ways, especially:

- anticipating future problems or things going wrong with the strategic project, and then working backwards to what caused this to go off the rails;
- within scenario analysis to examine the precursors of events which might produce a particular future external or internal environment. These events are often called 'transitional events' in scenario theory to indicate that they form the transitional link between one state of the world and another. Here we might determine The Event – like the price of petrol exceeding the equivalent of £5 a gallon – and then work backwards using fishbone analysis to identify both the necessary and sufficient causes of this transitional event;
- to analyse behavioural factors leading up to a particular organizational problem;
- to look at the consequences of the project going wrong. Here, the fishbone is reversed (a reversed fishbone analysis or 'bonefish' analysis) with the single cause (a project going wrong) leading into multi-consequences to the right. Figure 3.3 gives an example of this in action.

Amplifying this final point, it now becomes clearer that fishbone analysis is merely a way of depicting an ongoing cause and effect chain. Here, the latter effect becomes a cause of further effects, and so on. The most immediate practical use of reversed fishbone analysis is to identify the more critical interdependencies of the project and to identify the cost of getting it wrong. The cost of possible project failure is very useful in persuading top management to fully resource the project.

FIGURE 3.3: Bonefish analysis

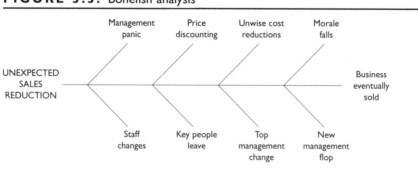

In chapter 4 we will go on to examine how projects can be evaluated and prioritized according to their attractiveness and implementation difficulty (or AID analysis). This can also be used to do a very initial prioritization of which of the various bones of the fishbone are most worthwhile addressing.

Sometimes it is relatively obvious what needs fixing after having performed a fishbone analysis. Sometimes it is easy to see one-for-one solutions for each one of the problem's root causes. Equally, sometimes a number of the bones might be addressed by a single intervention. Ideally, given the limitations and constraints on management time, it may be a better idea to try to solve several issues with one overall solution.

Sometimes it is better still to transcend the entire problem. Rather than trying to manage the situation as it is – however bad it is – it may be worthwhile looking for an entirely different approach. For example, at Hewlett Packard some years ago demonstration stock was causing a major headache as it was becoming increasingly difficult to manage a complex but vitally important flow of trial equipment to customers. Equipment had to be tracked and quality checked throughout the UK, which was decentralized to staff geographically who found the administration process a strain. A very long fishbone indeed (perhaps looking more like a centipede) is a sure sign that you need to reframe the problem.

The initial solution was to rationalize the demonstration staff and to centralize them, but this proved to be of somewhat limited attractiveness and also very difficult to implement. Then a newly appointed manager looked at the problem again without getting bogged down in the existing problem diagnosis and solved it with an entirely different strategy – she outsourced it!

A final point on fishbone analysis is that sometimes managers new to the technique feel that it is little more than a brainstorm. We are inclined to disagree. Whilst personally averse to much more structured fishbones and to structured diagnosis checklists, the fishbone does appear to perform a lot more than a loose brainstorm. In particular it helps to:

- visualize the problem in such a way that it is more likely to lead to diagnosing other potential root causes;
- share that visualization more powerfully then a simple list of bullet points with other managers;
- can be used to generate subfishbones and thus networks the web of causes;
- traces the apparent root cause back to the real root cause – a simple listing of causes is more likely to lead to a mixture of symptoms and root causes.

Of all the techniques, fishbone analysis is perhaps one of the most popular. Whilst its original background was in Total Quality Management (TQM), its possible application is much more diverse.

EXERCISE: FISHBONE ANALYSIS

Choose one project in your business which addresses a key organizational problem:
1   What is the main symptom of the problem?
2   What are its root causes? Go back, if necessary, to the ultimate root causes using fishbone analysis, subfishbones.
3   How might you dissolve or mitigate these problems, either for each of the bones or using a smaller, higher-level number of interventions?
4   What project would now address this situation? Define its objectives, scope and strategy.

Our final detailed diagnostic technique to help us scope the strategic project is performance driver analysis.

Performance Driver Analysis

Performance driver analysis is another way of performing business diagnosis as a means of diagnosing the project. This technique is highly complementary to fishbone analysis. The technique is particularly useful for business turnaround projects, diagnosing organizational issues and difficulties, and defining problems to improve business performance generally.

Firstly, begin by identifying the business or organizational area which is either the main focus of the strategic project or which may generate projects out of it.

Secondly, separate out the factors which are enabling the business or organizational unit to perform well (the key performance drivers). Draw them vertically as arrows (as per Figure 3.3) in proportion to their perceived relative strength.

Thirdly, identify those factors which are holding performance back, or which are actually reducing performance (the performance brakes). Again, draw them in vertically in proportion to their perceived relative strength.

Fourthly, step back from the picture and see whether, overall, the balance of performance drivers/brakes is strongly or weakly positive, neutral or negative.

Further areas to reflect on are:

- Are their linkages between the forces or patterns or underlying themes in them?
- To what extent are the key performance drivers external or internal?
- Do specific performance brakes warrant further diagnosis (possibly through fishbone analysis) in order to identify possible performance breakthrough projects?
- Or, might a single, well-focused project deal with many of these performance brakes with one hit?
- Could there be one or more breakthrough or continuous improvement projects aimed at strengthening existing, minor performance drivers, or even introducing new ones?

The performance driver analysis can either be done by mixing internal and external performance drivers, or these may be separated out to form two discrete outputs. Interestingly, managers generally find this technique more powerful than conventional strengths and weakness and opportunities and threats (SWOT) analysis, as it deals more directly with the variables impacting on performance rather than, for instance, 'nice-to-have' strengths.

In Figure 3.4 we see a business in a turnaround situation, one which was actually in the most attractive business of industrial sewerage (described as attractive because a business of this nature generally repels would-be new entrants.) Indeed, there would appear to be relatively little going for this business save for the fact that there was a great deal of regulatory pressure to ensure that industrial sewerage did not damage the environment (an external performance driver).

This business was in a state of strategic crisis. The existing managing director was replaced, and the business struggled on for nearly two years more before being closed down. This delay was perhaps a pity as

FIGURE 3.4: Performance driver analysis

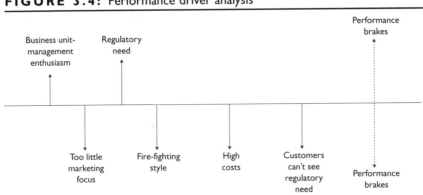

the performance driver analysis was so poor, and the fishbone analyses which underpinned the performance driver analysis were so extensive and formed an intractable labyrinth. Sometimes it is a kinder approach to deal more clinically with a turnaround project rather than struggle with one which is almost certainly terminal.

Performance driver analysis can also be used:

- to tease out deficiencies in organizational capability;
- to examine the strengths and weaknesses of a team before embarking on any team-building or management restructuring project;
- to assess staff at a micro-level who are underperforming, to establish a turnaround (or redeployment) project plan. Anyone who has experienced having a member of their staff undergoing a disciplinary process will know what is meant about this being a project – these situations are invariably complex, have a targeted result over a particular time, and are difficult and distracting.

Once again, performance driver analysis can be supplemented with prioritization techniques including:

- importance–influence analysis to identify which drivers can be worked on, and
- attractiveness–implementation difficulty (AID) analysis to identify which ones should then be focused on.

EXERCISE: PERFORMANCE DRIVER ANALYSIS

1   Identify one key business concern which you may wish to resolve, possibly through one or more projects.
2   What are the key external performance drivers and brakes, and how important are these?
3   What are the key internal performance drivers and brakes, and how important are these?
4   Which of these drivers would you like to focus on as one or more business projects, and what might the scope of these be?

Wishbone analysis

Wishbone analysis, although similar in shape superficially to fishbone analysis, is a quite different animal. Whilst fishbone analysis focuses on problems, wishbone analysis looks at opportunities. Not all projects, by any means, are primarily responses to problems. We therefore require a method of scoping out an opportunity.

With wishbone analysis we begin with some tentative form of a vision. This is drawn at the left-hand side of the page to signify that this is our starting point. To the right-hand side of the picture, again as a series of bones, we draw out all the factors which need to line up in order to deliver the particular vision which we started off with.

These bones not only give us the necessary factors (or preconditions) for success, but also the sufficient conditions. Another way of thinking about the wishbone factors is that they are the prerequisites of fulfilling your project vision or goal.

To illustrate wishbone analysis let us take a look at the first one ever drawn to understand how and why James Dyson's market entry to the carpet cleaning market was such a success – see Figure 3.5 (Grundy 1998). Figure 3.5 highlights not merely the more obvious preconditions of success (like the bagless technology and his patent) but also some less than obvious factors, including very clever (indeed cunning) marketing to his distributors.

The bones of the wishbone are not minor alignment areas, they are major. Indeed, where they are within the company's own domain of control then they are typically clever, innovative, if not downright cunning. Certainly they are not in any sense average.

This is a most important point and one which distinguishes wishbone analysis from other planning techniques and from a simple brainstorm. Wishbone thinking is very much an imaginative rather than a purely deductive activity.

To illustrate this, working with a major cellular telephone company's divisions, we drew up initial wishbone analyses for product launches. Initially, the wishbone looked very average: it had average product benefits, an average distribution strategy, average advertising and promotion, etc. Needless to say, these initial wishbones were produced in around 22 minutes.

We pointed out to the company's managers that when we looked at Dyson's wishbone, this was bristling with innovative ideas – and ones which were highly relevant. Very quickly their managers caught on and

FIGURE 3.5: Wishbone analysis

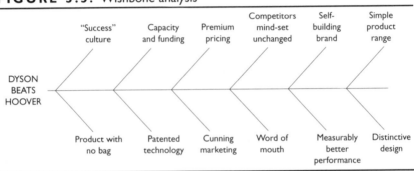

spent some further time to refine and upgrade their ideas, coming back with much more potent thinking.

Doing an effective wishbone is certainly not linear-like thinking. Instead, think of it as being more of an imaginative spiral upwards: take an idea, explore around the idea, then take it up one level of cleverness. Leave it perhaps for a while, spiralling up other ideas and then come back to it to see if you can develop it further. Review the new levels of thinking, seeing what new linkages can be made between the various different clusters of ideas.

This creative process has much in common with the notion of helicopter thinking which we explored in chapter 1. This helicopter or spiral thinking can be done at multiple levels: at the project concept level itself (what are we trying to do anyway?), at the high-level factors of alignment (per Dyson – cunning marketing or premium pricing), or even at a more micro level. Indeed, it is perfectly possible – and desirable – to do a mini-wishbone to support each and every bone of the wishbone.

So, for Dyson's word-of-mouth, a mini-wishbone analysis might include:

- advertisements showing the word-of-mouth effect (in 1997 I suggested to James Dyson he could run adverts on 'lend a Dyson to a friend', but the generous lender could never seem to get his/her Dyson back);
- founding a Dyson Members Club;
- offering a discount for a referral;
- an information card suggesting how the Dyson can be sold to friends and family.

As with fishbone analysis, it is a very sensible idea to perform this analysis on separate pages or flipcharts to avoid clutter. And in the same way as with the fishbone, you will need to stress that there is no particular order or structure to the bones of the wishbone – just let the creative flow develop. Usually there will be at least some indirect linkage between one bone of the wishbone and the others. Nor is there any special significance to what alignment factor you put at the right-hand side or the end of the wishbone.

Wishbone analysis can also be (in due course) prioritized. Various methods of prioritization can be applied using techniques which we develop later on in the book (chapter 4), particularly:

- attractiveness–implementation difficulty (AID analysis): this helps identify how feasible doing it is likely to be given our domain of influence and control.
- urgency–importance analysis: this helps to prioritize 'when we should do it and in which sequence'.

- uncertainty–importance analysis: this helps to evaluate the vulnerability of our wishbone strategy.

Clearly it would be excessive to use every single one of these techniques simultaneously on a project at this phase. Nevertheless, it is quite possible that two of these processes will help and also that at a later stage you will find it useful to try three or all four.

So, wishbone analysis is an imaginative way of using any strategic project as an alignment system. This system of alignment may well incorporate:

- factors both internal and external to the project,
- factors which are both easily controlled and less easy to control,
- factors which are in the present and in the future.

Besides being used to scope a project and also to flesh-out a product strategy – wishbone analysis is also relevant to developing project strategy (see chapter 4 for other techniques) – it can also be used to monitor the project. For example, Dyson's wishbone had a crucial alignment factor that 'competitors' mind-sets remain unchanged'.

For a period of time (around 1996–97) this certainly appeared to be the case. But, around 1998 both Electrolux and Hoover introduced a similar bagless technology to their machines: the single cyclone. This meant that at least from a customer perspective, Dyson's uniqueness was significantly reduced.

EXERCISE: WISHBONE ANALYSIS

Chose one strategic project in your business.
1   What is your overarching vision or goal?
2   What factors need to line up to deliver that vision?
3   Do you have high or low influence over these?
4   How attractive/difficult to implement is each one of the bones of your wishbone?

Gap analysis

A further diagnostic tool for project scoping is gap analysis – to help define the difference between where we are now and where we want to be in the future. Gap analysis is a classic, strategic planning technique (Ansoff 1965) which has become relatively neglected by managers. As an approximation, and based on running countless public courses on strategic management over the years, only about 10 per cent of managers have heard of gap analysis, and only perhaps 5 per cent have actually used it.

Many major companies, too, do not use gap analysis, even though there do not seem to be any other alternative techniques for linking strategy development, business breakthroughs, business plans and shareholder value creation.

Figure 3.6 gives us a classic example of a gap analysis. The horizontal axis is time and the vertical axis is always one related to business performance, in this case profitability. The base line of the business is, in this case, one of decline – which is typically the norm under a 'do-nothing' plan unless competitor conditions are actually relaxing.

The next planning line reflects projects under development. It would be an accident if the base line of the business plus projects under development (whether breakthrough or simply continuous improvement) happened to deliver business objectives (the top line in Figure 3.6). These business objectives, or strategic operations, are frequently of a higher order, basically due either to:

- the requirements to deliver growth in shareholder value anyway;
- the need to stretch managers' thinking about the art of the possible, making them more entrepreneurial and less bureaucratic in their style;
- the tendency for top managers to see their jobs as being one of 'artificial stretch' – so that to get a particular quantum of extra performance you need always to ask for twice or even three times that quantum to get what you want.

Certainly, the first two reasons for gap analysis above (shareholder value and creative stretch) are laudable. The third area (artificial stretch) is more dubious. Although one cannot change how organizations actually want to behave, it is worthwhile highlighting the downsides of artificial stretch in gap analysis. These downsides include:

FIGURE 3.6: Strategic gap analysis

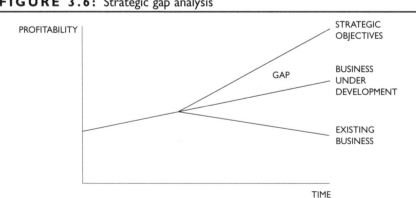

- managers taking stretch goals at face value, then trying to achieve them by trying to force the pace and by squeezing the results out of them, resulting in energy burn-out, a loss of commitment and enthusiasm;
- projects being taken on with stretch goals but which are doomed to delay or failure because of insufficient resources;
- the unreality of project goals causes a cerebral disconnection in managers – because they have been asked to do Mission Impossible, they never even get off the cerebral starting line of thinking, step-by-step, how they are going to get there and with what cunning plan or strategy;
- the organization as a whole may have taken on too many projects generally. Top managers themselves know in their heart of hearts that there is going to be strategic slippage (or 'strategic droop' [Grundy 1998]) across the piece. So, they start off too many projects in the hope that this will compensate for disappointing results. This culminates in harmful interproject rivalry, excess competition for resources, unhelpful politics and sometimes a performance inferior to that from doing even half that number of strategic projects.

Primitive gap analysis can therefore be most unhelpful, causing strategic panic in the organization as managers take on impossible or unrealistic challenges. Unless gap analysis is supplemented with solid, strategic thinking, especially on *how* the project will be delivered with competitor advantage, then gap analysis can be appropriately renamed CRAP analysis, or CReating Artificial Plans.

Having made these caveats clear, gap analysis – provided that it is well supported by imaginative strategic thinking and by well resourced implementation plans – is an essential technique. Gap analysis can highlight both the need for a strategic project and also give some idea of the scope of its outputs, also what is needed to be delivered and by when.

As gap analysis essentially focuses on the future, it does give a reference point from which to begin working backwards. For unless one has some framework for where one wants/needs to be and by when, the project may well be underscoped and underpositioned.

EXERCISE: GAP ANALYSIS

Choose one area of business performance, organizational change or operational improvement in your organization.

1   What is our current strategic position, operational performance or level of organizational capability?
2   If we do nothing (or do relatively little) where will it be in, say, in one, two or three years' time?

3   What existing projects or ongoing processes will mitigate any decline in position, performance or capability?
4   What are the strategic objectives – where do we really need/want to be in this area – again in one, two or three years' time?
5   What other options, other than this specific project, might close the gap?
6   What is the gap between the likely position without any new strategic project and our strategic objectives?
7   How will our project contribute to filling this gap, and will actioning it be both necessary and sufficient to bridge that gap?

The above exercise should generate much rich thinking, particularly about:

■ Where are we now? This is frequently far from self evident, and may require some more detailed analysis and research to establish the base position.

■ What is the likely deterioration in position with a 'do nothing' strategy? Here we need to evaluate the external pressures for change very thoroughly. This might be mitigated by minor investment or other improvements which might buy time. Whilst procrastination is not always a good policy, it may be possible to delay the project somewhat so that we are able to focus on fewer breakthrough projects at any one time. This, in turn, might allow us to perform a more effective implementation of this project when its time comes around. A critical part of the assessment here is that of the cost and risk of delay.

■ Are the strategic objectives realistic and reasonable given the industry we are in, given our strategic position in it, and also given the quantity and quality of resources likely to be available?

■ Is there a better way (considering other strategic options) of closing the strategic gap?

From-to (FT) analysis

From-to (FT) analysis is another useful tool for scoping strategic projects, especially for organizational change or for operational improvement. Where a development project has a significant impact on 'how we do things around here' or the 'paradigm' (Grundy 1993) then it is essential that at least a rudimentary FT analysis is conducted.

The paradigm embraces a raft of organizational processes, some of which are hard and tangible and some of which are soft and intangible.

For example, managers within Prudential Life Administration used a FT analysis based specifically on the paradigm to scope their organizational change project. This helped them to get their minds around the soft as well as the 'hard' factors, as shown in Table 3.3.

This kind of analysis can also be used to monitor the progress of a project, perhaps using a score of 1 to 5, with 1 being the 'from' and 5 being the 'to'. In some situations, however, we might well be starting off with better than a 1, as we might already have made some progress towards our goals, prior to embarking on the project. Equally, we might wish to go all out for a 5 as a 4 or even 3 score might be more realistic and acceptable, depending upon the situation.

The Prudential example of FT analysis is very much a more gourmet approach. We see a semi-structured approach being used to generate the key shifts which the strategic project is aimed at delivering. A simplified approach is to quickly brainstorm the From's and To's in a way much more specific to a particular project. The caveat here is that you really must think about the softer factors which are needed to shift, for example behaviours, attitudes and mind-set generally.

To perform a From-To analysis you need to carry out critical categories (what are you trying to shift?) and the horizontal from-and-to shifts (by how much are you trying to shift them?).

By now it may have become apparent to you that FT analysis is essentially an extended form of gap analysis (see our previous section and Figure 3.7). Because it breaks the gap down into a number of dimensions, it is generally more specific than gap analysis, and is frequently the next step on.

TABLE 3.3: FT analysis

Paradigm	From	To
Power	Restricted	Resides at the lowest appropriate level
Structure	Hierarchical	Flatter
Controls	Instinctive and spontaneous	Measured objectives
Routines	Retrospective looking	Live and forward looking
Rituals	Loose plans	Structured plans
Myths	The 'Mighty Pru', 'Life Administration is OK'	Real world
Stories	Our job well done	Delighted customers
Symbols	Status hierarchy	Rewards for performance
Management Style	Aloof	Open

EXERCISE: FT ANALYSIS

Choose one strategic project, in particular one for which there is already an existing state of affairs which you are trying to change or shift.

1   What are the key dimensions which you are trying to shift?
2   What are the extremes of these shifts – from left to right (i.e., where have you started from originally, and where would you like to end up ultimately)?
3   Where you are actually now? (Note: this does not have to be a 1.)
4   Where do you want to be as a result of this strategic project? (Note: this does not have to be a 5.)
5   What specific actions or interventions might make each shift feasible?

In our final question above we stray into project strategy. Indeed, like wishbone analysis, FT analysis can be a useful means of developing project strategy besides also scoping the project.

A common confusion which is well worth addressing at this point is about which tool to use and when. Managers are often unsure whether to use wishbone analysis or FT analysis in scoping their project.

First, and quite simply, do not attempt to use From-To analysis for an entirely new situation. For example, if you are launching a new product, setting up a new office or penetrating a new distribution channel, you will not have a 'From'. In this situation, just use wishbone analysis.

Only where you feel it is worthwhile reflecting upon your existing competencies before you do something quite new is it worthwhile doing a FT analysis.

Where you have an existing situation, a number of choices exist:

- do an FT analysis (as above);
- where the future is more important than the legacy, go directly to wishbone analysis

FIGURE 3.7: Using FT analysis

	FROM			→ TO
	1	2	3	4	5
Structures*					
Goals*					
Behaviours*					
Cost base*					
Responsiveness*					

*You will need to identify shifts relevant to you

- where you are not very clear about where you are now, why you are there, and what might have gone wrong in the past – begin with a fishbone analysis, then, either move onto a wishbone analysis (to develop the future vision and factors of alignment), or move from the fishbone analysis directly into FT.

Really, the tools are highly flexible and providing you are following a logic and the techniques do seem to fit with and be coping well with the context, then just follow their natural flow.

A good rule of thumb is to think for a few minutes before you actually use any technique and ask, 'If I use this technique or this logic, what is likely to come out?' as a reality-test before committing time to analysis. By doing this, around 90 per cent of moments of frustration will be avoided.

Identifying the project's key objectives

Now we have thoroughly diagnosed the context for the project using a selection of project diagnosis tools, we can now set the project's key objectives with greater clarity. Whilst this may seem to be an obvious and self-evident part of the process, it is often not. There may be several dimensions of the project's objectives, including strategic, operational, organizational and financial objectives.

For instance, strategic objectives might include:

- penetrating a market to gain a certain percentage of market share,
- gaining a particular competitive position,
- creating new opportunities for strategy development,
- generating tangible synergies or spin-offs in other areas of the business.

Operational objectives might include:

- improving efficiency levels,
- resolving performance difficulties or bottlenecks,
- simplifying operational processes,
- achieving world-class operational standards,
- achieving very high customer service standards, or zero defects,
- developing new processes.

Organizational objectives might include:

- building existing competencies,
- creating entirely new competencies,

- improved teamworking,
- increasing organizational responsiveness and flexibility,
- simplifying the organization,
- creating specific behaviours, for example leadership, creativity, strategic thinking,
- shifting the organizational mind-set,
- making it a genuinely international organization.

Financial objectives might include:

- improved rate of return on assets,
- improved return on sales or margins,
- reduced costs,
- payback over a particular period (for an investment),
- net present value (the economic value of the future volume of net cash flows less investment).

Whilst every project will have its core objectives (usually multiple), there will almost certainly be some secondary objectives. Although a subset of these objectives may be reasonably self-evident, there will be some ambiguity about what the strategic project is actually about. It is therefore imperative to define the primary and secondary objectives explicitly rather than leave them to the risks of miscommunication and misunderstanding throughout the organization.

For example, taking the key objectives of developing a corporate strategic plan for a major services company with over £1 billion turnover, we see the following.

Strategic objectives:
- To define the strategic position of the group and of its individual divisions.
- To identify and diagnose the key strategic issues at both the divisional and corporate levels.
- To define and prioritize a number of areas for strategic breakthrough and to evaluate the key strategic options facing divisions and the group.
- To help us to manage our external stakeholders more effectively, particularly institutional and major private holders of shares.

Operational objectives:
- To provide a better framework for operational decision-making.

Organizational objectives:
- To help define key skills gaps (present and future) as input to organizational development.
- To help us reexamine our mind-set of 'who we are, what are we here to do and how?'

- To build strategic thinking capability at business, divisional and corporate levels.
- To allow high potential managers to participate in the debate about the future of the group, both to develop them for the future, and to enthuse them.

Financial objectives:
- To provide a framework for strategic financial management of the group.
- To provide input to the strategic and financial three-year plan.
- To estimate investment requirements
- To help prioritize investment – organically in alliances and in organic development.

The above is quite a long list but by making these objectives explicit we can then go back and later ask the question, 'To what extent did the project meet, or not meet, its key objectives, and if it fell short, why?'

Also notable about the above example is that the strategic review had a number of softer or organizational objectives. Arguably, if these are met they might have, in the longer-term, equal or more impact than delivering a formal strategic plan which would, over time, be somewhat less relevant.

EXERCISE: DEFINING YOUR PROJECT'S KEY OBJECTIVES

I   What are the current objectives of one project which you are currently dealing with? How do these objectives cover the following different types:
- strategic objectives?
- financial objectives?
- operational objectives?
- organizational objectives?

2   Did breaking down these objectives in more detail help you to really think about the full rationale for doing the project?

Having established greater clarity on project objectives it is then worthwhile to go back to our earlier diagnosis, whether this was achieved using fishbone, wishbone, FT or performance driver analysis. At this earlier stage, the probable scope of the strategic project should have begun to emerge, potentially in the shape of an embryonic strategy. This scope can then be tested against the project's objectives, for example to address these questions:

- Will achievement of the objectives deal fully or only partly with the problems or potential opportunity unearthed in the diagnosis phase?

- Are the objectives sufficiently complete to achieve this?
- Are the objectives becoming so complex that we may well need to think of splitting the project into separate projects, or at least into subprojects?

The clearer the project's objectives are then the easier it is to interrelate the project to other projects, and also to begin to compile a business case for the project. It also becomes easier to decide on the most appropriate project management skills that will be required. Also, control measures can be more readily derived. Finally, it becomes much easier to communicate the project and to position it with key stakeholders.

Having now covered the project's objectives we can now move onto positioning the project, and particularly to think about its key stakeholders.

Identifying the project's key stakeholders and difficulty

Whilst a more detailed account of stakeholder analysis awaits us in chapter 6, it is necessary to touch on stakeholders. A stakeholder can be defined as 'an individual or a group of individuals with an influence over the strategic project' either through:

- being a decision-maker,
- being an adviser on the decision,
- being a user or victim of the project, either during implementation or on project completion.

Clearly a particular stakeholder might fall into two or even three of these categories. For example, a decision-maker may be involved in implementation, and also as a potential user. Or, an implementer might also ultimately be a user. Overlaps like this are often helpful as otherwise the decision-making can become dislocated from the implementation reality.

Stakeholders can be either internal or external to the organization. Whilst external stakeholders are frequently important, it is often the internal stakeholders that are the really crucial players. Therefore it is to the internal stakeholders our attention most frequently turns.

At the project definition stage, the minimum we should do is to identify the likely stakeholders. This can be done by preparing a very simple stakeholder periscope picture. Draw three concentric circles on a flipchart with the centre containing core players, the second circle containing secondary players, and the third circle containing peripheral players.

Next, place Post-it notes of key players according to whether they are likely to fall into the three categories. Within each circle place stakeholders most likely to be on board at the top with those less likely to be on board at the bottom. Those we are unclear about will be placed in the middle. Figure 3.8 gives a quick illustration.

This pictures does not discriminate between the levels of influence of primary and secondary players (for that see 6), nor does it dig deeper down into their agendas. Nevertheless, it gives a good first cut of where stakeholders might be located, at least in sufficient detail to help identify to whom the project needs to be communicated.

EXERCISE: USING THE STAKEHOLDER PERISCOPE

Choose a strategic project of your choice, and use the stakeholder periscope picture.

1   Who are the primary stakeholders?
2   Who are the secondary stakeholders?
3   Who are the peripheral stakeholders?
4   For each of these, are they likely to be for, neutral or against the project?
5   Are any of the stakeholders likely to shift over time, either from one category of stakeholder to another, from positive attitude to negative, or vice versa?

Having identified the project's objectives and the likely stakeholders, it is now possible to define a most appropriate communication message and strategy. If this is done effectively there will be a number of benefits:

FIGURE 3.8: Stakeholder periscope

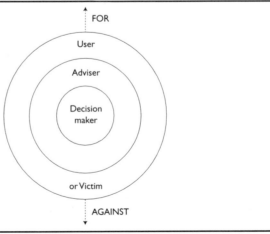

- the project will be better understood, and misunderstandings avoided;
- opinion should be premobilized in the project's favour;
- objections or reservations about the project will be surfaced and can be headed-off;
- implementation issues might also be revealed.

Nevertheless, at minimum we should think about:

- What are the key phases of the project?
- During which phases will we encounter the most/least difficulty?
- Why?

As a quick-and-dirty technique for surfacing difficulty, hold the technique of fishbone analysis in your mind whilst you try to sense the future.

EXERCISE: ANTICIPATING IMPLEMENTATION DIFFICULTY

Choose a new strategic project:

1 Using fishbone analysis, what are the most probable sources of its likely difficulty?
2 Have you done similar projects in the past, and what have the difficulties been? Are these likely to add to the difficulties you have identified above? If so, extend your fishbone.
3 Where you have had little experience of projects like this in the past, might this lack of experience in itself generate difficulties? If so, add to your fishbone.

Conclusion

Project diagnosis is a crucial phase in Strategic Project Management. If sufficient time and thought is spent at this phase there is every chance that we will be doing the right (as opposed to the wrong) project, and that we will have fully understood its scope.

The diagnosis techniques for the current position, together with objectives setting and preliminary thinking about stakeholders and implementation difficulty, should stand us in good stead for our next phase – developing project strategy and plans.

Finally, as a gentle reminder to the reader – have you spent time on the exercises of the first three chapters?

References

Ansoff, H.I. (1965) *Corporate Strategy*, New York: McGraw Hill.

Grundy, A.N. (1993) *Implementing Strategic Change*, Kogan Page.

Grundy, A.N. (1998) *Exploring Strategic Financial Management*, Prentice Hall.

CHAPTER FOUR

Developing project strategy and plans

Introduction

In this chapter we look more specifically at project options and their initial prioritization at a strategic level, using the strategic option grid. We also examine different options for implementing them.

Our next major phase is to explore more detailed methods for prioritizing different projects which compete against each other at a more operational level using attractiveness-implementation difficulty (AID) analysis. In order to explore their difficulty in more depth, we look at force-field analysis and the supporting techniques of stakeholder analysis.

Once the project strategy has become clearer we are able to move into much more detailed project planning and programming. The key activities of the project are then scoped out using how-how analysis (or work-breakdown). We then plot activities over time using Gantt chart analysis. We examine the project's critical path through mapping which projects are interdependent with others and the order in which these need to be implemented.

We then touch on uncertainty analysis using the uncertainty grid to test out the likely robustness of implementation. This helps us to check out and adjust, if necessary, the critical path. This process is supported using importance-influence analysis to target the uncertainties which we can do most about.

Developing project options and strategies

Whilst it is perfectly possible to evaluate a number of project options in one's head, the task becomes more difficult as the number of project options increase and as more than three major criteria need to be considered. This moves from 'very difficult' to 'Mission Impossible' when working with a team of managers, especially ones with strong egos and strong views about most areas of strategy and strategic projects generally.

Some more formal way of prioritizing strategic options needs to be found, and this is manifest in the strategic option grid (see Figure 4.1) which looks at a number of options against the following generic criteria:

- strategic attractiveness: this depends upon the strength of the factors driving growth and competitive pressure in a particular market, and existing and future competitive position;
- financial attractiveness: this is determined by the value and cost drivers underpinning the strategic move which drive cash inflows and outflows and the relative investment at stake;
- implementation difficulty: this is the cumulative difficulty over time;
- uncertainty and risk: these are the fundamental assumptions upon which the strategy is founded and their degree of sensitivity to external and internal shock;

FIGURE 4.1: Evaluating strategic options

Options Criteria	Option 1	Option 2	Option 3	Option 4
Strategic attractiveness				
Financial attractiveness*				
Implementation difficulty				
Uncertainty and risk				
Acceptability (to shareholders)				

* Benefits less costs – net cash flows relative to investment

- acceptability to stakeholders: this is the level of existing and probable future support for the strategy, given the agendas and influence of the key players with an impact on it.

The strategic option grid is completed by discussion prior to defining any further detailed investigations required to collect more data. Even at this stage, creative options can be identified (see the various columns – Option 1, Option 2, Option 3, etc. We sometimes refer to this as the Thunderbird 1, 2 or 3 option, from the television show.)

Each of these options is then evaluated either as:

✔   attractive

✔✔   fairly attractive

✔✔✔   very attractive.

Remember that 'very difficult' and 'very uncertain' will count as one tick.

The strategic option grid thus leads to a much more focused, well-informed discussion relative to that which occurs normally.

CASE STUDY – THE BIRTH OF THE STRATEGIC OPTION GRID

In the mid-1990s, the last parts of British Rail (BR) were still being privatized. BR then had a centralized marketing business which had its own in-house advertising agency, telephone answering service for train enquiries and other sundry activities.

BR commissioned a strategic project to review options for the marketing business – especially for the telephone answering service. Unfortunately, this business had losses which were a substantial percentage of turnover. As the business was not very large in BR terms, an answer on what to do with the business was needed – fast.

A workshop was scheduled between 9am and 3pm with the objective of creating and evaluating as many turnover options as possible. Suitably energized, the small team set about scoring as many goals (identifying and evaluating strategic options) in the six hours available. The team actually identified nine and worked through a complete analysis using the strategic option grid, which had been invented between 9 and 9.30am out of necessity.

A combination of option two (cost reduction), option three (increased pricing) and option six (greater subsidy from the train operating companies) actually helped to save the organization. Instead of closure, 50 jobs were saved and the public were spared the disruption of no longer having a centralized system.

Since its invention to help save this part of British Rail, the strategic option grid has proved to be a most valuable tool for appraising options for strategic projects and has evolved in its effectiveness, particularly through additional questioning.

Key strategic questions to ask yourself about each strategic option follow.

Strategic attractiveness

- What are the key growth drivers (the factors causing the market to grow) impacting on your strategy?
- How are these likely to change in future?
- What is the overall level of competitive pressure in the market? Consider buyer power, supplier power, threat from entrants, rivals, substitutes.
- How might this change?
- What is our competitive position (relative value added to customers compared to costs), and how is this changing?
- How can we innovate to shift the attractiveness of the industry?

Financial attractiveness

- What are the key value-creating activities in the business and which add the most/least value?
- How do these activities interact with one another?
- What are the key value and cost drivers within these activities? Value drivers are those things inside or outside of the business that directly or indirectly generate cash; cost drivers are those same things which produce cash outflows.
- How can we squeeze more value of the business without undermining its competitive pressure?

Implementation difficulty

- How inherently difficult is the strategy to implement over time?
- Do we have all the key competencies to implement it?
- Is this the kind of strategy we naturally do well?

Uncertainty and risk

- What are the key external uncertainties and risks?
- What are the key internal uncertainties and risks?

- How might some uncertainty/risk factors compound with others to undermine the strategy and impact on shareholder value?

Acceptability to stakeholders

- Who are the key stakeholders with an influence over the strategic decision and its implementation?
- What, given their agendas, are the patterns of stakeholder influence overall?
- Given this, does the strategy have sufficient commitment to succeed?

EXERCISE: STRATEGIC OPTION GRID

Choose one strategic project area of your choice.

I   What are the key strategic options (either for what you will do or how you will do it)?

2   How attractive do these score on the strategic option grid?

3   Could any of the strategic options be revised to perhaps yield a higher attractiveness?

The strategic option grid can be used at potentially two levels:

- The competitive strategy level (what we will do)
- The implementation level (how we will do this).

Whilst there are typically quite a number of options for what you might do, typically there are even more options for how you might do this. It might be said that the Kama Sutra is a legendary example of this; having identified what you might do, there are at least a hundred ways of doing it.

The variations on implementation can include for instance:

- the timing of implementation,
- the duration of implementation,
- the phases of implementation,
- who to involve and when,
- the amount of resources generally,
- the positioning of the project,
- whether to rely exclusively on external resources or whether to contract out (either in part or in whole),
- the style of implementation.

The final point on style of implementation brings us to the possibility of either a push strategy or a pull strategy, or perhaps a mix of both. A push strategy is one where a number of key stakeholders are not involved in formulation of the project strategy. A pull strategy is where all stakeholders are involved in the strategy to maximize their buy-in. These strategy typologies were used by the Central Culture Team at BP during Project 1990 to help senior managers think through the most appropriate change strategy.

In a push strategy there is a very strong organizational imperative to deliver a particular change, not merely in terms of the result but also its timing and even, potentially, in its manner. In a pull strategy there is much less, if any, sense of coercion. Here the project strategy is seen as being arrived at by as much consensus as possible, with enthusiasm being generated from within the ranks of the stakeholders upon which the change (or the project) impacts.

Both push and pull strategies derive from change theory. In change theory the style of implementation is prescribed differently, depending upon the situation (this being called a contingency approach). Generally speaking, however, most strategic projects can and should incorporate a mix of both push and pull elements. It is perfectly possible and desirable, for example to have a project objective laid down fundamentally as a push strategy, whilst the means of the implementation is left more open as a pull strategy.

Also, one may well need to use a different mix of pull vs push strategies during different phases of the project. At an early stage of an organizational change project, for example, one might seek input to future style, skills, etc, at a participative level (through a pull strategy). Next, one might communicate the overall future shape of the organization as, more or less, a given (or as a push strategy). Finally, one might run workshops with staff in their new positions to get them to think about how the new organization can work best (shifting to a pull strategy once more).

Having examined a powerful, if sophisticated, way of prioritizing strategic projects at a macro level, let us now look at more micro-level project prioritization.

AID analysis

By looking at a project's relative attractiveness and its implementation difficulty one can now begin to evaluate projects at a micro level from a number of perspectives:

- one can prioritize a portfolio of projects, any one of which can be undertaken;
- mutually exclusive projects can be prioritized;
- different options for implementing the same project concept can be evaluated;
- the different parts or activities within a project can be prioritized.

The AID analysis grid subsumes both strategic and financial attractiveness into the vertical dimension of attractiveness. Implementation difficulty and stakeholder acceptability are combined in the horizontal axis of implementation difficulty. See Figure 4.2.

Beginning with the vertical dimension of attractiveness, one can now expand on the final bullet point above.

Only uncertainty is left out of the AID grid – so we have a much simpler prioritization technique but one that does, however, omit uncertainty.

The strategic option grid and AID analysis are not mutually exclusive. The option grid can be used first to evaluate different strategic options (either for different projects or for different ways of doing a specific project). Then the AID analysis might evaluate and prioritize subparts.

It is sometimes the case that some parts of a project can be undertaken without doing others. For example, buying a business is a project, but the constituent parts of the business can be regarded as subprojects to be retained or possibly disposed of.

Even where a project does consist of a number of subparts, which are not discretionary (such as a training programme), it is still possible to display their individual positionings on the AID grid. Without doubt some parts of the training will be more difficult to implement than others – and will thus have different positionings horizontally on the AID grid.

Thinking now about the vertical dimension of attractiveness, each part of a training project may vary in its relative benefits and cost. Table 4.1 demonstrates a possible profile for a training project.

The attractiveness-implementation tool (AID grid) enables tradeoffs to be achieved between projects. The vertical dimension of the

FIGURE 4.2: AID analysis

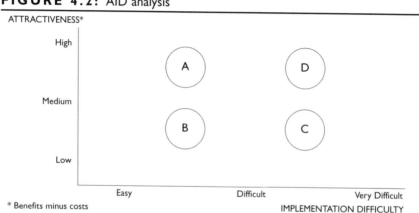

* Benefits minus costs

picture focuses on benefits less costs. The horizontal dimension represents the total difficulty over time. This includes the time up until delivery of results and not of completion of earlier project phases. This tool enables a portfolio of possible projects to be prioritized. Figure 4.2 illustrates a hypothetical case.

Project A is seen as being both very attractive and relatively easy to implement. This project is noncontentious and will probably be given the go-ahead. Project C is relatively difficult – it will probably end up being zapped unless it can be reformulated to make it both a lot more attractive and easier.

Project D presents the biggest dilemma of all. Although it appears to be very attractive, it is also very difficult to implement. Yet managers will tend to focus on the attractiveness of the project rather than its actual difficulty. That can occur even though they have gone through the IMF and stakeholder analysis thoroughly.

When using the AID tool at Hewlett Packard this happened twice. Quite separately, two D-type projects were identified, and as managers spent more time analysing them, commitment to action levels built up.

Although neither of the projects went ahead in their existing form, both Tony Grundy and the then-internal facilitator Stuart Reed, had to be relatively strong to convince the teams that some further refinement was necessary.

Stuart Reed commented at the time:

> I had gone through with them [the managers] both the implementation forces and the stakeholders. Although it did seem to be an attractive project, our two organizational tools were telling us 'it is not going to happen'. I think because the managers were going through the analysis tools for the first time (and hadn't actually tried to implement the project), they hadn't quite realized that it really wasn't going to happen.

TABLE 4.1: An example of AID analysis on training

	Benefits (B)	Costs (C)	Attractiveness (B) – (C)
Pre-diagnosis	High	Medium	Medium
Pre-work	Low	Low	Low
Main programme	High	Medium	High/Medium
Interim support	Medium	Low	Medium
Follow-up programme	High	Low	High
Ongoing support	High	Low	High

Projects in the north-east zone of the grid present some interesting management dilemmas. Following up one HP school of thought (No. 1, as above), one viewpoint is that it is unlikely to be worthwhile doing these projects realistically as the organization will lack the commitment to drive them through. However, a second HP school of thought is that such projects merely represent a challenge for creative thinking – as long as they are potentially very attractive, it may be very fruitful to do this.

At HP another senior manager reexamined a project which Grundy had been involved in 18 months earlier. This potential project concerned a business process change and restructuring. At the time, the position of this project was due east on the AID grid, i.e. medium attractive and very difficult.

This project went into suspended animation for approximately 18 months. Then the new senior manager had solved the problem both creatively and decisively by out-sourcing the process rather than by internal reorganization. The project thus shifted from due east to north-west – high attractiveness and low implementation difficulty.

Another school of thought appeared within Pioneer UK, the hi-fi company. Its Japanese managing director said, 'Perhaps we should do that project *because* it is difficult'.

Initially, we wondered whether this was perhaps an example of management heroism. On reflection, however, this philosophy fitted in well with the notion of breakthrough management, or *hoshin*. Here a breakthrough is frequently something that is both highly attractive and very difficult to implement. Whilst breakthroughs do not have to be very difficult to implement – just hard for others to imitate – they frequently are.

A particularly cunning plan is to target projects which are likely to be between very difficult to Mission Impossible for others to implement but easier for us. Here Mission Impossible is just off the page to the east of the AID grid.

If we do decide to target projects which are very difficult, then following the *hoshin* philosophy it is important to narrow the focus to a very small number of projects within a specific period of time. It is very unlikely that more than three can be undertaken simultaneously without distraction of organizational attention and loss of energy generally.

The positionings on the AID grid are likely to be relatively tentative unless tested out using other techniques. For example:

- The attractiveness of the project may require further analysis using value driver and cost driver analysis (see chapter 5). Ultimately, this attractiveness can be financially quantified, albeit perhaps approximately.

- The implementation difficulty can be tested out using force-field analysis and stakeholder analysis (see later on in this chapter).
- The difficulty over time can be visualized using the difficulty over time curve (see chapter 6).

A useful rule of thumb for the less experienced user of the AID grid, or for those who have not used force-field and stakeholder analysis to check out their horizontal positioning, is:

- if you think the project is easy, it is probably difficult;
- if you think the project is difficult, it is probably very difficult;
- if you think the project is very difficult, it is probably Mission Impossible.

Another technique is to tell scenario stories about the evolution of the project over time. This may help to tease out its likely trajectory on the AID grid. For example, many projects start out with an assumed north-west position (very attractive and easy), but then zig-zag south and east to the south-east (low attractiveness and very difficult).

A final point on AID analysis is that this technique can be used to prioritize each of the bones of the fishbone or, indeed, the wishbone. This can be done either using a separate AID picture or (and this is neat) actually along the edges of the fishbone, as mini-AID pictures with a cross drawn of the positioning. Let us now illustrate the technique with a consulting experience of one of our authors.

CASE STUDY: PROJECT COLOMBIA – THE PROJECT FROM HELL

In early 2000 I was invited to teach strategic management for a Colombian organization via a training channel in the UK. My UK channel had worked with the Colombians before, but due to a recent staff changeover knew very little about the project.

I was given scant details about the project other than that 'these are middle managers' and the fee was rather attractive.

My first view of the project was that it was very attractive – especially as I wanted to rebuild links with this particular channel – but at minimum difficulty. On the other hand, I felt that Colombia might be an interesting place to visit, increasing its attractiveness. I set about project managing the task and, through my UK channel, e-mailed a long list of questions to scope the project. The project's parameters for the programme included:

- six four-hour sessions, Monday to Saturday, which approxi-mated to a week's work, allowing for the spread over six days;

- to be delivered in the evenings from 6 to 10pm;
- with up to 80 managers.

This shifted the project to very difficult (at minimum or beyond) to nearly Mission Impossible, and at the time I began to question if I should do it. Whilst 80 managers would be a tough assignment, they could hardly demand individual attention, making it maybe doable. Also, I had in the past successfully taught 65 students on an evening MBA. By breaking much of the evening activity into working groups of perhaps six or seven managers working on cases it did not look beyond possibility.

The evening work was an unfortunate feature. However, I do like to relax, and the idea of five evenings back-to-back with a Saturday morning was a turn-off. The upside was that I could perhaps sightsee or write this book during the day. Nevertheless, attractiveness declined slightly.

As the project came a bit closer, and I had already done some design work, my channel suddenly discovered that they had not been paid for their last programme six months before. I immediately reopened my diary for other bookings but, as luck would have it, I did not fill the week with other work and the Colombians – almost irritatingly – sent an advance payment to cover my fee.

Nevertheless, the uncertainty caused significant psychological cost and time spent discussing should we/shouldn't we go ahead with my channel. The project's attractiveness declined further, although this became a 'sunk cost' in the period immediately before going. A sunk cost is a cost no longer relevant to decision-making.

About two weeks before going, some timetables for the programme were e-mailed from Colombia. These appeared to show that I was being asked to do two eight-hour day classes as well for the same fee. It was then confirmed that they did want me to do these, and, oh dear, had forgotten to tell me. The last tutor sent to Colombia had also apparently done the day class, but this was before the new staff at the channel arrived on the scene. Obviously this made the project low/medium attractiveness, and at least very difficult – making a no decision.

I now faced the choice of wiping out a whole week's diary or going ahead with my trip to Colombia, donning my Superman outfit and doing it anyway. But as a strategist, I reasoned that this would damage the Colombians even more than me, as I could always find something else to do. Meanwhile, they would be faced with handing back all of their fees to the local managers.

So, I decided to insist on a larger fee to cover the extra time being requested. Whilst this increased fee was not proportionate to the extra hours, it did put my project on the borders of break-even, at medium attractiveness and very difficult. Another incidental benefit was that I would be travelling business class both ways so that I could perhaps do some writing of this book in hopefully ultra-pleasant conditions.

Unfortunately, my experience of Colombia was a very mixed one. There were few sights to see, and one was even closed for renovation. The pollution deterred me from going out, and the hotel lacked the swimming pool that I had mistakenly expected. It rained heavily during the day, and as we were 6000 feet high, it was never going to get hot anyway, besides making breathing difficult, especially with the traffic fumes.

Further, course administration was not quite up to European standards, because I had to speak through an interpreter all week. By Friday I was in the land of Mission Impossible.

To firmly drive the project further south (into low attractiveness on the AID grid), my promised business class ticket on return from Colombia failed to materialize (as the local organization gave me an economy ticket pretending it was business class), leaving the project off the page to the east on the AID grid (see Figure 4.3).

Besides illustrating the importance of AID analysis in antici-pating and monitoring projects and also of scenario storytelling, this case illustrates the need to avoid strategic projects where com-mitment escalates. Frequently, projects which start off as marginal end up as 'lobster pot' projects – once into the project it is very hard, and perhaps impossible, to get out.

FIGURE 4.3: AID analysis – project Colombia

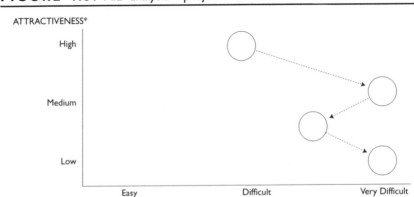

ATTRACTIVENESS*

High

Medium

Low

Easy   Difficult   Very Difficult

* Benefits minus costs   IMPLEMENTATION DIFFICULTY

EXERCISE: AVOIDING MISSION IMPOSSIBLE PROJECTS

Think back through your career.

1   With hindsight, which project(s) counts as Mission Impossible?
2   To what extent could you have anticipated this outcome through scenario storytelling?
3   Once the project was under way, what specific danger signs or indicators gave you advance warning that the project might be about to become Mission Impossible?
4   What degree of influence did you really have in protectively putting the project onto a different trajectory? For instance, as in my Colombian experience, I could have pulled out three weeks before; I could have raised the fee, as I did, or I could have walked out at the beginning of the fourth day when told I was working an extra hour more than contracted, which I very, very nearly did.

Having dealt thoroughly with AID analysis, let us now turn to force-field analysis, which assesses project implementation difficulty.

Force-field analysis

Force-field analysis is one of the oldest management tools available and is derived originally from Lewin (1935).

Force-field analysis can be defined as the diagnosis and evaluation of enabling and restraining forces that have an impact on the implementation of a strategic project.

Force-field analysis is a technique which brings to the surface the underlying forces which may pull a particular change forward, prevent progress or even move the change backwards. These forces can be separately identified as enablers or constraints. But neither set of forces can be adequately identified without first specifying the objectives of the strategic project or programme which we focused on in depth in the last chapter.

When managers first see force-field analysis, they often read it as being some form of extended cost-benefit or pros-and-cons analysis, which it is definitely not. Force-field analysis is simply concerned with the difficulty of the journey which the strategic project is likely to make throughout its implementation.

The difficulty of this journey, like that of any other journey in life, has nothing to do with the attractiveness of reaching the destination. As we have already seen when learning about AID analysis, attractiveness is quite a different concept from difficulty.

The only sense in which it is permissible to incorporate the perceived benefits of the strategic project as a force-field enabler is insofar as:

- there is a actually a genuinely attractive business case for the project and one which has turned on key stakeholders;
- key stakeholders are attracted by the project for other reasons.

Turning back now to force-field analysis, the most effective way of evaluating the forces enabling or constraining achievement of the strategic project objective is to draw this pictorially. This picture represents the relative strength of each individual enabling or constraining force by drawing an arrowed line whose length is in proportion to that relative strength.

A horizontal version of force-field analysis is depicted in Figure 4.4. Note in this case that, on balance, the enabling forces appear less strong than the constraining forces. This particular analysis is for a telecommunication company's strategic plan. It shows that although many of the plans, processes and programmes had been put in place, it was nevertheless difficult to envisage implementation being a complete success. Subsequent events suggest that implementation difficulties at the company were very severe.

The example of the telecommunications company highlights one important truth about force-field analysis: the degree of ease of the strategic project is only in proportion to the extent of your preexisting cunning implementation plan.

Managers who have not already thought hard about the phases of difficulty (see our last exercise in chapter 3), and about options to get round potential hurdles (for example, push vs pull strategies) may be doomed to suffer a very difficult project.

As a rule of thumb, one would wish to see the enablers outweighing the constraints by a factor of at least 1.5 to 2 overall, in accordance with the principle of military dominance. Otherwise, we should be concerned and potentially worried that implementation droop will set in.

FIGURE 4.4: Force-field analysis – telecommunications company

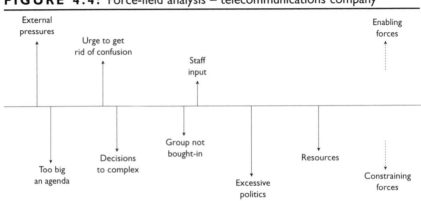

Also, any stoppers really must be addressed, otherwise implementation really won't happen. During (and before) implementation the key implementation forces should be continually monitored to ensure that none threatens to 'go critical' and becomes a stopper.

The next issue that arises is how to evaluate the relative strength of the various forces. Two methods used successfully in the past include:

- scoring each force as having high, medium or low impact;
- scoring each force numerically on a scale of 1 to 5.

Where a team may wish to change its mind (and does not wish to spoil its artwork), then by using Post-it notes the length of the arrows can be changed.

Most groups of managers work comfortably by using the high, medium or low scoring method. In exceptional cases (for example where managers have scientific backgrounds or have an inherent love of quantification), the numerical 1 to 5 scale appears to fit more comfortably.

One of the common objections to force-field analysis is that the whole scoring exercise is highly subjective. This feeling normally occurs within the first ten minutes or so of any analysis exercise. It arises usually because all managers have done is to identify that a force is an enabler or a constraint without exploring questions including:

- Why is it an enabler or a constraint?
- How important an influence is it on the change process (and when)?
- What underlying factors does it depend upon in turn?

This highlights that any force-field analysis is dependent on many assumptions, many of which are implicit. A more successful and less subjective analysis will have brought to the surface, shared and agreed these implicit assumptions.

A number of pitfalls need to be avoided in the use of force-field analysis for strategic project management, which include:

- focusing primarily on tangible, as opposed to less tangible, implementation forces;
- missing out major constraints because the team wishes to paint an ideal rather than a realistic picture of the change (we return to these issues in a moment);
- failing to identify a 'stopper', that is, a change which has such a powerful impact that it is likely to stop the change in its tracks. Stoppers should be drawn either as a thick black arrow or, alternatively, as an arrow which goes right to the bottom of the force-field analysis and off the page. (This assumes that you are using the vertical format for force-field analysis.)

A stopper can be defined as an influence or change which will effectively put an end to the initiative either through direct confrontation or passive resistance. Initiatives may fail because of 'limpet management' – just as one constraint is loosened another in effect reasserts itself. Also, there may be cases where a specific enabling force can be made strong and prove decisive in moving the change forward. This kind of force may be described as an 'unblocker' and can be drawn as a very long (or thick) positive line upwards on the force-field picture.

There may also be instances where a negative and constraining force can be flipped over to make a positive force, and in so doing transform the picture. For instance, if an influential stakeholder (who is currently negative) can be turned around in favour of the change, this can provide a major driver in the strategic project's progress. To prioritize which force to focus on, begin with the most presently limiting or constraining factor. This is the first key tenet of the Theory of Constraints (Goldratt 1990).

A useful tip is to look beyond the existing enabling forces to the context of the project itself. Within that context, ask yourself whether there are some latent enablers which, if brought to the surface, could be used to unlock organizational energy. For example, if staff feel over-burdened with work then a restructuring which is geared not so much to reducing cuts but to reducing organizational stress and strain is likely to be most gratefully received.

Using a pull strategy to get staff's ideas on future organizational processes in advance of a restructuring might flush out some really good ideas for simplification. It might also get staff on board as they see these ideas already incorporated in the plans for the new structure.

This is the second, major tenet of the Theory of Constraints, which is that within any really difficult situation there is buried somewhere within it some latent, naturally enabling force.

It may be helpful to use the following checklist to brainstorm the enabling or constraining force. This is structured as five categories (based on Peters and Waterman's [1982] original seven S's):

- strategy
- structure
- style
- skills
- systems.

Strategy
- Do we have a simple and clear objective?
- Is this supported by a coherent plan?
- Does this plan fully address the key implementation issues?

Structure

- Are the roles of the key implementers sufficiently clear and well communicated?
- Have they got sufficient power and influence to achieve results?
- Does the project impact on a number of business and/or functional areas? If so, will it be effectively co-ordinated?

Style

- Does the project require new behaviours in the organization or changing old behaviours? If so, will these behaviour shifts materialize?
- Is there sufficient commitment to the project, and will this commitment be sustained?
- Does the project team itself have appropriate leadership and members – with suitable interpersonal and political skills, not just technical?

Skills

- Does the project require new skills within the organization, and is this being effectively addressed?
- Does the project develop skills which may in turn generate or enable future strategic development opportunities to be detected and exploited?
- Does the project create skills bottlenecks which might either throw other projects off their critical paths, or create internal conflict, or both?

Systems and Resources

- Does the project require new systems or processes to achieve success, and will this infrastructure be in place?
- Does the project require significant changes to existing systems or processes and are key stakeholders (the guardians of these systems) on board with all of these changes?
- Are there actually sufficient resources?

CASE STUDY: STRATEGIC PROJECT FOR AN MBA PROGRAMME

A successful MBA programme which focused on part-time study began to explore new ways of reaching its students and to achieve substantial growth. The MBA board seized on the idea of launching a distance learning MBA. Using the above checklist, a number of enabling and constraining forces were identified. The enablers were:

- strategy – pressure from the top business school management to expand and failure of other strategic growth initiatives.

The constraints were:

- skills – skills in preparing distance learning materials are under-developed;
- systems and resources – systems and processes currently don't exist, and the budget is woefully inadequate to achieve success.

The force-field picture for this project is shown in Figure 4.5. Fortunately, this project was abandoned (but this was only after market research had been conducted. Often it pays to do the implementation analysis before doing expensive, external analysis.) A better option was then floated which survived the force-field test much more effectively.

Let us now summarize some of the key do's and don'ts of force-field analysis. Do's include:

- brainstorm all the key tangible and less tangible forces impacting on the strategic development process;
- include key forces drawn from your FT analysis (see our last chapter), and the stakeholder analysis (coming in our next session);
- test your judgements by questioning why a force is strong or weak by reference to the strategic implementation objective and by thinking about its constraints within the overall process;
- do the initial force-field analysis on an 'as is' basis – show the warts and be prepared to be provocative;
- where a major constraint exists, draw this in as a stopper (that is as a very long downward arrow) to draw attention to its role in braking the change process;
- use the tool throughout the strategic project management process as the forces will change over time;
- use the force-field for both different subprojects or activities (as the degree of difficulty will vary) and for separate phases of project implementation;
- involve others to test and provide input to the analysis.

Don'ts include:

- don't confuse force-field analysis with simple cost-benefit analysis. Benefits should only be included as a force if they are perceived by and owned by key stakeholders. Often, these benefits are in the eye of the programme initiator and are neutral in driving the change process forward;
- don't use force-field analysis as a tool just to describe the current position. Force-field analysis should be used actively to reshape your

FIGURE 4.5: Force-field analysis – distance MBA

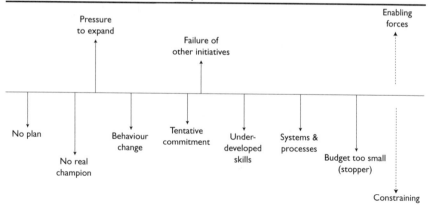

implementation plan to optimize the effect of enabling forces and to neutralize or flip-over the constraining forces to become enablers.

■ don't get bogged down in attempts to evaluate the forces precisely – force-field analysis is a soft science.

Force-field analysis can be used in a number of ways. First, it can be used very formally, either within a team or individually. Or, it can be used intuitively – in effect as a form of organizational radar. In fact, having used force-field analysis formally a number of times enables it to become unconscious. However, there are situations when you really do need to revert to a formal picture, if only to get a clearer mirror of your own intuitions.

Stakeholder analysis

Stakeholder analysis is another major tool for analysing the implementation difficulty of strategic projects (Piercey 1989 and Grundy 1993).

Having already defined stakeholder analysis at the end of chapter 2 (and given a preliminary analysis using the stakeholder periscope), we can now focus on its use. The steps for performing stakeholder analysis are:

■ First, identify who you believe the key stakeholders are at any phase of the process, possibly using the stakeholder periscope.

■ Second, evaluate whether these stakeholders have high, medium or low influence on the issue in question. You need to abstract this from their influence generally in the organization.

■ Third, evaluate whether, at the current time, they are for the project, against it, or idling in neutral.

In order to estimate where a stakeholder is positioned approximately, you will need to see the world from that particular stakeholder's perspective. From experience over the years we have found that the best way to convey this is to ask managers to have in effect an out-of-body experience – but not quite literally, of course.

This involves not merely trying to sense the surface attitudes of stakeholders about a particular issue but also the deeper-seated emotions, focus, anxieties and even prejudices.

We will reserve a more detailed treatment of how to do this in our later chapter 7 on people and behaviour. In this chapter we will illustrate how a specific stakeholder's agenda can be mapped using stakeholder agenda analysis, which is another application of force-field analysis.

From experience, managers who literally do take the perspective that 'I am the stakeholder' are typically at least 50 per cent more accurate in their analysis.

The above-mentioned three steps give a good first cut of the pattern of stakeholders. The cluster of stakeholders depicted on a stakeholder grid (see Figure 4.6) should then be assessed to see what the overall picture looks like, particularly:

- Is the project an easy bet?
- Is it highlighting a long slog?
- Does this seem like Mission Impossible?

For instance, if most of the stakeholders are clustered towards the bottom part of the stakeholder grid, then you clearly have a Mission Impossible on your hands, unless the stakeholders can be repositioned.

Another difficult configuration is where there is an equal number of supporting stakeholders with lower influence (i.e., in the north-west of the picture) to those against but having higher influence (in the south-east). Once again, this means that the strategic project is likely to experience major implementation difficulties.

Finally, where you have a large number of stakeholders floating in neutral in the middle of the picture, this very neutrality can present major problems due to organizational inertia.

It is a particularly useful idea to position yourself on the stakeholder grid, especially if you are the project manager. This helps you to reexamine your own position and underlying agendas, which may be mixed.

Following your tentative, first-cut analysis you should then move on to the next phase:

- First, can new stakeholders be brought into play to shift the balance of influence or can existing players be withdrawn in some way or be subtly distracted?

FIGURE 4.6: Stakeholder analysis

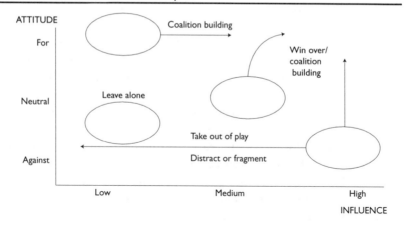

- Second, is it possible to boost the influence of stakeholders who are currently in favour of the project?
- Third, is it possible to reduce the influence of any antagonistic stakeholders?
- Fourth, can coalitions of stakeholders in favour be achieved so as to strengthen their combined influence?
- Fifth, can coalitions of stakeholders antagonistic to the project be prevented?
- Sixth, can the project change itself, in appearance or in substance, to be reformulated to diffuse hostility to it?
- Seventh, are there possibilities of bringing on board any negative stakeholders by allowing them a role or in incorporating one or more of their prized ideas?
- Eighth, is the pattern of influence of stakeholders sufficiently hostile for the project to warrant its redefinition?

Once you have done the stakeholder analysis, it may well be worthwhile revisiting the force-field analysis to either introduce one or more new forces, or to revise earlier views. The force-field analysis will now incorporate all of the enabling and constraining forces, including some of the more political and the less tangible ones.

Often a particular stakeholder may be difficult to position. This may be because his/her agendas might be complex. It is quite common to find that it is only one specific blocker which has made a stakeholder into an influential antagonist.

Where there are very large numbers of stakeholders at play on a particular issue, this may invite some simplification of the project. For instance, the project may need to be refined, perhaps even stopped and then restarted, in order to resolve an organizational mess.

In order to use stakeholder analysis effectively you may need to set some process arrangements in place where a team project is involved. First, the analysis may be usefully performed in a workshop environment so as to give the analysis a reflective or learning feel. This will help to integrate managers' thinking on a key project. It may also be useful to devise code-words for key stakeholders in order to make the outputs from this change tool feel safe. On several occasions managers have decided to adopt nicknames for the key players. An element of humour will help to diffuse the potential seriousness of performing stakeholder analysis.

So far we have used stakeholder analysis in a relatively static manner. But obviously key stakeholders are likely to shift over time – and early support for the project may therefore evaporate. A number of things need to be anticipated:

- senior managers' support is likely to be very sensitive to the perceived ongoing success of the strategic project as it evolves. Any signs of failure are likely to be accompanied by suddenly diminishing support;
- new stakeholders may enter the scene, and others might disappear;
- certain stakeholders may increase or even decrease in influence;
- where the project changes in its scope or in its focus significantly, stakeholders will then change their positions.
- stakeholders' own agendas might change due to external factors outside this particular project. For example, other projects might distract them or result in a reprioritization of agendas and of this project in particular.

Due to the above it may be necessary to review stakeholder positions at least several times during the lifetime of the project.

FIGURE 4.7: Stakeholder attitude and influence-over-time curves

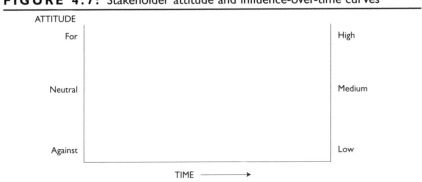

As a final note, obviously the stakeholder tool should not be used for covert personal and political purposes. Its purpose is to help get things done in organizations and not to obtain personal advantage for its own sake.

For further analysis it is possible to examine how stakeholders may change over time by plotting their attitude over time (ranging from 'against' through to 'for') and their influence over time (ranging from 'for' through to 'against'). This is depicted in Figure 4.7.

Also, it is possible to prioritize which stakeholders to focus on by plotting their level of influence on this issue and your degree of influence over them.

In Figure 4.7 two axes are plotted. Note that one should try to evolve strategies for gaining more influence over those stakeholders who are most influential and who one currently has least influence over.

In Figure 4.8 is a force-field analysis-type picture used to represent the turn-ons and turn-offs within a single stakeholder's agenda. This is not only useful to do for others but also for yourself.

As a final note, each stakeholder is not to be thought of in isolation. Frequently, one stakeholder's positioning is interdependent upon the position of others. This can be drawn out by clustering independent stakeholders on a flipchart and then drawing lines between those who are most interdependent with one another.

How-how and activity analysis

So far we have been working at the project level. Whilst we may have thought in broad terms about a project's overall implementation, this may well not have been broken down into detailed actions. This task can be achieved by how-how analysis. This is sometimes known as 'work

FIGURE 4.8: Stakeholder agenda analysis of a new job

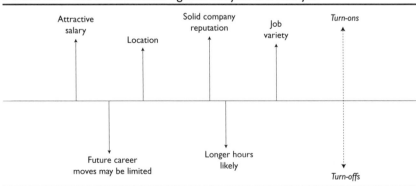

breakdown' – a distasteful term as it sounds rather mechanistic. This might also fail to imply that one needs to be highly imaginative in detecting all the tasks needed to achieve the result, as opposed to the just more obvious activities.

How-how analysis works by starting off with the core task, such as to turn around a business (see Figure 4.9). This begins at the left-hand side of the page. By working from left to right, one repeatedly asks the question, 'How is that particular task to be achieved?'

This produces more and more detail until a complete listing of activities is created. Whilst at this stage these activities are not phased over time, this should give a really detailed idea of project activities.

With how-how analysis it is crucial to expand the activities to those softer areas which may also be required to achieve the required result. This might entail training or other support for behavioural or mind-set change.

Once the major activities have been generated, the next stage is to begin to think about their phasing over time. This can be done in either of two ways:

- with a project with relatively few interdependencies in the sequencing of activities one can go directly to a Gantt chart – which displays activities over particular times;
- with a project where there are likely to be extensive interdependencies in the sequencing of activities one might seek instead to develop the activity network.

FIGURE 4.9: How-how analysis

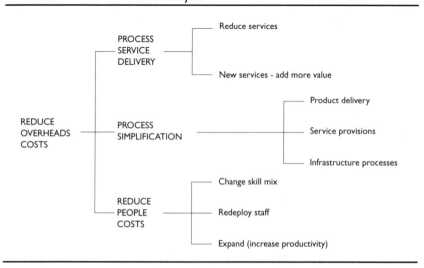

A Gantt chart (named after its creator) is shown in Figure 4.10 – for the business turnaround project which was plotted earlier. Note that many of the activities occur in parallel with one another.

Gantt analysis is normally very easy to use. Even where there might be a complex underlying network of opportunities it may still be worthwhile doing a quick Gantt chart to get a feel for when things may need to happen by.

Once again, we should not see Gantt analysis as a mechanistic process, for there are frequently many possible phasings of these activities. Even where there are well-trodden ways of doing particular kinds of projects, such as clinical research projects in the pharmaceutical industry, there are still often choices as to when activities can begin and in what order.

For example, at the point of writing this particular book, there had been no formal publishing contract, although there was a publisher who wished to publish the book in principle). Normally, one would not entertain moving beyond chapter 1 without getting a publisher's advance, but because of a confidence in the need for this book and a wish to shorten timescales, it was decided to bring forward writing the core of the book. This reduced timescales to publication by around three months.

Interestingly, the book was written in about the same length of time that the publisher turns the completed draft into the final thing – something which has always puzzled us. Have most publishers applied the techniques of project management and simplifying business processes as effectively as they might?

This also raises the interesting issue of strategic project management as a way of increasing time-based competitive advantage (Stalk 1990). In most industries it is becoming increasingly important to accelerate the implementation of business strategies.

FIGURE 4.10: Gantt chart – business turnaround

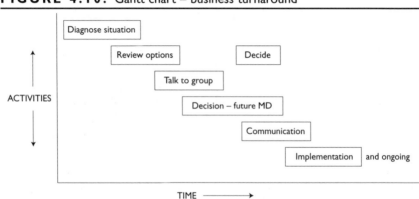

For example, with the advance of Internet-based marketing, many companies are in danger of being left behind in the race to revolutionize communication with, and transactions between, buyers electronically. Here, being six months late to market may well mean the difference between spectacular successes and abject failure. As such, it is crucial to parallel-work as many activities as practical in order to accelerate implementation.

To illustrate, one senior Tesco manager once said, 'What we are trying to achieve in two weeks is what we and others used to achieve in three to six months.'

Projects, as we have already defined them, are all about achieving a pretargeted result in a specific time and at a specific cost. It is therefore imperative to see what we can do (through Gantt chart analysis, the activity network and the critical path) to accelerate these.

A very solid rule of thumb which might help to achieve this is try to do activities sooner than you might otherwise think of doing. This applies especially to activities which are more likely to be on the critical path and those which are most constraining.

A practical example of this was when one of the authors had a Japanese client, TDK in Luxembourg, some years ago. After the end of the first workshop he had to shake hands with the key stakeholders in the client (rather than just disappear at the end). This took considerable time, and he well remembers that by the time he caught a taxi to the airport he was running very late. The taxi, an elderly Mercedes, was driven by an even more elderly Belgian driver. The driver seemed fixed on going 40 miles per hour.

Anyway, he missed the plane, and had to wait four hours for the next flight to Stansted London. During that time he became tired, and it was just around that period that he believes he contracted the flu.

The next time he went to Luxembourg he therefore determined to project manage saying goodbye to people. This meant that if he could, he would shake hands with the senior managers around lunchtime so that he could make a very fast getaway.

Besides parallel working activities and accelerating the start of activities, it is also perhaps possible to split the activity up into at least two phases. The most obvious phases are planning and implementation. For example, even if you cannot do an activity now, you can certainly create a plan for it.

As a practical example, one of the authors recently returned from Colombia to the UK. On his journey out he had approximately 90 minutes to pack everything – workshop materials, clothes, CDs, personal things, diary, phone, etc. This could easily have taken him 2-and-a-half hours to do. He knew he was time-constrained so spent ten minutes just doing a checklist of things he needed, grouped according to where they would be in the house. He then ordered these groupings so he would not be dashing around the house. He completed the whole exercise in around 50 minutes. He saved around 60 per cent of the time he would normally have spent.

At this point, Laura Brown would like to add a quick commentary:

> Tony is not kidding when he says he project-manages virtually every-thing. It is truly awesome and I have learnt a lot about being really, really focused. But at the same time this also means not losing sight of the big picture. Tony really does not like losing sight of this big picture by getting absorbed in very specific (and not so important) details, the rabbit holes. He even told me that in his 50 minutes he project-managed a crucial ten minutes of quality time saying goodbye to me!

Accelerating activities works up to a point but only provided that the quality of the process can be maintained. For example, in the above project (going to Colombia), because he was interrupted halfway through his 50 minutes he forgot to transfer to his travel bag £60 of phonecards that he had bought especially for the journey. This caused not only extra cost but no end of problems in getting through to the UK from Colombia when he arrived there.

Accelerating projects seems therefore to behave as follows. Up to a certain point there are some very real cost savings (due to time and resource saved) as you accelerate activities. But after that point, the costs go up, sometimes quite disproportionately, as errors are made and costs are generated elsewhere or later, or because resources get in the way of each other. Another rule is: if you accelerate, then you really must simplify.

Another possibility in activity analysis is delay. Whilst this may not be an obvious strategy sometimes it may be wise to delay an activity if there are simply too many activities happening at once. When you try to do a number of things simultaneously, efficiency quickly declines after a certain point.

If, therefore, particular activities do not need to be done at the present time, a temporary delay may actually help to accelerate other activities disproportionately.

Indeed, there is invariably a good deal more flexibility within the activity analysis of when things need to get done by. The major con-straining factors are not so much performing the activities but the availability of data, decisions being made, resources being made actually available and sheer physical constraints. These factors are most con-straining for the strategic project rather than necessarily the activities themselves. For example, physical constraints rendered it impossible to go back from Colombia to get the telephone cards in order to communicate quickly and cheaply with the UK. This means one needs to anticipate the most critical constraints whilst performing activity analysis and focus on those, rather than necessarily working on refining an exact activity phase.

Another word from Laura Brown:

> Tony is right about those physical constraints. When he was in Colombia it was virtually impossible to get in contact with him. As he could not easily ring me (without spending £4 a minute), I tried to ring him. The only person I could get through to was a Spanish-speaking (only) receptionist. At the time I was suffering some major disruptions at work and needed to talk to Tony – as a matter of some not insignificant urgency.

Critical path analysis (and uncertainty)

Critical path analysis is at the very centre of traditional project management. Whilst being absolutely imperative for complex, technical projects, it needs to be set in context amongst the other tools in its degree of importance when considering a strategic project. Whilst there is, invariably a real critical path for a strategic project, this is frequently likely to crystallize during the project rather than before it.

If you have already done an approximate Gantt chart this will give you some strong clues to the likely structure of the network of activities of the project. Essentially, you will need to decide which activity needs to be done and in what order. So, for each activity you need to work out which activities had to have been completed already in order for this activity to be started. Quite quickly a chain or network of activities can

FIGURE 4.11: Urgency-importance grid

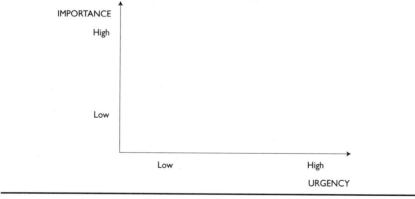

be built up. One useful way of doing this is to write each activity on a Post-it note and then simply placed in the appropriate order on a flipchart. Then, once you have the order sorted out, draw in the arrows to represent the activity path through the activity network.

Alternatively, the Post-it notes can be arranged on an urgency–importance grid (see Figure 4.11), which is another classic, quick and dirty way for prioritizing activities. With this grid it is important to avoid overfocusing on the most urgent at the expense of the most important. The grid can also help you in time management. For example, spend 80 per cent of your time on the few, really important projects, focusing on them all at once. Then spend the remaining 20 per cent of your time (on dedicated days or half-days) to specialize in clearing the less important projects before they become too urgent and distracting.

Using Post-it notes is a good way of testing one's assumptions about the relative order in which the key activities need to be carried out. Using this process one is often able to parallel work activities which might previously have been assumed were strictly sequential, for instance. Figure 4.12 shows a network of activities for a business turn-around plan.

Turning to the critical path of the project, it is necessary to identify that sequence of activities which, if subject to any delay at all, will delay the whole project itself (i.e., its critical path). This is actually what the critical path really is. So, for example, in Figure 4.12 we now see the duration of activities and that path A is therefore the critical path.

With strategic projects (as opposed to more technical ones), it is less obvious that not only which sequence of activities is the critical path

FIGURE 4.12: Project network – a business turnaround

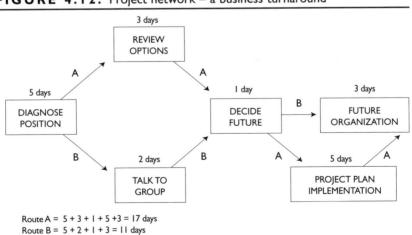

Route A = 5 + 3 + 1 + 5 +3 = 17 days
Route B = 5 + 2 + 1 + 3 = 11 days

but also how determinate this path will be. In real life the critical path will shift considerably for a strategic project, operating in an incremental and often turbulent organizational environment.

Whilst it is useful to have some view as to what the most likely critical path is for a strategic project, it is equally important to:

- monitor the key uncertainties,
- identify the most constraining factors of data, decisions, resource and physical constraints,
- be aware of whether any activities can be accelerated internally to make up for the delay,
- be aware of whether deploying additional resources (possibly out-sourced) can be brought in, in order to accelerate key activities,
- be aware of which activities frequently take longer than assumed – especially softer activities like shifting mind-set and behaviours.

This makes critical path analysis a much more flexible process for strategic projects. Indeed, it becomes just as much a soft, intuitive process as much as an analytical process.

In order to assess the relative difficulty of specific activities, it may well be useful to draw up a mini-force-field analysis to get a better feel for this. This will help to identify those activities which may require either more time, more resources or simply more thinking through (bringing us back once more to the cunning plan).

Moving now onto uncertainty, our classic technique for managing and monitoring this is Mitroff's uncertainty grid (see Figure 4.13). This grid can be used for a variety of strategic projects, including:

- new market entry and new products,
- acquisitions and alliances,
- business process reengineering,
- organizational restructuring and change.

FIGURE 4.13: Uncertainty-importance grid

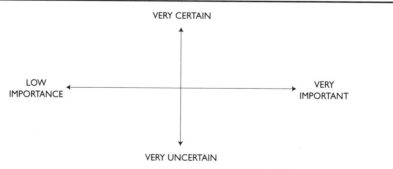

We will return to the grid in chapter 5 on strategic project evaluation.

The grid is used specifically for surfacing the assumptions underlying the particular activity. The grid plots the degree of importance horizontally against degree of uncertainty vertically. Once again, use Post-it notes to represent the key assumptions and then position them on the grid.

Probably the majority of your chosen assumptions will end up between the centre and the right of the grid – that is from medium to high importance. This is not a problem as long as you do capture some of the assumptions which are of lower importance. Quite frequently these lower importance assumptions increase in importance either as you think harder about their implications for the activity or just as they shift during the project.

Not only might the assumptions shift from left to right, but they are also likely to move from top to bottom as uncertainty increases. The most dangerous assumptions are obviously in the south-east: both most important and most uncertain.

In defining your assumptions the usual convention is to think of the world as 'going right'. In other words, these are the assumptions which need to be fulfilled in order for project success to be successful. From experience, many managers seem to find working with assumptions like this surprisingly difficult. To some extent this is due to the in-built optimism that managers have a culture of 'before it goes wrong, our only assumption is that it will go right'. This seems also coupled with the phenomenon once described as the Nietzsche Syndrome, or the will to power. That is, if it goes wrong we will just get on and fix it. Nietzsche was a famous German philosopher who focused on mental strength as a source of power.

Probably Mitroff's most practical grid dates back to the 1960s when sociologists were keen on examining taken-for-granted assumptions. These taken-for-granted assumptions give one a sense of a coherent social reality. Challenging assumptions can be a strenuous process and thus not in keeping with normal management activity which focuses principally on getting things done, as opposed to thinking about what things should be done and how (or helicopter/strategic thinking).

Returning now to activity analysis, activities which have a heavy concentration of assumptions in the danger zone (or south-east of the uncertainty–importance grid) are very likely to suffer:

- delays,
- uneven delivery of results,
- additional costs,
- knock-on difficulties onto other activities or even other projects.

The uncertainty grid helps to identify the really hot-spot activities throughout the project, enabling one to helicopter over it.

The uncertainty grid can be used to check the robustness of the critical path analysis. For example, what happens to the critical path if hot-spot activities exceed their projected durations by 20 per cent or 30 per cent? This enables almost certain blockages to be foreseen, along with their knock-on effects.

Clearly, only a foolish project manager would operate with no slack to accommodate for activity overruns. It is essential, one way or another, to build in some oxygen, or float, to the project. Float is defined as the amount of time allowed for overrun of activities.

This float can be built in either as a final activity to the project (explicitly), or by particular generous time allowances for one or more activities. Another approach is to deliberately front-load the time pressure on early stage activities so that should slippage occur then you are still actually on schedule. Minor apparent slippage actually has the effect of stimulating concentration and effort which, if it is not present at the early stages of a project, is hardly likely to be there at the later stages.

It is wise to invariably practise this approach of front-end loading when running strategic projects. This means that if activities extend or if new activities occur then one has some time resource.

Tighter targeting of time for activities seems to have a number of effects, which are very evident when running workshops, namely:

- set-up time (getting started) is much reduced;
- talking around more peripheral issues is also minimized;
- managers are more likely to devise a process to get to their targeted result;
- they will be much more conscious of time.

If one allows deliberately more time for a project activity then there is an opposite result. Not only this, but it is almost incredible how wasteful managers can be if given luxurious time targets.

For example, one workshop facilitator mistakenly gave a team not 45 minutes to achieve a task but an hour and a quarter. After about 15 minutes (one-third through the activity), hardly anything had been accomplished. In fact, the managers kept drinking coffee for five minutes. After half an hour the teams had just got started and were rambling around the issues.

When the facilitator prompted them about progress, they simply turned around and said 'well, we have 45 minutes to go'. The moral: if you give people a lot of time then they will take it.

CASE STUDY: CRITICAL PATH ANALYSIS AND TIME ABUSE

Another example of what came to be called time abuse in a Japanese company (as opposed to time management) was the management course I ran for 80 or so managers in Colombia. Each day's class officially started at 5pm except on Friday when it started at 6pm. The class times had been changed at short notice from 5pm so it was not too surprising that I never really got started until around 5.35 to 5.40pm.

I also observed that about five to ten minutes after I started, I always got a surge of another 15 managers. And it did not seem to matter when I started, this always happened. But I still hadn't understood what was really going on.

On the fifth evening I arrived at 6pm promptly and was surprised that no-one was there. It was like an action replay of the other nights, except lagged by an hour. I waited until 6.25pm and then started, with only 25 managers there. At 6.30 another 20 managers appeared and at 6.35 another 15 surged in. I then discovered what had been going on.

Apparently the Colombian managers were chatting with each other in the bar downstairs. That night many of them were enjoying beer. When I actually started the signal was sent down (I was teaching on the seventh floor) via the lift that the evening had started. This, I found, was a most interesting culture of 'just-too-late' management as opposed to 'just-in-time' management. Whilst I had been waiting for them, they had been waiting for me.

Clearly, if I had known this before I would have devised a rather different process to influence their behaviours, for example starting at a particular time regardless and arranging for sign-in lists to be taken in after a certain time (for instance half an hour after I had started).

However extreme, this example highlights the need to attend to the behavioural aspects of critical path management. I knew I would get some value out of my Colombian experience of a non-financial kind – here it is.)

Returning now to critical path analysis, project software (like Microsoft Project) is of some value in helping work through the potential implications of project delay. But a big word of warning is needed here. Managers who are inexperienced in project management, or those who are not so familiar with the special challenges of managing strategic projects, may become too engrossed in playing with activity spread-sheets. It is all too easy to make project management into rocket science, which it rarely needs to be.

Critical path and activity analysis leads naturally to the topic of resource management. One can produce a fabulous-looking project plan, but also one that is hopelessly unrealistic considering resource con-straints, for example, a situation where a number of activities may have been scheduled in parallel within a certain time period. At the mid-point of the activity there is a big resource gap which, if not fulfilled, could lead to a significant delay in the project. Indeed, available resource may not necessarily be constant, but undulating and changing over time, depending upon:

- holidays, sickness and training,
- new joiners or leavers,
- staff working on other projects elsewhere,
- the ability to source-in extra skills from outside, either as consultants or as subcontractors.

Again, project software (with suitably injected intelligent assumptions) should reveal any resource gaps – at least in terms of quantity (if not the quality) of skills missing.

We should now add a final note on activity and critical path analysis. Highly elaborate project plans (especially those compiled using computer software) can give the impression that everything will just happen on time. But one of the most critical assumptions is the actual release of resources to the project on a just-in-time basis. Where these resources come from a general pool of resources or from another specific department then one cannot simply assume that staff will be available to start on time. Even where they work on projects within the same department, they may be delayed in completing other projects.

So, one needs to establish checkpoints in the project plan to double-check that future resources will be available as and when assumed. This will not only highlight potential bottlenecks in advance but may also help accelerate activities in other projects so that staff can be made available as has been assumed.

Often the process of resource allocation will not go wonderfully smoothly. There will be real conflicts which may not be resolved by mere horse-trading. This problem underscores the importance of prioritizing projects effectively, and also the assessment of the costs of delay.

'Costs of delay' is a fundamental concept for strategic project management. Costs of delay can be defined as the total costs, both directly and indirectly (and tangible and less tangible) of delay in a project relative to each unit of time.

FIGURE 4.14: Project interdependency map

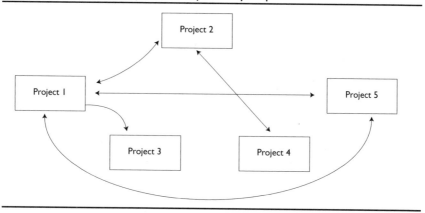

Costs of delay are well understood in at least some industries, such as in oil exploration (where delay exacts penalty charges) and in major construction projects. But other industries have yet to catch on to the importance of this concept when performing project prioritization and planning. Here the relative costs of delay are an essential measure to enable at least some organizational politics to be dissolved.

Ironically, in some industries, such as the pharmaceutical industry, the costs of delay are understood, especially for the launch of a new drug. However, an assessment of these costs does not seem to be used extensively during earlier stages of the drug's developmental cycle. Some projects are therefore starved of resource, resulting in significant delays, especially during clinical trials of new drugs.

Project interdependencies

Finally, it is crucial during the project planning phase to perform an overview of the key interdependencies which each strategic project has on others within the organization. This can be achieved by again writing down on Post-it notes the names of key projects and then clustering them on a flipchart. The strong interdependencies between projects can be drawn in as thick, bold arrows, whilst the weaker interdependencies are drawn in as dotted arrows. This process was used by the London Metropolitan Police to map out the interdependencies between projects to implement its Organization and People Strategy. An example of a project interdependency map is illustrated in Figure 4.14.

Conclusion

Developing project strategy and plans can be a relatively complex process, even once the project's overall scope has been defined. This phase of strategic project management necessitates drawing together traditional techniques of project management (such as activity and critical path analysis) with the more strategic techniques of AID analysis, force-field analysis, stakeholder analysis and the uncertainty grid.

We have now seen how strategic project management is very far from being analytically straightforward, even when deploying the additional techniques which have been run through.

To perform a more detailed project evaluation, however, additional techniques from scenario development and from finance and shareholder value theory are needed.

References

Goldratt, E.M. (1990) *Theory of Constraints*, Massachusetts: North River Press.

Grundy, A.N. (1993) *Implementing Strategic Change*, Kogan Page.

Lewin, K. (1935) *A Dynamic Theory of Personality*, McGraw Book Company.

Mitroff, I. and Linstone, H.A. (1993) *The Unbounded Mind*, Oxford University Press.

Peters, T and Waterman, R.H. (1982) *In Search of Excellence*, New York: Harper & Row.

Piercey, N.P. (1989) 'Diagnosing and Solving Implementation Problems in Strategic Planning', *Journal of General Management* 15(1):19–38.

Stalk, E. (1990) *Competing Against Time*, New York: The Free Press.

CHAPTER FIVE

Strategic project evaluation

Introduction

Strategic projects are inevitably subject to the compounding effects of uncertainty over time. This makes it more difficult to perform an effective appraisal of them, especially in financial terms. Paradoxically, the traditional approach of finance theory has been to pretend almost that such uncertainty does not exist. By focusing almost exclusively on the need to quantify value with precision, financial theory has turned the financial appraisal of strategic projects into a ritual.

In the past, strategic management has, with certain exceptions, gone into a retreat, allowing a financial perspective to become too dominant. In this chapter we seek much closer integration of strategic and financial appraisals.

Sooner or later, most strategic projects require a considerable amount of investment, whether this is capitalized on the company's balance sheet or not. Often managers see doing the business case as a chore, especially when they have already gone past the point of no return in their minds as to whether to do it or not. Where there is a lag between making the strategic commitment and the preparation of a business case, this may put a further psychological distance between the strategic thinking and the financial analysis. This implies that both strategic and financial appraisal of projects needs to be fully integrated within a single decision-making process.

In evaluating any strategic project the decision-making process must be scrutinized. Here and in Figure 5.1 is a brief summary of the stages of a more complex project:

- Definition: define the scope and focus of the strategic investment project, including its strategic objectives and context (as seen in chapter 3).

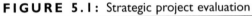

FIGURE 5.1: Strategic project evaluation

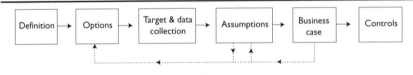

- Options: explore critical options for the decision and also any options which it forecloses (see chapter 4).
- Targeting and collecting data: target data required after a first-cut review of the kind of external and internal assumptions which will need to be made about key value drivers.
- Assumptions: collect and evaluate data through formulating the external and internal assumptions. Test these assumptions and revisit the key options and work-up contingency plans.
- Business case: present the business case and, where feasible, refine the programme to add more value at less cost and at lowest risk.
- Controls: translate the business case into monitoring measures and controls.

But before we examine this process stage by stage, we need to examine in more depth about how value is created in business as part of a system which we can call the business value system.

The business value system can be defined as the set of interdependent situations within a business which either directly or indirectly adds value to the customer and ultimately generates a net cash inflow.

The business value system provides a key link between competitive strategy and shareholder value. Besides this, it also provides a better context against which the value of strategic projects can be assessed. Whilst the business value system bears some resemblance to Porter's value chain, the latter concept is perhaps less flexible and less easily tailored to the variety of the modern business.

The business value system is also more informative than simply talking about a 'business model', as it focuses explicitly on value, on value creation as a system, and it specifically sets out to exploit interdependencies.

An example of a business value system is drawn from the football industry (see Figure 5.2). Whilst the centre of the picture revolves around traditional value-creating activities (ground takings, player acquisition and disposal, etc.), the periphery contains more novel activities. As we saw in an earlier chapter, at the project level these embrace a whole raft of new value-creating activities.

FIGURE 5.2: Business value system – football clubs

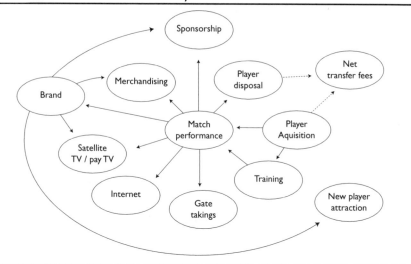

By mapping out the business value system and showing where a strategic project concept impacts both now and in the future, we can more easily understand how the project adds value.

We will return to the business value system during our later discussions of assumptions surrounding the declining base case.

Once we have worked through each stage in the appraisal process we can then examine how strategic project management techniques can be used to reappraise a business as a system of projects through the Rover case.

Stages in strategic project appraisal

In this section we go through each one of the stages in the earlier strategic project appraisal process.

Project definition

We have already explored project definition extensively within chapter 3 on strategic project diagnosis. But now we need to explore the relationship between this definition and financial appraisal.

First, if we examine the definition of the decision or programme more clearly, we soon realize there are many problems in defining the unit of analysis. Is it a particular strategic project or a more broadly based programme? Where there are many and complex interdependencies it is frequently easier and better to evaluate the financials at the level of a set of projects – the strategic project set (see Figure 5.3). (Remember that we examined key project interdependencies at the end of chapter 4.) This requires analysis of the project in relation to other areas of the business. For example, if we were examining the incremental value of a new design of supermarket trolleys, then we need to look at the project in a wider context due to close interdependencies of this project with other efforts at service differentiation.

So, if we were looking at an investment in an innovative fleet of supermarket trolleys, one would need to ask, 'What is the most appropriate unit of analysis of the investment project, or programme?'

Although the costs of a new trolley fleet could be quantified, the benefits might be less tangible, for many of these benefits relate to customer value. The effectiveness of a supermarket trolley is of importance from a customer perspective. But this importance is part of the 'total service' effect in combination with other programmes, including the level of staff service and friendliness to customers generally and the provision of other physical conveniences to support the shopping experience (including creche, cafe and hygiene facilities.

So it would be inappropriate to consider the investment in supermarket trolleys in relative isolation. Thus the project aimed at improving the total customer service package is the strategic project set.

One of the biggest traps in analysing strategic project decisions is analysing projects at an inappropriate level. Figure 5.3 suggests that you first need to question whether the project is self-contained or not. Only if

FIGURE 5.3: Defining the strategic project set

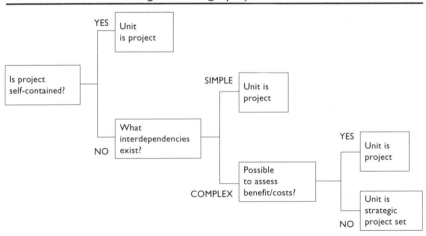

it is self-contained can you, at that point, determine that it should be analysed as a distinct project.

Next, you need to ask whether there are many interdependencies. If so, are these simple (thus enabling them to be analysed as a discrete project) or complex? If they are complex, then the final question is, 'Is it easy to do a cost/benefit analysis of them?' If it is not easy, then you should not analyse this as a separate project. Instead, you should analyse it amongst part of a higher level set of projects, or the strategic project set which we described earlier.

For instance, investment by a major brewery in a strategic change programme for its senior and middle managers was seen as being a discrete training or skills-based investment. But when this was examined more closely, the main value of the programme was realized through a number of strategic changes in the business being subsequently led by those managers rather than merely handed over to management consultants, such as business restructuring.

EXERCISE: DEFINING THE LEVEL OF EVALUATION FOR A STRATEGIC PROJECT

Choose one strategic project you are involved in or have been involved with in the past year.
1   Is the project relatively self-contained or not?
2   Are their many interdependencies which impact on its value?
3   Are these interdependencies simple or complex?
4   Are these interdependencies feasible to quantify?
5   Should we appraise the project at the level of the strategic project set or as integral with the business strategy?

Options for defining the project

As we saw in the early part of chapter 4, there are invariably many different options for defining a strategic project – all of which have major financial implications, for instance:

- Should the strategic objective be achieved through organic or through acquisitive activity?
- Is it more appropriate to move forward on the project very quickly or slowly?
- Is it worthwhile piloting its development prior to making a bigger commitment?
- Should commitment be delayed until there is a sufficiently strong implementation capability, enough resource and perhaps better timing?

- With a market-focused project, should a number of product/market routes be pursued simultaneously (thus perhaps spreading resources too thinly), or should one major project be progressed at a time?
- Can the project's key objectives be fulfilled at lower cost or with greater flexibility through an alternative option?
- If we go ahead with this particular project, what other options (present and future) does this decision foreclose?

The strategic option grid from chapter 4 is a useful way of scoping options and their potential attractiveness prior to getting involved in more detailed analysis.

Targeting and collecting data

Once you have identified one or more options you should then identify the data required in order to assess the cash flow impact of any investment in the project.

Data can be collected from a variety of sources, externally and internally.

Externally
- Data from external customers facilitates understanding whether any project or service meets the needs really important to them better than your competitors' products do.
- Consulting regulatory authorities will reveal whether your project is likely to infringe regulations.
- Investigating whether competitors are likely to be launching a competing product or service in the near future.

Internally
- What is your operational capacity likely to be over time from internal staff?
- What are levels of likely efficiency, operational flexibility and quality – again from internal staff?
- How high are unit cost levels? From financial spreadsheets and other estimations, how will these vary according to levels of activity?
- What are the skills requirements in both quantity and cost – from human resources and operations?

At some point this data needs to be converted into cash flows, but this should wait until we have formulated the key assumptions which will underpin the project.

Evaluating the assumptions

Defining the assumptions requires considerable debate and is a challenge in providing a realistic basis for a business case. For example, if we go back to the new project in the subsection on project definition, we might identify a number of key assumed/value drivers, for instance:

- the new product adds superior customer value, enabling it to sustain volumes in existing customers and increase margins (slightly);
- this enables new customers to be penetrated;
- the level of competitive rivalry is a value driver as this might increase or reduce prices.

Cost drivers also include the unit costs might be influenced by levels of activity through economies of scale, and the cost of new product development is a key cost driver.

Here a value driver can be defined as anything either externally or internally within the business that might directly or indirectly generate positive cash inflows.

A cost driver can be defined as anything either externally or internally within the business that might directly or indirectly generate negative cash outflows.

An example of a value driver is that of customer loyalty. Projects can be targeted specifically at improving customer loyalty, such as Tesco's Clubcard. An example of a cost driver is the amount of time dissipated to little benefit in management meetings. A project targeted at managing down costs of meetings would be to train managers in value-based time management, including the concept of the value over time curve (see chapter 6). To illustrate the business value system and value and cost drivers, let us look at an illustration of certain strategic projects on a major theme park, Alton Towers.

CASE STUDY: ALTON TOWERS

In the early 1990s Alton Towers, a major UK theme park, launched a major new attraction, the Nemesis. Nemesis was a costly, multi-million pound ride which catapulted its riders to speeds of over 60 mph through a gorge.

The ride proved so popular that it produced queue waiting times of up to two hours. It even skewed demand in the park away from existing rides.

A more modest ride, say at half the cost, might have produced little of these effects, highlighting the need to achieve a critical mass not only for this particular project but for projects generally. On top of this, Alton Towers revenues in total actually increased – even during the very deep recession of the early 1990s. Whilst its base case would inevitably have been one of decline, the ride had dual benefits of repositioning Alton Towers as a world-class theme park and protecting the park against the recession.

As time moved on, Alton Towers needed another ride to reinforce its strategy and to satisfy the demand for even more exciting experiences. In the late 1990s, the Oblivion opened. Oblivion involved a sheer drop (again at up to speeds of 60 mph) and then a journey with three gravities of weight through a terrifying tunnel in pitch black.

Alton Towers drew even bigger crowds. Whilst Nemesis continued to draw the customers, Oblivion attracted existing customers who might otherwise have tired of riding Nemesis time and time again.

These two major projects at Alton Towers highlight the need to look at project evaluation in a combined strategic and financial context – linked with an appreciation of critical mass and also of the base investment case – which may frequently be in decline.

Frequently, business cases omit or take for granted many of the implicit external assumptions. Although incremental sales volumes, prices and margins are invariably spelt out, things like competitive behaviour and customer value are less thoroughly examined.

Questions which help to test out the external assumptions for a strategic project are related to the competitive environment, and customers and market trends

The following questions give managers checklists for evaluating any kind of strategic project.

The competitive environment (for externally facing projects)

- What assumptions about the competitive environment are implied by projected volumes, prices and margins? How do these change over the life-cycle?
- How might specific competitors be either addressing the same opportunity already or might they be able to respond quickly to your move?

Customers and market trends

- How do customers perceive the value of any end product or service upon which the opportunity depends? Consider perceived image, cost savings, risk levels.

■ How important is this value creation within the customer's own business value system, and what interdependencies is this contingent upon?

■ How powerful are customers relative to the company and to what extent is the additional value created harvested by customers vs the company?

■ In addition you need to consider any life-cycle effects associated with market change for any externally facing projects.

EXERCISE: THE EXTERNAL EVALUATION OF A STRATEGIC PROJECT

Choose one project which you are currently considering undertaking.

1   What do the checklists on the competitive environment and on customers and market trends tell you?
2   What key questions now remain to be answered about these external aspects?
3   How can you answer these questions with appropriate research within least time and cost?

To test the internal assumptions underpinning a strategic project the following questions should be asked. These deal with investment, costs and implementation assumptions.

Investment-linked assumptions

■ What capacity levels are assumed and are these assessed in relation to the operating cycle over a whole annual period?

■ What unforseen areas of investment may be required either of a future or indirect nature (e.g., expansion of office space) not currently included in 'incremental' cashflows?

■ What investment is implicitly required by customers (either in capital or non-capital)? What is the perceived return/risk to them and over what timescales? Consider here the investment required to switch sources of supply.

■ What hurdle rate of return is appropriate for this project?

Examining the last question more closely, this does not mean that the cost of capital (which is the cost of funds from shareholders and other long-term sources) should be increased where the risk specific to a project appears to be high. This riskiness should be incorporated into the uncertainty analysis and sensitivity analysis, otherwise there is a danger of double-counting risk. For if a project's cash flows are discounted at a project-specific risk premium and then also subjected to a testing sensitivity analysis, the resultant financial sensitivities will have been, in effect, adjusted for risk twice.

The cost of capital will be more important where cash inflows from investment decisions are relatively long-term (particularly over five years) and competitors might have access to cheaper sources of capital (for example, if they are based in Germany or Japan).

For projects with shorter time horizons and paybacks, other issues such as uncertainty, intangibles and interdependencies probably will be much more important.

Cost assumptions

■ How have incremental costs been defined and how do cost apportionments incorporate a fair allowance for direct and indirect resources absorbed by the activity?

■ What further technical breakthroughs are assumed in order to support assumed levels of productivity?

■ What are the likely effects of reducing unit cost through gaining assumed economies of scale? To what extent are unit costs increased if volumes are significantly less than 'most likely' assumptions?

TABLE 5.1: Cash inflows and outflows for a new product

	Year 0 £'000	Year 1 £'000	Year 2 £'000	Year 3 £'000	
Cash inflows – revenues					
Extra sales volume: existing customers		750	750	750	
Extra sales volume: new customers		150	250	400	
Less sales volume from old product withdrawn		(650)	(600)	(550)	
Total inflows (1)		250	400	600	= 1250
Cash outflows – costs					
Extra cost of sales		530	580	670	
Less cost of sales of old product withdrawn		(520)	(480)	(440)	
Product launch costs	350				
Total outflows (2)	350	10	100	230	= 690
Net cash inflows/ (outflows) 1 – 2	(350)	240	300	370	
Cumulative cash inflow/outflow	(350)	(110)	190	560	= 560

In using discounted cash flow, future cash flows are adjusted for the cost of capital to give a present equivalent. After deducting the outlay, this gives a measure of value added by the project, or its net present value (NPV).

Implementation assumptions

- Are timescales for implementation realistic?
- Are there adequate operational resources to implement the project, especially where this relies upon scarce management and technical skills?
- Is the area of opportunity one where the organization and key individuals have both the capability, the commitment and, where relevant, the appropriate culture to make it a success?
- Who are the key stakeholders in the investment project, are they in favour, neutral, or intangible, and what is their relative influence?

EXERCISE: THE INTERNAL EVALUATION OF A STRATEGIC PROJECT

For the same project as earlier that you are considering undertaking, answer the following.

1   What do the internal assumption checklists tell you about the durability of the project?
2   What further data do you now need in order to formulate a robust business case?

Once the key assumptions have been defined, the next step is to begin to quantify the incremental cash flows associated with the project. A conventional process of cash flow evaluation is shown in Table 5.1.

The investment shown in Table 5.1 has a short payback period (payback occurs early in the second year), and there is a healthy return. The investment also has a most attractive 'net present value' or NPV which represents the present worth of future cash flows, having taken into account the company's cost of capital. The cost of capital is discussed in the next section.

In the following calculation we do not need to adjust the outlay for the cost of capital as it occurs now. In theory, this cash would be simply handed back to the shareholder – it has not been exposed to risk. But cash inflows at points in the future are not only worth less (because they occur at some future date) but also they are exposed to risk. Therefore the providers of finance require two compensations for risk: a risk-free return plus a return to allow for risk. Both returns are contained within the cost of capital. See Table 5.2.

TABLE 5.2: Allowing for risk

	£000	Discount factor (B)	Present value (A x B)
Time 0	(350)	$\dfrac{1}{1} = 1.10$	(350)
Year 1	240	$\dfrac{1}{(1.12)} = 0.89$	213
Year 2	300	$\dfrac{1}{(1.12)^2} = 0.80$	240
Year 3	370	$\dfrac{1}{(1.12)^2} = 0.71$	263

Net present value = 366
(assuming a cost of capital of 12 per cent)

Analysing importance and uncertainty of assumptions and project scenarios

Whilst the above illustration is a well worked through example of financial appraisal, it is only as good as the assumptions on which it is based.

One way of testing the external and internal assumptions for the project is by using Mitroff and Linstone's importance-uncertainty grid from chapter 4 (see Figure 5.4). Using this analysis grid, managers can plot key assumptions driving the value of the strategic project decision. These can be external and internal, and soft and hard assumptions.

Having selected a subset of these assumptions, these are now prioritized by using the grid. Once assumptions are carefully and skilfully defined, it is possible to debate the relative importance and uncertainty of these various assumptions, as seen in chapter 4.

FIGURE 5.4: Uncertainty-importance grid – new product launch

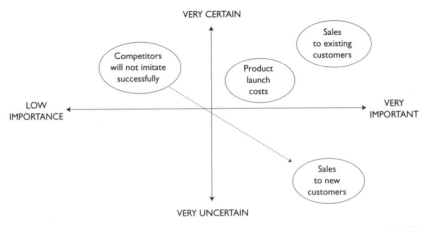

At the beginning of the investment appraisal, key assumptions are likely to be mapped in the due north and north-east quadrants. Upon testing, it is quite common to find one or more assumptions moving over to the danger zone in the south-east.

Figure 5.4 actually relates to the new product launch in Table 5.3. The extra sales volume from existing customers is very important but also considered relatively certain. Sales to new customers are considerably more uncertain but also very important, as shown in the south-east of the grid in Figure 5.4. Product launch costs are somewhat less important and also reasonably certain, shown just slightly north-east of the centre of the grid.

In Table 5.3 payback is defined as the period of time over which the initial project outlay is recouped.

In this sensitivity analysis, payback now occurs later on in Year 2 than in Table 5.1. Also, the net present value is reduced, as seen in Table 5.4, which is under half the NPV in Table 5.2.

Interestingly, a more fundamental assumption , which is implicit in managers' minds but brought out by discussion of the grid, is that competitors will not produce a cheaper and better product in Year 2.

TABLE 5.3: Sensitivity analysis for a new product launch

	Year 0 £'000	Year 1 £'000	Year 2 £'000	Year 3 £'000	
Cash inflows – revenues					
Extra sales volume: existing customers		750	675	675	
Extra sales volume: new customers		150	112	180	
Less sales volume from old product withdrawn		(650)	(525)	(455)	
Total inflows (1)		250	400	600	= 912
Cash outflows – costs					
Extra cost of sales		530	507	554	
Less cost of sales of old product withdrawn		(520)	(420)	(364)	
Product launch costs	350				
Total outflows (2)	350	10	87	190	= 637
Net cash inflows/ (outflows) 1 – 2	(350)	240	175	210	
Cumulative cash inflow/outflow	(350)	(110)	65	275	= 275

Sensitivity analysis needs to be done not merely on assumptions impacting on the more obvious value and cost drivers but also on the less obvious. In this example (which is based on the assumptions in Table 5.1), the impact of imitation of the new product in Year 2 has dramatically reduced the NPV.

TABLE 5.4: Allowing for risk

	£000	Discount factor (B)	Present value (A x B)
Time 0	(350)	$\dfrac{1}{1} = 1.10$	(350)
Year 1	(240)	$\dfrac{1}{(1.12)} = 0.89$	213
Year 2	175	$\dfrac{1}{(1.12)^2} = 0.80$	140
Year 3	210	$\dfrac{1}{(1.12)^2} = 0.71$	149

Net present value = 152
(assuming a cost of capital of 12 per cent)

In this case, the assumption is shown as beginning life just west of the product launch costs assumption (relatively certain and less important) but actually heading south-east.

The uncertainty-importance grid is therefore a vital tool for evaluating assumptions prior to undertaking key financial sensitivities on the project. This tool helps focus these sensitivities towards the critical uncertainties (for example, to new competitor entry). A 'sensitivity' is defined as being the financial impact from a change in either a value or cost driver. For example, following on from the uncertainty-importance grid, successful imitation of the new product by a competitor might well reduce prices by 10 per cent in Year 2 and Year 3, and reduce the volume sales to new customers by half. This would produce the sensitivity analysis in Table 5.3.

Strategic projects with particularly long-term horizons or which are impacted by major competitive or other environmental change, present their own challenges. This calls for a slightly more sophisticated approach, as follows.

Understanding the dynamics of uncertainty and scenarios

Here the uncertainty-importance grid needs to be accompanied by some intensive thinking about the system which drives key uncertainties for the strategic project. This can be represented as the uncertainty tunnel (see Figure 5.5). The uncertainty tunnel is depicted as a tunnel bound by constraints on what is possible within a project's environment. Essentially, uncertainty is seen as driven by unpredictable change.

In Figure 5.6 unpredictable change is explored by looking at its precursors (that is, what has affected the project previously from its environment). Secondly, managers analyse these factors either amplifying or dampening a particular unpredictable change.

FIGURE 5.5: Uncertainty tunnel

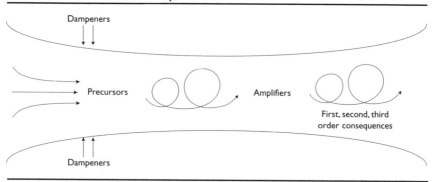

Following this analysis we then examine the immediate vs the long-term consequences of change on the project, perhaps discriminating between its first, second and third order consequences. This enables the effect of customer and company learning, and competitor responses to be brought into the equation.

Of course, there may not be a single uncertainty tunnel but more than one. For instance, if a particular type of technology begins to percolate through the larger computer system market, it may go through two phases of uncertainty:

- initial take-up by companies and application ('Future 1');
- learning about how the new systems add, dilute, or destroy value, and additional investment to develop new computer platforms ('Future 2').

In this example, the uncertainty tunnel would allow managers to build up shared mental maps of how value would be created for a strategic project. Note here the need to distinguish between not just a single future but a number of futures.

EXERCISE: USING THE UNCERTAINTY TUNNEL MODEL

Chose one project that you are contemplating.

1   What are the precursors to the project?
2   What factors might amplify uncertainty?
3   What factors might dampen uncertainty?
4   What are the potential first, second and third order consequences of a shift in the project's internal or external environment? Allow yourself to tell scenario stories at this point.

FIGURE 5.6: The effects of the declining base

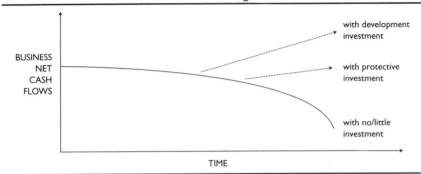

Exploring the base case

Before we leave the topic of assumptions for the strategic project we also need to explore the 'do nothing' or base case option (Grundy 1998).

The base case is what might happen without the investment decision. Traditional financial theory teaches us to evaluate incremental cashflows – 'incremental' meaning the difference between net cashflows both with and without the investment project.

A major problem with the base case is that of predicting the rate or pace of decline. This is inherently difficult to predict. Some managers may then try to shield financially suspect projects behind the argument that unless the project is implemented, the strategic and financial health of the business will be irreparably damaged. See Figure 5.6 for a classic illustration of a declining base case.

The important thing to remember with the base case is that you need to spend almost as much time thinking about the world in which one does not do the investment as the world in which one does.

The base case is reminiscent of the Alton Towers illustration earlier, where without the investment cash flows the project might well ultimately have deteriorated.

EXERCISE: EVALUATING THE BASE CASE FOR A STRATEGIC PROJECT

Choose a project where, in a 'do nothing' situation, the business revenues are in decline.

1   What is the likely pace of decline?
2   What might accelerate this pace of decline?
3   What other measures, besides incremental investment, might mitigate the decline?
4   Is the decline sufficiently cataclysmic to suggest that it may even be worthwhile exiting this business rather than investing more in it?

Returning briefly to the AID grid from chapter 4, there are interesting implications of doing vs not doing the project. Figure 5.6 shows the 'with the project case' as only marginally attractive and also relatively difficult. But the 'without the project case', the business is actually in decline (and thus has negative attractiveness), and is very difficult.

Although going ahead with the project does not look particularly wonderful on a 'with the project case' only, considering the negative base case that is avoided, it actually does become attractive. The value of this kind of project is thus protective rather than offensive.

These characterizations of value are just two of many possible examples of how projects can be segmented. For example, projects can have an 'opportunity' value – in opening up doorways to future value. Or, they might have a 'synergistic' value – along with other projects. They might also be of 'sweat' value – simply squeezing more out of the same or out of less resource. Finally, they may be of 'deliberate' or 'emergent' value – emergent value being value which was not actually anticipated but which came out of unexpected alignment.

Intangibles and interdependencies

Dealing first with intangibles, strategic projects add value only insofar as they are part of the business value system. Interdependencies thus need to be explored because they are essential in understanding how the business operates as a total competitive and financial system.

Interdependencies exist in a variety of forms. Some interdependencies are external and reflect the impact of one external assumption on one another. For example, a resurgence of economic growth may increase the size of a particular market and also attract new entrants.

Many of the internal assumptions depend upon external variables, giving rise to even more interdependencies. For instance, competitive rivalry may lead to a high incidence of price discounting and thus to lower margins.

Many of the more interesting interdependencies are those within the architecture of the business strategy itself. For instance, one product may benefit or suffer due to the introduction of a new product. FMCG companies realize this and also supermarket chains opening superstores – these companies are acutely aware of cannibalization effects. This is not so commonly appreciated in many other industries.

The analysis of interdependencies should follow on from the analysis and testing of the external and internal assumptions. Where the decision process is of a less formal nature, analysing interdependencies should be integral with the evaluation of assumptions.

EXERCISE: INTERDEPENDENCIES OF A STRATEGIC PROJECT

Choose one strategic project of your choice.

1   What are the key interdependencies between this project and other projects within the business, or other business activities generally?
2   What interdependencies are both most important and uncertain? (You may wish to use the uncertainty-importance grid at this point)
3   What would you need to do to align these interdependencies, and what might this cost?

Intangibles are one of the main curses of strategic project appraisal. For many managers, intangibles have become the 'no go' zone of financial analysis. Although these are areas of value extremely difficult to quantify in financial terms – and perhaps impossible to quantify with precision – there are invariably ways of defining intangibles better. This can be done by looking at the project from different perspectives:

- Competitive: impact on customer perceptions of value or in measurable improvement vis-à-vis competitors.
- Operational: performance improvement or flexibility of operations.
- Organizational: impact on morale and, indirectly, on motivation.
- Opportunity generation: the opportunity which might be opened up or explored as a result of the investment project.

The first step with intangibles is to ask, 'Why is the value thought to be of an intangible nature?' This may be because:

- The benefit accrues to the customer rather than directly to the company. However, there may also be indirect benefits to the company via reducing the customer switching its source of supply, or through increased orders and volume, or through increased prices, or through protection against discounts. For example, when Hewlett Packard tried to appraise the value of attaining a particular quality award, it found that most of the value came relatively indirectly and could not be harvested in a simple or direct way.
- The benefit may be of a future and essentially contingent nature. This may be contingent because a future state of the world is required to crystallize a market – this may require alignment of a credible product offering, customers recognizing the need exists, potential demand actually crystallizing. Even in this situation, your particular company needs to be credible as a supplier to generate value.
- The benefit accrues via a number of internal interdependencies with other areas of the business, or these may occur because the project is essentially part of the business infrastructure.

- The benefit comes due to the project being essentially protective or defensive in nature.

A process for dealing with intangibles is:

- to identify why the value is of an intangible nature;
- to seek possible alternative measures to help target and provide indicators of alternative measures to those of purely financial value (see Table 5.5);
- through management consensus, to compare what value managers are prepared to put on the intangible.

An example of managing intangibles can be drawn from ICI's expansion into the international seeds business in the 1980s and 1990s, with which we started this book. A number of acquisitions of family-owned seeds businesses had been made, with ICI paying significant sums for goodwill. These businesses were held at the time to have considerable intangible value, particularly:

- through providing the platform to exploit new breakthroughs in genetic technology (but what was the likelihood of this breakthrough, how would ICI capture its value in the market place – using these companies, and for how long?);
- by achieving operational synergies with the other newly acquired companies (but who would harvest these synergies, how and when?).

In the event, these intangibles proved elusive for ICI, the moral being: do not hide behind the difficulties of evaluating the intangibles.

EXERCISE: INTANGIBLES

Choose one or more area of intangibles, use Table 5.5 to examine the basis of its value.
1   What is the underlying nature of the intangible?
2   How might it be measured or how might its key indicators be monitored?
3   Ultimately, if its full potential for cash generation is realized both directly and indirectly, what might its value be worth?

We now develop a heuristic for managing intangibles. This takes us through the following stages:

- Why is the value intangible (e.g., is it future and contingent? Is it generated by value-sharing, eg with customers? Is it protective value? Is it created by synergies within the system?
- How is it created?

Table 5.5: Types of intangibles and possible measures

Types of intangibles	Related to other appraisal problems	Possible focus for measurement
Product image	Customer value	Customer views of product
Reduced customer product and service	Customer value	Customer views of costs and risks
Customer loyalty	Customer value	Estimated revenue and likelihood of switching
Protection of business	Protective investment	Monitoring incidence of existing loss of business
Spin-off opportunity	Contingent value and interdependency	Specify conditions under which opportunity arises and is harvested
Flexibility	External and internal interdependency	Specify conditions under which flexibility will add value
Cost savings elsewhere	Internal interdependency	Before and after measurement of cost drivers and of impact
Alignment of external and internal factors	External and internal interdependency	Specification of conditions under which alignment may occur and probable value

- When will it be created?
- How will it be captured?
- And by whom?
- How much value will be created, and at what cost?

Moving on from intangibles, let us now examine what should be in a business case. When someone says the words 'business case' managers often think of a weighty, detailed document with lots of hard facts and financial numbers.

But the real point of a business case is to gain more clarity about the objectives of the project, its implications for the business and particularly to expose and test the key assumptions which drive value. This can be achieved in a very succinct way, for instance by restricting the business case to a maximum of eight pages, as noted below (often less will suffice):

Format for a business case
- Executive summary (one page)
- Project definition, objectives and scope (one page)
- How the project adds value – new opportunity, tangible synergy, defensive or protective value (one page)
- Key external and internal assumptions – with an evaluation of importance and uncertainty (three pages)

- Implementation issues (one page)
- Summary financials (one page).

This brings the total length to eight pages plus detailed appendices containing technical details, detailed financial and non-financial measures and milestones, detailed financial sensitivities, detailed resource requirements – possibly another seven pages. This brings a typical case to just 15 pages.

EXERCISE: THE BUSINESS CASE

Use the above format for a business case for an existing project proposal in your business.

1   What key questions remain to be answered about the value of the project?
2   What data do you now need to answer these questions (and at least cost)?
3   What process of management reflection, learning and review would now help to refine a most robust but realistic business case?

Some practical tips on putting together a robust business case include:

- Involve a good spread of managers in project definition, option generation and data collection in a targeted way. This will ensure your assumptions get a good reality check and you identify a good range of options, implementation constraints, and begin to position your project for endorsement.
- Be disciplined in data collection. Only collect data which will help you make the critical assumptions which the project depends on. This actually means spending less time on those assumptions which are less critical, such as more minor internal costs.
- Integrate the data in a preliminary workshop to evaluate options and assumptions in a creative way. Do not lose focus in a series of meetings spread over time.
- Take the point of view of other stakeholders in the organization. Consider which assumptions are most important to them, where will their judgements differ from yours, and why. Experiment here with the 'out-of-body' experience – imagine you actually are those stakeholders: what attracts you towards or repels you away from the project?
- Do not try to obscure or conceal the project's downsides. An astute review panel will quickly identify issues which you have glossed over. Your 'out-of-body' simulation will equip you to have a balanced debate on the merits of the project.

Business cases will only add value if:

- they are clear, succinct, and written in a jargon-free style;
- they expose the most important and uncertain assumptions, and also address these both in the sensitivity analysis and via contingency planning;
- they do not fall into the trap of seeing the financial numbers as absolute measures of value but instead use these creatively. For instance, in dealing with less tangibles it may be fruitful to put an illustrative value on 'what these might be worth', so that a more balanced, overall appraisal of the project can be achieved.

We have argued throughout for the need to understand the key value drivers and to expose and challenge the key assumptions before undertaking the sensitivity analysis, as we saw in the new product launch in Table 5.3. 'Better practice' means doing very rigorous testing of those key variables which are likely to be most uncertain and most important.

It is only by working this way around that true sensitivity analysis is performed, otherwise all you end up with is insensitivity analysis – playing with the assumption set to get the right answer, such as a positive net present value (NPV), which in this case means no more than 'numbers prevent vision'.

Having worked through the appraisal process we can now illustrate this with reference to the Rover case, which is replete with lessons for evaluating strategic projects. When you are reading this case study please bear in mind the earlier checklists for external and internal assumptions.

CASE STUDY: ROVER 2000

Background and brief history

Until 1987 Rover Group was owned by the British government. Over the previous two decades Rover had seen a very large amount of government investment but had struggled to produce a profit. Rover's models were not noted for their success.

The Austin Allegro is a well-documented example of product design compromise resulting in marketing disaster. Even Rover's best-selling model, the Mini, is reputed never to have made a significant profit due to underpricing. Rover's reputation for quality was poor both at home and internationally, resulting in its marque being adversely regarded in some countries. To improve standards and to spread the burden of investment over a larger number of units, Rover forged an alliance with Honda for technology transfer.

By the late 1980s Honda had been so successful that its growth made it an unequal and dominant party in the alliance. In industry circles, Rover was said to be 'Honda's most profitable overseas operation', even though it was not under Honda's control. The relationship, although successful operationally, was described as 'The Honda Bear-hug'.

In 1988, the Thatcher Conservative government had Rover as an ongoing headache until British Aerospace (BAe), an industrial conglomerate, offered to take it off its hands. Rover Group was sold to BAe for under £200 million, and BAe managed to recoup most of its outlay by selling off its Trucks division.

Whilst BAe had attained Rover Group for free, over the next five years it had to invest in Rover Group and manage it through the most difficult recession since the 1930s. It is unlikely that BAe made significant shareholder value out of Rover.

By the early 1990s BAe itself was in serious trouble both in its civil and military aerospace operations. Its new chairman, an accountant from the financial conglomerate BTR, had no compunction but to sell Rover Group at the earliest opportunity.

BAe had agreed to hold onto the Rover Group for at least five years but in late 1993 the Rover time bomb was due to go off.

The BMW takeover

In early 1994 Rover Group was sold for approximately £806 million to BMW, snatched from under the nose of Honda. Although Honda knew the group intimately, their belated offer of around £500 million was uncompetitive, and BMW became Rover's new owners.

At 1994 Rover's business portfolio could be viewed as a bundle of strategic projects, including:

- the elderly, larger, executive car – the Rover 800;
- the more successful, midsized, executive car – the Rover 600 (built on a Honda platform);
- the smaller Rover 400 and Rover 200;
- the less fashionable, small car, the Metro;
- the Mini;
- the successful sports car – the MGF;
- the highly successful four-wheel-drive (4WD) range of Land Rover, including the Discovery;
- the technology transfer agreement with Honda.

Using the AID analysis a quick and dirty analysis of the then-Rover portfolio can be done. To counter the suggestion that this was with hindsight, earlier articles at the time (Grundy 1995, written in 1994) coincided closely with these views.

The 'difficulty' dimension here reflects both the external difficulty of achieving a successful market position and the internal difficulty of sustaining that position. We have thus tailored this dimension as 'competitive difficulty'.

Figure 5.7 represents these strategic projects.

In the highly attractive and easier north-west section of the AID, we see just two projects: the Discovery 4WD and the MGF. In the east section of the AID we see the Mini as moderately attractive and as very difficult. The Rover 600 lies at the bottom left of the grid – the costs of the technology agreement with Honda materially reducing its attractiveness to low.

The Rover 200 and 400 are positioned to the south as low attractiveness and difficult. These smaller car markets are highly competitive and Rover, once again, because of its size, found it a struggle to compete. The Rover 800 was in the south-east of the grid. Sadly, the Metro is off the page – both Mission Impossible and of negative attractiveness.

Honda's technology agreement, whilst being 'easy' was also of low attractiveness, due to their negotiating power.

When BMW acquired Rover it might have tried to renegotiate the agreement with Honda to put it on a fairer basis. Whilst Honda would have resisted this, they would have stood to gain from a continued, although more balanced, arrangement.

BMW was (according to industry sources) uninterested in continuing the relationship with Honda. This meant effectively wiping out two south-east zone strategic projects: the Rover 600 and the technology transfer agreement.

BMW continued production of the south-zone Rover 200 and Rover 400, hoping to hang on until their natural replacement cycle. It continued manufacture of the Rover 800 and the Metro right through to the late 1990s. BMW decided to gamble on replacing

FIGURE 5.7: AID analysis – Rover cars portofolio

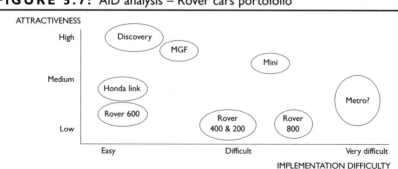

the Mini – a project that might be positioned anywhere from south-east to north-east, or even off the page to the right, depending upon BMW's marketing concept for the Mini.

If we look at Rover's business as a portfolio of strategic projects using the AID analysis, an alternative approach for BMW might have been:

- to return and develop the Discovery 4WD and the MGF into a more extensive sports car range, echoing Mazda's success in that niche but capitalizing on the MG's Britishness;
- to dispose of Rover's executive cars, the 600 and the smaller 400 and 200, to Honda, or to another volume car producer – even if this meant selling those for free or at negative value. Including the Mini marque in the disposal would have been helpful. Or BMW could have formed a separate company with Honda for this operation;
- to halt production of the Rover 800 and the Metro to help avoid future investment costs and to help upgrade the Rover marque.

But instead of being selective in its strategy, whether immediately or over a period of time, BMW took to its new offspring with enthusiasm across the piece.

By late 1999 BMW had invested over £3 billion in Rover Group. But instead of seeing a profit from Rover, Rover began to run up appalling losses. Whilst approximately half of those losses of around £908 million were attributed to the much-strengthened pound, nevertheless by stripping out these losses one would have hoped for at least some return to even begin to justify this enormous investment.

By 1999 even BMW's major shareholders, the Quandt family, began to lose patience with its management. As early as 1997 rumours surfaced in German newspapers that the family's patience was wearing thin. By 1996 BMW management realized it had a real problem on its hands and put in new management at Rover. But the integration delay had been costly and constant battles raged within BMW at very top levels as what to do with Rover.

Over the period 1996–98 there were numerous rumours that BMW would be selling Rover's volume car business to another car company, possibly to Chrysler, but no deal ever emerged.

In early 1999 the internal battle over Rover's future spilled over into the public domain. BMW's Chairman and his deputy were both fired because of their publicly visible disagreements.

By 1999 Rover's new product range was now launched aggressively onto a highly competitive market. The Rover 75 replaced the old 800 and 600 series – a welcome rationalization. But the 75 was overpriced for its traditional market segment and failed to appeal to a younger market segment in the UK. As the flagship of the new Rover portfolio, the Rover 75 appeared to be sinking rapidly.

Once again, the Rover 45 and 25 were sent out to fight in a highly competitive British and world market.

Incredibly, by the summer of 1999 the new Chairman of BMW (recruited from academia) publicly endorsed Rover Group's existing strategy. But internally – and especially from the mounting pressure from the Quandt family – the long overdue move to restructure the Rover portfolio was building.

But by late 1999 BMW management still had not bitten the bullet, although the obvious options to deal with the Rover project portfolio were to:

- dispose of the Rover 75, 45 and 25 to another car producer at either nil or at negative price (but perhaps with guarantees to protect employment at certain plants);
- to rationalize Rover and simply harvest the existing portfolio of vehicles, avoiding major new investment;
- to shut Rover down completely;
- to retain the Discovery range.

Alchemy and Phoenix – the Death and Rebirth of Rover

In March 2000 an announcement by Alchemy, a venture capital company, and BMW stunned the public, the government and all of Rover's employees. A hitherto almost unknown venture capital group was to restructure Rover Car Division.

Alchemy was to acquire Rover cars on the understanding that the costs of major redundancies would be borne by BMW and also short-term operating losses.

Alchemy was to continue production of Rover cars for the time being but at much lower volume levels. It would rationalize plants and rebadge the Rover products as 'MG'. Ultimately, it would hope for a disposal of the business once turned around.

BMW was to keep the Mini. But the big shock was BMW's decision to sell off Land Rover and the Discovery range to Ford. Once billed 'the Jewel in the Crown of Rover Group', this did appear to be a strong move, to say the least.

The disposal proceeds were to be around £1.8 billion, but it soon transpired that GM of the US would have been willing to pay £2.4 billion. Clearly, BMW felt it could no longer afford any significant connection with the Rover Group and had decided to cut its losses – at virtually any cost.

Ironically, Alchemy never actually succeeded in buying Rover Group. In Spring 2000 another consortium, Phoenix, led by Rover's former CEO John Towers, miraculously obtained sufficient finance to acquire Rover Cars. The UK government, which had been highly embarrassed by BMW's disposal and closure plans, obviously had a big influence in diverting Rover's fate. Whilst Phoenix stated its intention to maintain car production at 200,000 vehicles per annum, by June 2000 it appeared to do a U-turn on this as immediate production plans were set at 100,000 – as the 200,000 target was merely 'for the future'. Perhaps this was merely a presentational issue, but will Rover now dwindle incrementally into a black hole of non-existence?

Key Lessons from the BMW/Rover Case Study

- The assumptions made about the external environment (for example growth rates, competitive pressure, exchange rates, etc) can have a profound impact on the value of a strategic project.
- The assumptions about your own competitive position can equally have a strong bearing on this project (witness Rover's weakness as a small car company dependant upon Honda – with a UK-focused brand).
- The internal assumptions are also critical (for example, your assumed cost base, lead-times to implement the project, and organizational capability).
- The investment required to achieve the project's goals may be far more than initially anticipated (in Rover's case this was a multiple of past levels).
- Politically, strategic projects can easily run into the mire, and top management's commitment may eventually dissipate.
- The business case for acquiring Rover Group would have benefited greatly from working through the issues with the strategic project management techniques, including the assumption grid, value and cost drivers, AID analysis, force-field and stakeholder analysis, FT analysis and the uncertainty tunnel.

Conclusion

Project evaluation is not just a matter of number-crunching cash flows in order to justify investment in the project. It is a very thorough testing and in many cases a reformulation of the project strategy – and even of its scope and main focus.

Project evaluation brings together analysis of both the external and internal environment and assumptions about that environment, and translating this picture into value and cost driver analysis. Only when this is done is it feasible to begin a detailed financial appraisal.

References

Grundy, A.N. (1998) *Exploring Strategic Financial Management*, Financial Times Publishing.

Mitroff, I.I. and Linstone, H.A. (1993) *The Unbounded Mind*, Oxford University Press.

CHAPTER SIX

Strategic project mobilization, control and learning

Introduction

In this chapter we look at the steps needed to flesh-out implementation plans and how they can be monitored more effectively as follows:

- project mobilization and roles,
- project milestones and indicators,
- project learning,
- project dynamics.

To illustrate this phase of strategic project management – and also to review the total process to date a substantial case study of project managing strategic change at a very large UK insurance company, the Prudential, will be discussed.

Project mobilization and roles

Diagnosing a project, defining its strategy and evolving a project plan are merely the precursors of actually beginning a project. Projects necessitate action, and action is the vehicle for crystallizing strategy. But, unfortunately, many managers get caught up in the reflective mode of strategic or tactical thought and become incapable of taking the first steps into Action. Just like the American hero in the film *Baby Steps*, who became a guru by encouraging people just to take the very first step towards the goal, however distant, just making the very first step in a project will, given a robust strategy, probably take you, in effect, one-third to a halfway to its completion.

In fact, at one major telecommunications company one manager actually joked out loud that, 'When someone calls something "strategic" around here it means that it is never going to happen.'

For us, strategy is, and must be, about *action*. But mobilization implies some degree of commitment, and that potentially means some exposure to risk. Even if the first steps are taken in a project, energy can quickly dissipate. Continual management and monitoring of the energy is required. Alongside the energy exhibited by the project team one can begin to draw curves over time, particularly of energy-over-time (see Figure 6.1) and commitment-over-time (see Figure 6.2).

By anticipating and monitoring these variables over time it is possible to gain a greater influence over the softer aspects of the project management process.

The curves in Figure 6.1 and Figure 6.2 can be used for a variety of purposes, particularly:

- to anticipate future energy and commitment within the project,
- to monitor where the project is now,
- to reflect upon (and learn from) past experience of the project.

Interestingly, one group of managers in the pharmaceutical industry found it very difficult to identify the energy level in a project team as their everyday activity involved moving from one project to the next incessantly. The consequence of this was that they hardly had any energy at all – which was telling about their process.

Project roles are equally vital in securing the achievement of milestones. For each milestone the project plan needs to specify who will be delivering it. This may fruitfully distinguish between the individual(s) who is actually going to ensure that project activity has delivered it vs those who have provided an input to the process. It may also distinguish (in organizational terms) between:

FIGURE 6.1: Energy-over-time curve

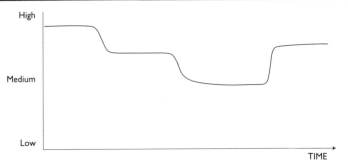

- the end users of the project,
- the project team and leader,
- the project sponsor.

An obvious point – but one which needs spelling out nevertheless – is that roles should be allocated not to who happens to be available to the project but only to those who fit project roles. Too often people get allocated a project because they happen to be around but either lack the technical, managerial or political skills, or the appropriate management style to really make the project a success.

For genuinely strategic projects it is imperative to get a main board sponsor for the project, otherwise the project may lack appropriate positioning in the organization or may lack a sufficient power and influence base.

The sponsor must not be someone who holds this role as an ornamental responsibility. He/she must have a genuine passion for the project and be visibly active in championing its cause.

Project milestones and indicators

Milestones form the key methodology for project control. A project milestone can be defined as the time by which some specific project deliverable has been achieved.

When planning a project one normally works backwards from the milestones to the present, rather than vice versa. This means that one is less inclined to indulge in spurious or dilutive activity.

Project milestones are typically a combination of quantitative and qualitative targets. For example, the authors' goal was to complete the

FIGURE 6.2: Commitment-over-time curve

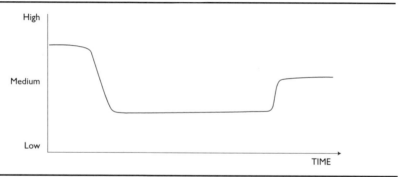

first draft of this entire book to a standard that required minimal prework by mid-September 2000.

Sadly, many managers become overly preoccupied by project milestones and neglect the 'how' of the project – its project strategy and plan. These are crucial and to some extent are more important than the project milestones themselves. Remember that the whole point of a project is to achieve the result in least time and cost.

EXERCISE: MILESTONES

Choose one project, which you are currently managing.
1   What are the milestones for each key stage or activity of the project?
2   Do these milestones actually specify both the quantitative and qualitative aspects of key deliverables?
3   Is this sufficiently clear so that an alien (as it were) could understand it and thus know what was expected out of the project and by when?

Where a project fails to achieve its designated milestone, then the next step is, unsurprisingly, to do a fishbone analysis of the root cause of its failure.

Besides specific project milestones for certain projects (like change management) where it is harder to define more specific milestones, it is as well to also specify some key indicators. Key indicators are some of the softer and more qualitative deliverables of the project. So, for example, with a culture change project we would need to examine each of the key shifts which were the goal of the project and then ask, 'What are the key indicators for this shift to have actually occurred?'

A guiding principle overall is to ensure that project milestones and indicators do not become a bureaucracy. Their whole purpose is to energize, mobilize and focus, not to become ends in themselves.

Project learning

Throughout the project a great deal of learning can be gained both for the project manager and for the team generally. This learning can take many forms, including learning about:

- the feasibility of achieving project goals (the 'what'),
- the project process (the 'how'),
- capability and effectiveness of the project team,
- the organization itself,
- the environment external to the project.

Sadly, many managers are not so good at learning, particularly as there is much potential learning to be gained from mistakes. Many managers will retract into a defensive mind-set when confronted by a mistake. One approach to counter this is to secure the opportunity to conduct a 'strategic amnesty' of the project. This may require explicitly laying down that any mistake and its root causes (again, see fishbone analysis) can be reexamined openly – and without fear of incrimination. At Mercury Communications, for example, a formal, strategic amnesty session was used to reexamine some of the key reasons for past project failure in the domain of new business development (Grundy 1993). Surprisingly, managers got far more out of this exercise than the facilitator had ever imagined. Indeed, one particular director became almost overzealous in describing past project disasters. His criticisms of project failure were both highly humorous and scathing. It was only afterwards that one of his managers privately told the facilitator, 'I can hardly believe that he [the senior director] said those things, as it was actually he himself who perpetrated them in the very first place!'

Paradoxically, the more vulnerable the project is to failure, the worse a team's ability to learn is inclined to become, as they become clogged-up in a defensive mind-set. There are few teams of managers who can run counter to this tendency. Unfortunately, the brighter the managers, the more prone they tend to become to closing down the learning. Very bright people can be perfectionists and may well become 'allergic' to recognizing errors in judgements in strategic projects.

One way to counter this is to establish a balanced team (see chapter 7) with a relatively detached chairman-type player who can be more objective and dispassionate about the project.

Project dynamics

Finally, turning to project dynamics, there are very many ways in which a project can be tracked over time. For example, to what extent does it have a deliberate, an emergent, a submergent, emergency or detergent project strategy? Also, as we see in the next chapter, what is its difficulty over time? Upon fleshing-out the AID analysis picture, we can also ask, 'What is the likely value-over-time of the project?' Figure 6.3 illustrates the value-over-time curve for a typical strategic project. Note that the value-over-time accumulates as the various set of activities produce aligned deliverables, representing between them more than the sum of their original parts (Grundy 2000).

We have already touched upon the other curves for projects, particularly the energy-over-time curve of the project team (Figure 6.1),

FIGURE 6.3: Value-over-time curve

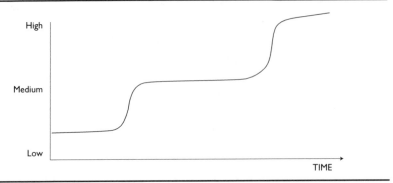

and the commitment-over-time curve (Figure 6.2). Other curves over time which can be useful are:

- belief-over-time curves (that the project will be a success),
- confusion-over-time curves,
- frustration-over-time curves,
- value-over-time curves (Figure 6.3).

Ideally, the project manager will tell scenario stories (in his/her head) about the future evolution of the project, and also use these visual curves to monitor where the project currently is against these scenarios.

CASE STUDY: PRUDENTIAL LIFE ADMINISTRATION

Introduction

In the following case we illustrate how the implementation process of a strategic change project may need to be managed. Our case study involves major, internal strategic change at the Prudential. The case study shows how strategic change needs to be managed by a stream of interdependent strategic projects rather than by a single, big-bang initiative of the kind popularized in the 1990s (for example Project 1990 at BP and 'Simply Better Way' at SmithKline Beecham).

Notice that through the entire case study there is very little mention of hard critical path analysis and Gantt charts. Whilst clearly these were used as part of the daily task of moving the project forward, they were far less important than softer indicators of the progress of this challenging project.

Prudential's Life Administration was the administrative centre which serviced the its direct UK sales force in the 1990s. The Prudential had been famous for many decades for 'The Man from the Pru' who called into UK households on a regular basis. With its direct sales force, the Prudential serviced a large market share of the UK life insurance market via its Home Service division. This generated a large workload of administration which was serviced from Life Administration at Reading – an important part of Home Service division.

This case focuses on a major change project in the 1990s to make Life Administration more responsive, effective and less costly. This involved transforming a traditional, somewhat inward-looking organization of some 2000 staff into a flatter, fitter and faster organizational unit. This project is described as follows:

- the context for project change,
- project mobilization,
- reflecting on the change project – midcourse correction,
- making structure and style work,
- project review and learning,
- summary of outputs and outcomes and lessons.

The context for the change project

During the 1970s and 1980s the life insurance market grew substantially, with the Prudential maintaining a strong position in this market. This was helped by its substantial direct sales force. But in the late 1980s a number of factors began to have an impact, which were to reshape the industry, particularly:

- an economic boom fuelled by a variety of social, monetary and political factors,
- deregulation in the financial services industry generally,
- competition intensifying from UK banks and building societies,
- fiscal encouragement by the Conservative government to encourage saving and wider investment in shares, personal pension schemes and other savings vehicles.

By the early 1990s the external environment for Prudential Home Services appeared to become more mixed. There was a surge of growth in the life insurance industry generally, but the sustainability of that growth, as well as the relative market shares of key players, was looking increasingly uncertain. This was particularly true in relation to personal pensions following legislation changes which made these much more attractive to customers.

It might, therefore, have been easy to continue to seek improvements within Life Administration as a service function within

Home Service on an incremental basis, without considering more fundamental change. But senior management within the Prudential believed that Life Administration was of such strategic importance that a steady improvement policy would be inappropriate. There was also concern that in order to compete effectively it was crucial to improve the quality of service and to improve its cost effectiveness. This suggested the need for a major change project to make Life Administration a leaner, effective and efficient organization.

There were more specific internal triggers for intervention. Prudential had launched a number of new products and demand outstripped expectations in the heady economic climate of that time. Almost overnight, Life Administration was faced with major increases in throughput, putting strain on its processing capability. In the short run, this led to operating difficulties and temporary backlogs which underlined to senior management the need to improve responsiveness of the organization. There was also a feeling that the error rate associated with transaction processing, although acceptable in the past, was in excess of that required to compete effectively given the improvements which competitors would certainly be making.

The task of the change programme was of major proportions. Life Administration then employed 2000 staff in a relatively complex and hierarchical structure. The culture of Life Administration was said to be 'traditional' and 'paternalistic', which could result in considerable inertia or even active resistance in the face of a sustained change intervention. The task of shifting Life Administration into a flexible, responsive, quality-led yet cost-effective organizational unit appeared daunting.

The key objectives of the change project were to:

- turn Life Administration from being an average performing administrative centre to one excelling in service quality, yet at a low cost as the 'engine room of the Prudential';
- to retain key elements of the culture which made Life Administration an attractive place to work; however, the emphasis would be on attractiveness in terms of challenge and fun rather than cosy and secure;
- to effect this change while ensuring continuity of Life Administration's operations – the change would be conducted with least disruption.

Project mobilization

In common with many strategic change initiatives, a key signal of pending change was the appointment of a new head of Life Administration. In his mid-30s, with a background as an economist and actuary, Tom Boardman was given the daunting task of moving Life Administration from a 'me-too' organization to a centre of excellence, in terms of both quality and efficiency of service.

Tom Boardman was an enthusiast for using best management practices to drive the change process. Over a period of three years he and the management team initiated a number of major change thrusts which included:

- devising a mission for Life Administration which would provide a focus for the change. This was developed by a group of managers who went away for nearly a week to think about quality, out of which came the key ideas within the mission;
- learning more about perceptions of Life Administration by undertaking detailed market research and continuing to track these perceptions as a control for change;
- launching a major quality programme with the aim of creating a measurable quantum shift in the quality of the organization's outputs and processes;
- refocusing business plans in order to drive change through performance measures to replace existing budgets for 'more of the same'. Quality measures were to provide the heart of the business plans;
- installing a project management process for managing specific areas of change.

Besides these change thrusts, a number of new managers were brought in at both senior and middle levels to inject new ideas and energy into the management team. A number of these new managers were young and had joined the Prudential in recent years.

The quality programme was, therefore, an important plank in the strategic change project. In order to provide a solid foundation for the programme, surveys of how customers saw Life Administration were conducted. The results provided reinforcement to internal messages of the change imperative, as well as a means of ongoing measurement.

Linked to the concept of quality was a major effort to measure the efficiency and effectiveness of service to customers and of internal operations. This involved a project aimed at strengthening the business planning unit to co-ordinate market research, performance measures and the quality programme. By focusing these key initiatives under one manager, it was possible to bring much greater cohesion and singularity of direction to the change process.

So far, the scale of the strategic change programme which was being contemplated may seem nothing extraordinary. However, to underline the magnitude of the change task it is worthwhile to reflect on the sheer size of the Life Administration machine. Some salient facts which highlight the scale of activities were that Life Administration:

- serviced 15 million policies each years,
- handled 18 million items of mail annually,
- received 100,000 telephone calls each month.

This workload was achieved through a highly complex set of systems and administrative processes with a traditional workforce and many tiers of management. This highlighted the scale of the task of transforming the organization (with least disruption) into a fighting force.

It is hardly surprising, therefore, that it took the best part of two years to mobilize fully for the change project. This was, in part, due to the decision to phase structure changes after the start of the quality roll-out, as it was feared that to push forward on both initiatives simultaneously would have been counterproductive. The new management team, under Tom Boardman, also probably underestimated the time and sustained effort required to mobilize for this change. Indeed, it was not until around two years into the process that it became apparent that there was still a long way to go in sustaining intended change initiatives so as to reap the underlying benefits of the whole programme. As was put subsequently by Kippa Alliston, Tom Boardman's successor:

> A lot has been achieved in the last 18 months in moving Life Administration towards a total quality, customer-led culture where we're selling not just a product, but service excellence itself. It will take another three years or so for that culture to put down deep roots.

It became clear that the really sticky areas of change were of a more behavioural rather than of a more tangible nature. Although the initiatives co-ordinated by the business planning unit were beginning to bear fruit, a number of symptoms of barriers to change began to become apparent. For instance, during the first business planning cycle managers lapsed into their old budget games –

putting in excess and spurious bids for resources which they knew would be negotiated away. This was despite Tom Boardman clearly laying the ground rules that budgets would be based on business rather than territorial needs. Although the quality programme was making headway, there also seemed to be some quite major blocks within the management team itself which inhibited this initiative from being taken seriously.

Tom Boardman felt that it was now time to up the ante and looked to focusing an attack on behavioural style through a Managing Change Programme, outlined below.

Reflecting on the change project – midcourse correction

A small team of management developers within the Prudential then began to think about staging an organizational change and learning project in Life Administration. This was aimed at producing an 'organizational shock' which would unblock the barriers to change through a top team learning vehicle. The task of co-ordinating this project was given to an external consultant and an experienced management developer familiar with the problems and opportunities of linking management development and organizational change. The initiative was focused on overcoming the blocks to change, and it highlights the difficulties of managing blocks and barriers. This was merely a part of the overall change dynamic.

Through previous work in using change and learning projects as vehicles for triggering organizational change, the consultant was acutely aware of the potential limitations of this approach. Where only some rather than all of the management team are involved, there would be uneven ownership of new concepts, beliefs and behaviours. Individual learning (a key project output) can also rapidly fold back on itself (the unlearning process) unless some active experimentation with change frameworks is undertaken.

An action-based change and learning programme was therefore set up. This involved a number of key inputs both to steer the project effectively and to build ownership. This involved:

- extensive discussions with Tom Boardman (as key stakeholder) to focus the programme, to determine desired learning and behavioural change, to identify key strategic change issues and areas where specific action would be necessary;

- interviews with half a dozen of the management team to include both the new and old blood;
- design of a two-day workshop (run twice for a dozen managers in each workshop) on managing change. All of the top management team attended this workshop programme. On the second day of each workshop a set of change issues were input (distilled from preinterviews with Tom Boardman and with a representative sample of the management team) to stimulate debate on a strategic vision for Life Administration. These issues were at the core of the workshops. Prior to this these had been more implicit and less than fully shared within the management team;
- four learning and change projects (see Figure 6.4) were devised for managers to work on as joint change and learning vehicles. These incorporated similar issues to those which had already been addressed by the business planning unit whose head, Andrew Budge, provided helpful ammunition for the learning and change workshops. (This was an excellent example of internal and external change catalysts working in close partnership.) The 'problem' within each project was then preidentified by Tom Boardman with some external input. Each of these four projects involved group work in workshops by a team of six managers over a two-month period meeting
- a two-day Change Project Conference was run for all the management team, over 21 managers. In these two days the output of each learning and change project was presented and debated. The conference was attended by Tom Boardman's boss, a senior director of Prudential Home Service.

During the short design phase, Tom Boardman quickly realized the potential of the programme. Although the programme was

FIGURE 6.4: Learning and change projects

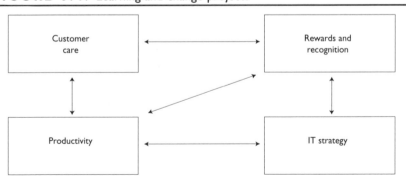

initially viewed perhaps as a pure learning programme, the benefits of addressing live critical business and organizational issues came quickly to the fore. Not only did this involve running an individual development and team-building programme, it also involved analysing and moving towards resolving some key change issues. As these were both pressing and, in part, tangible, they enabled blocking management behaviours to be flushed out and made visible.

In mobilizing for change generally it is essential to link change initiatives and projects explicitly, rather than to assume these linkages are apparent. This enables the change to be time-compressed – otherwise initiatives may meander towards their goals. During the Life Administration change workshop it was remarkable (even to the consultant) how much the change process could be accelerated through an organizational learning hothouse.

For instance, during the second two-day workshop a new change project emerged during the analysis. One syndicate group had been given the task of analysing the issues associated with changing the roles of the firstline supervisor. From the top team's perspective, this area of change had been recognized but had not been (at that point) seen as having both a high impact and being extremely difficult to implement. The syndicate performed a force-field analysis and reported back with a diagram which was more adverse than the one which they had done for a 'very difficult change'.

Several of the managers were physically shaken as they came out of their syndicate room – clearly a key insight, however negative, had emerged. The rest of the management team were able, through using the force field analysis tool, to share the syndicate's vision of the change and to confirm that this appeared both vitally important and also uncertain. The force field also highlighted the process levers which would help the change move forward. These included defining the change objective more tightly and deriving a strategy for change which built ownership rather than alienated key stakeholders.

By 9.30am on the Monday following the second change workshop (Thursday and Friday of the previous week), Tom Boardman had set up a new change project based on this syndicate's output – the Structure Project. This was to be managed by an experienced change manager seconded from his line role on a full-time basis.

Other key insights also emerged which were promptly set in action. For instance, although Life Administration had set up a project management process, the linkages and interdependencies between change projects were initially implicit rather than explicit.

A second key task of the manager of the Structure Project was to map these interdependencies, to identify any overlaps and to, where necessary, reconfigure projects. Surprisingly, this took several weeks to accomplish, highlighting how important it is to identify inter-dependencies between change projects from the outset.

In the past Life Administration had held an annual conference which was, typically, an inward-looking event, focusing on opera-tional issues. It had been planned to run a one-and-a-half-day feedback workshop to end the Change Programme. Tom Boardman saw the opportunity, however, of achieving two objectives with one vehicle and announced that the annual conference would become a Change Project Conference. The two-day event would then be facilitated externally.

Managers are often attracted to content-led issues and it was determined, therefore, that to balance this, equal emphasis on process during the conference was essential. This would include the project team's reflections on their own learning process, such as openness to change. A critique was made not only on the content of their projects but also on how they worked together as teams – in other words, their process. This enabled the top man-agement team to gain an insight overall into their openness as an organizational unit to learning and challenge. By playing back external impressions it was possible for the facilitator to act as a neutral organizational mirror – without being unduly provocative. It may be tempting for a facilitator to exaggerate weak-nesses, but this is a dangerous process as the facilitator quickly becomes the target for externalizing the team's feelings. It also produces a distortion in what the team sees like the crazy mirrors one sees at amusement arcades. Exaggeration of this kind is seldom appreciated.

The four learning and change projects included a project focusing on customer care, one on productivity, one on rewards and recog-nition, and one on IT strategy. Three out of four of the projects were relatively uncontentious in content terms, save one. It is interesting to examine this closer in order to understand the underlying process at work.

One of the learning and change projects dealing with infor-mation technology was focused on a current change thrust which had been launched some time ago. This was of major impact on Life Administration and there was a significant degree of commit-ment to a particular path of action. One group highlighted that, on the face of it, there were some significant short- and medium-term problems in achieving change milestones. These milestones were critical for improving operational performance.

When the project teams presented their findings, a vigorous debate began about whether these problems did or did not exist. This surfacing of contentious issues was very healthy, but the project team members felt that problems were being underplayed by members of top management.

This episode highlights a number of key lessons:

- Top management may well find it uncomfortable at times to have core business problems of a sensitive nature probed through organizational learning workshops of this kind and revert to defensive routines.
- Middle managers may assume that it is top management's job to have 'all of change problems in the project' well covered all of the time. Yet, the complexity and ambiguity of change, especially when this involves wholesale change throughout the organization, make this an impossible task.
- When a major issue emerges, it is easy for managers to revert to looking for someone to blame rather than being open. The ultimate test of openness involves openness during attack. When a vigorous critique is bearing down on you, it is hard to remain receptive.
- Before this incident, the learning and change programme had actually run too well and too smoothly. Unless some really contentious issues surface to test managers' behaviour then the programme has not really dug down to the sharp realities of managing change.

The true test of capability to manage change is not whether a management team acts defensively or openly during a workshop. It depends upon whether it subsequently goes on to reshape how it implements change. Following the early Change Project Conference, the above issues were rapidly addressed.

Making structure and style work

Following the Change Project Conference, it was necessary to face the considerable difficulties of implementing change, both in organizational structure and in supporting management style. Some of these changes may have been prompted, in part, by the Change Project Conference and learning programme and some by ongoing thinking by the top team – change strategies are often the result of an intermingling of ideas.

Dealing first with structure, some major changes were made, including:

- The Life Administration structure needed to be refocused to be more outward-facing. At senior management level, one manager was responsible for interfacing with outside locations and one on internal services. Both managers were on the original management team.
- The number of senior and middle managers was reduced considerably from about 25 to 12. This involved some redeployment to other parts of the Prudential, which had been preplanned. But this still left existing managers competing for a smaller number of jobs.
- At the firstline manager level there were some major changes too, as about 100 people from existing roles competed for 70 jobs within the new structure. This change was conducted in parallel with a rigorous recruitment and selection process including psychometric testing and counselling of all candidates. The new roles were genuinely of a 'managerial' nature as opposed to supervisors/technocrats.
- At the clerical level, staff were to become multiskilled so that they would be able to do work without having frequent recourse to their supervisors to check what they were doing. As Boardman's successor, Alliston describes it, 'If ten people are all delivering one small part of the total product and it goes wrong, nobody feels accountable. If one person is accountable for all of it, you get quality and service excellence.'

A number of the above points can be amplified. First, the choice of who would become members of the new senior team was decided by a meritocratic approach. Previous incumbents were invited to apply for the new jobs. Although these changes involved considerable pain, they were accomplished with some sense of perceived fairness which did much to ease the transition.

Second, the rationale for the changes was communicated vigorously throughout the middle and lower levels of the organization. This rationale lay in a) the rate of change in the external market; b) the need to focus on the customer; and c) the harsh financial realities which needed to be faced up to. Life Administration brought in a senior lecturer from Manchester Business School, Dr John Westwood, to give a presentation on changes in the financial services industry generally. These sessions were attended by all the administrative staff over many half-day sessions. Even so, it proved necessary to rent Reading Town Hall to accommodate the numbers of staff at each session. This emphasizes the importance of spending time and effort (often lavishly) in the communication of the rationale for change.

Westwood reflects on his sessions at Reading:

> Let's not beat about the bush – before the days of Kippa Alliston and his predecessor Tom Boardman, if you put a foot out of line at Reading, you got stamped on... If you said, 'I don't know why I'm doing this – isn't there a better way?', you got squashed. All the ideas, the enthusiasm, the energy were suppressed... Kippa's going to release them. I talked to people after the sessions, and I found they were already coming up with good ideas. If you can mobilize 80 per cent of 1800 people, you're going to get a hell of a lot of good ideas for turning Life Administration into the best and cheapest engine room in the industry.

Third, the approach taken to achieving change at the clerical worker level was one of trial and learning. Rather than impose a rigid framework of change, a degree of diversity was allowed so that the multi-skilling could be tailored to different job areas. One issue which emerged was how this diversity could be managed and monitored so that Life Administration's way of doing things (its paradigm) did not become too diverse and fragmented.

The multi-skilling approach demanded a major investment in training. This ran against the earlier tradition in Life Administration: 'You don't get to do a senior job here unless you have proven yourself for years'. By intensive training, however, it proved possible to shortcut this artificially long path up the hierarchy. Training, therefore, emerged as a key vehicle in turning Life Administration into a flatter structure.

Much of this discussion has centred around structure rather than style. The philosophy adopted within Life Administration was that structure and style issues were inextricable, and changes in structure were necessarily bound together with major shifts in management style. But style was found to lag behind structure change. This was highlighted in the Change Project Conference where 'paradigm analysis' suggested that, in terms of style, the organization was only perhaps one-quarter of the way towards achieving its desired shift. A further review of progress to internalize a 'quality culture' also identified some remaining gaps in attitude and behaviour, although there was some dispute as to whether this was unduly pessimistic.

Given the scale of the change task already described, this pace of progress does not seem surprising. But where progress in tangible areas of change (especially in systems, structures and processes) can be achieved relatively rapidly, management becomes disappointed when soft areas of change lag behind. This may raise doubts about whether more could have been done earlier in attempting to shift style, and whether the critical path for change had been fully thought through. But had Life Administration chosen to focus on less tangible areas of change first and deferred change in more tangible areas, many of the 'hard' drivers of change would not have been engaged. This highlights the difficulty in trade-off change priorities and, equally, the sensitivity of progress to choice of where to focus, when and in what order. Alliston looks back on this change:

> Take a culture where people weren't allowed, or didn't feel empowered, to contribute – one that rewarded long service rather than ability, one that did not have a clear focus on the customer – on whose processes were designed to satisfy internal requirements... and then you have all the attributes of the old Prudential.
>
> Not enough attention was paid to the customer, whether [they were] policyholders or those very significant other customers – the agents in the field, who in the old culture were thought of as interruptions, intrusions, people who got in the way of work, rather than as people we serve.

Project review and learning

After three years of the start of the various initiatives, the key plans of change were firmly in place. The management team had been slimmed down, the roles of firstline managers had been refocused and considerable progress made towards expanding the role of clerical workers. The quality programme was well bedded in and Industrial Branch, a key part of Prudential Life Administration, won a national award for quality. Life Administration continued to perform regular market surveys to test whether perception of its customers and its responsiveness had changed.

Boardman then moved to another major change project within the Prudential. Alliston, who had joined the Prudential from IBM, was determined to press on with the change programme.

Boardman's main achievement was to create a reversal of culture in Life Administration from one which was resistant to change. He succeeded in weeding out much of the old organizational paradigm. His management style, which was supportive and based on team-building, fit extremely well with this phase of change. Boardman's particular contribution was to get management and staff to reflect on their own the need for change.

Alliston's style had a marked contrast. Alliston promoted a culture of leading from the front. It was based on intense challenge without fear of causing pain to others and himself, seeing it as the necessary price of moving forward quickly.

Already, mainly through natural wastage, the number of staff in Life Administration was reduced from 2000 to about 1600, while continuing to serve similar levels of workload. The rates of error in clerical work and turnaround times were also halved over the same period, even though there was a major decrease in checking.

If Boardman was prepared to address change in a proactive way in Life Administration, Alliston was equally direct and explicit in taking the same programmes forward. This involved a further phase of review of progress towards meeting change objectives.

First, there was a review of the quality programme to establish the remaining gaps. As Alliston put it:

> We need to find out what our customers want and how they want to be served – and one thing I can predict is that whatever the customer wants, we will provide it. I want to build on the basis of customer satisfaction surveys and service-level agreements and to continue to focus all our efforts on the customer.

Second, all employees went through a two-day customer service workshop followed up by a detailed attitude survey by external consultants. The majority of the workshops were attended by Alliston.

Third, managers benchmarked how Life Administration was tackling the problems of making it an outward-facing, responsive and low-cost administrative service centre. Alliston described his vision as:

> Change into what? I describe Reading as the engine room of the division. That engine room, relative to its competitors, must become the lowest-cost engine room in the UK and with the highest quality...
>
> I am determined that Reading will become the service excellence centre for administration, both in terms of price and quality. I want success and I'm not prepared to have failure.

The two-day customer service workshops were well received – principally because there were no holds barred – all staff were encouraged to 'tell it how it is' in the debriefing session with their managers after each workshop. This input, and particularly the follow-up survey by external consultants, was able to highlight and amplify a number of major tensions which were at work beneath the organizational surface produced by the rapid pace of change. Some highly contentious issues emerged, such as leadership style, genuine commitment to openness and a perceived bias towards productivity rather than service quality.

The content of these findings was fed back to staff in a four-page newsletter whose frankness might have stunned managers in cosier environments. These issues were then distilled into the dozen or so key projects which would focus change over the following two to three years.

The next part of securing Life Administration's current position to achieve that goal was done by establishing contacts with a number of other leading organizations with similar administrative functions undergoing parallel change. In this benchmarking exercise, the new management team began by posing a dozen key questions which focused on both the content and process of managing change in a complex administrative centre. These questions were also used in the similar organizations prior to establishing firsthand contact. The posing of these questions, in itself, served as a powerful method of reflecting the progress of change to date. Examples of some of these questions included:

- How do we manage our (internal or external) customer from a distance and remain responsive?
- How do we learn from the process of change when a diversity of approaches appears to develop?
- What changes in culture are implied by this series of changes and how are these managed?
- How is the change in activities linked to present and future system development?
- Looking back on the change to date, how could we have done things better?

A number of important lessons were gained from setting up this exercise:

- Companies are eager to share experiences and approaches with indirectly competing companies. This applies not merely to implementing strategic change but to a variety of other important management issues.
- Companies are reluctant to seize this opportunity because of the psychological hurdle of making first contact and also of

handling the experience in a structured way. By using an external facilitator it is often possible to both identify target companies and contacts relatively quickly with which to network cross-organizationally as well as to establish contact.

■ Much of the balance of the exercise lies in the critical internal benchmarking which is of great benefit in its own right.

■ When visiting other companies, managers should look for subtle differences in management processes and styles which may be critical and not just hope to come away with relative performance measures such as 'better than', 'same as' or 'worse than'.

Over a three-month period, six of Life Administrations' senior managers visited four major organizations in pairs, along with an external facilitator who set up contacts and structured visits. The four companies included a building society, a bank, a telecommunications group and an oil company. The issues and lessons in managing change were remarkably similar, not only within financial services but also within the other industries that were networked into.

Some early insights from this benchmarking project were that Prudential Life Administration needed to seize the opportunity in moving to a new building (which it subsequently did) as a way of consolidating culture change. Also, some method of harmonizing change in a number of process areas, which had hitherto been empowered to seek their own solutions, needed to be applied. A renewed and more thorough attack on business process redesign and simplification was also necessary. There were also insights gained in how to channel the results of the employee survey into positive change and a host of indirect spin-offs on operational issues.

To conclude this case on project managing change at Prudential Life Administration, the most important lesson is that a clear rationale and strategy for the project must be established. This may need considerable time, effort and skill to mobilize. Besides having adequate 'change project hardware' in terms of resources, project management processes, change and quality programmes, it is equally important to have 'change project software'. This includes firm leadership which is prepared to be open to continuous learning; it also includes well-focused communication effort. There also needs to be some higher element to alleviate the feeling that change is burdensome. Where the organization is shedding some of its old, bureaucratic skin in favour of greater autonomy, challenge and fun, these benefits must be continually sold to all staff.

Another central lesson is that key planks of the 'change message' such as the 'mission' need to be as simple as possible. Although the stated mission – 'delighting our customers by delivering a quality service, in a cost-effective manner, through the contribution of everyone' – may seem to be simple and clear to senior managers intellectually, it is not so easy to transmit this to all levels without some loss of impact.

Another important lesson was that managers felt they had 'communication well covered', for example through regular business plan updates. But what was perhaps missing, with hindsight, was what the implications were from a recipient's perspective.

The journey for Life Administration is far from over. As Alliston describes it:

> It really becomes an increasingly uphill battle from now on. We have bitten the bullet on productivity and this means there really isn't the slack which we once took for granted. People are being asked to work a lot harder, and for some of the staff this has proved overwhelming. In the most distant past we allowed people to drift through the levels, but that is gone for ever.
>
> Unfortunately a lot of people joined for the old values of security and stability, and to them the change project has come as a painful experience. But you just can't duck that pain.
>
> What will really help is when we get for ourselves a lot slicker set of processes. That involves stopping doing some things, for example one of our staff had been producing a report for many, many years. Recently she said, 'Why are we doing it?" It turned out that the report didn't really add a lot of value. There are those stories. But in the end we will need these systems – you can't just go around beating people up for productivity. The real challenge is to rekindle enthusiasm and build on those areas where people are doing outstanding jobs and where they really hold onto targets, rather than looking at them.'

The contributions of both Boardman and Alliston to achieving change in Prudential Life Administration are summed up by John Westwood of Manchester Business School: 'While Tom got people to think the unthinkable and got the ball rolling [project mobilization], Kippa Alliston picked up the ball and kicked it.'

Despite some difficulties which are currently unresolved, the fact that Life Administration is moving into the later stages of this major transition without serious disruption in continuity of services or in performance bears testimony to the persistence and stamina of the evolving management team. No doubt the use of project management tools like force-field analysis and stakeholder analysis combined with a quality initiative, performance measures and enlightened human resources practices played an important role. But this role would not have been effective without the refreshingly proactive style of top management and their enthusiastic endorsement of strategic project management.

Key lessons from the case

A number of key lessons can be distilled from the case of project managing change at Prudential Life Administration:

- Mobilizing for change may take a considerable period to achieve, especially where culture is traditional and operations are complex. For this process strategic project management is imperative.
- If a strategic change project is managed piecemeal and incrementally, in this context it is likely to falter.
- Each aspect of any strategic change project and subproject needs to be monitored – not only through explicit, tangible milestones but also by softer indicators, perhaps using FT analysis.
- Deliberate project strategies may appear to work for a period but may then begin to get more fluid and emergent. Periodically, change projects may become submergent or exhibit emerging strategies, and then enter the detergent phase of the strategy mix. See Figure 6.5 for a graphic illustration of this process.
- Effective management of this kind of change requires parallel attention to both structure and culture alongside change in operational processes.
- A number of reinforcing projects are needed to shift the paradigm. These need to exist in reality and be practiced by senior management rather than merely talked about.
- Differing styles of project leadership are called for by different phases of strategic change.
- Quality and customer care may provide the core of these changes but need to be supplemented by changes in business planning, performance measurement and appraisal, external benchmarking, project management and workshops to share issues and mobilize for change.
- This shift in paradigm requires continual and genuinely open internal review and learning.

FIGURE 6.5: The evolution of project strategies

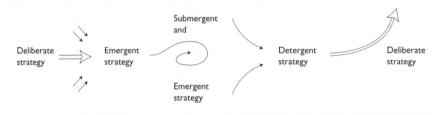

- The impact of internal review is much bolstered by external benchmarking projects if suitably focused and followed through.
- All of this effort needs to be brought together within a clear and complete strategic vision embodied in firm but supportive project leadership.

EXERCISE: PROJECT MOBILIZATION

Choose a project you have been or are currently involved in.
1   What are (or were) the very first steps in mobilizing the project?
2   How effectively were these taken, and why?
3   What are the likely or past:
   - energy-over-time curves?
   - difficulty-over-time curves?
   - value-over-time curves?
   - frustration-over-time curves?

Conclusion

All projects require skilful monitoring and control of their dynamics throughout implementation. Moreover, it is imperative to anticipate these dynamics before the event rather than just to accept things as they are when they occur as an organizational given.

As a critical part of anticipating the dynamics it is essential to think about potential changes in stakeholders and in their attitudes and agendas for good or for bad, as these will play a decisive role in shaping the dynamics.

The Prudential case study underlines the need to cope with, and to anticipate, the organizational flux with which projects can be affected.

References

Grundy, A.N. (1993) *Strategic Learning*, McGraw Hill.
Grundy, A.N. (2000) 'Strategic Project Management and Strategic Behaviour', *International Journal of Project Management* 18:93–103.

■ CHAPTER SEVEN ■

Influencing people and behaviour

Introduction

In this chapter we now look at some of the softer aspects of strategic projects – especially in terms of managing and influencing people and behaviour. This involves:

- diagnosing the system of strategic behaviour impacting on a project,
- diagnosing team roles in strategic projects,
- specific techniques for managing strategic behaviour in projects,
- illustration with a major case study at Champneys Health Resort.

A number of analytical techniques that help with strategic project management have already been discussed, including:

- fishbone or root-cause analysis,
- how-how analysis,
- FT analysis,
- force-field analysis,
- stakeholder analysis,
- attractiveness-implementation difficulty,
- assumption analysis/uncertainty
- importance-urgency analysis.

Whilst often associated with managing the more tangible aspects of projects, these techniques can be used as effectively for the softer aspects of influencing people and behaviour. For example, fishbone analysis can be used for diagnosing behavioural difficulties or constraints. How-how analysis can be used to identify strategies for influencing key stakeholders. FT analysis can help establish to what extent staff have gone through a tangible culture shift. Force-field analysis can help uncover the purely behavioural aspects of influencing stakeholders. Attractiveness-implementation difficulty (AID) can help prioritize which stakeholders are best to try to influence. The uncertainty grid assists in surfacing assumptions about the intentions and agendas of stakeholders. Finally, urgency-importance analysis provides a focus for prioritizing the influencing efforts over time.

Nevertheless, the above techniques deal primarily with the more analytical aspects of managing strategic projects. The authors' research into the behaviour associated with strategic projects has led to the conclusion that equally important are the behavioural aspects of strategic project management (Grundy 1998).

Practising managers will easily recognize that the conduct of strategy itself is a battleground, given the considerable turbulence which surrounds both external and internal strategic moves. Strategic projects, however well intentioned, become easily buffeted by strategies which are highly emergent and unpredictable. The more difficult of the influences are frequently behavioural in nature. There appears to be great merit in incorporating techniques for surfacing behavioural issues in project management, especially for the more strategic projects, which will be called 'strategic behaviour'.

Strategic behaviour is the cognitive, emotional and territorial interplay of managers within or between groups when the agenda relates to strategic issues.

Our definition of strategic behaviour stresses the extent to which cognitive, emotional and territorial perspectives and agendas of managers are interwoven. We are thus more able to understand those aspects of strategy implementation which are perhaps less easily discussed by managers. This difficulty could be due either to the fact that they involve power or because of emotional sensitivities.

EXERCISE: STRATEGIC PROJECTS AND STRATEGIC BEHAVIOUR

Choose one strategic project you have been involved with in the past.
1 What were the key behaviours both within the project team and around the rest of the organization which either
   ■ facilitated the project's implementation?
   ■ constrained the project's implementation?
2 For one or more significant constraining force:
   ■ Why did this exist? Use fishbone analysis.
   ■ What could be done to ameliorate its effects?

Two examples of strategic behaviour are illustrated by the following strategic projects.

A financial services company has a project to reduce its business complexity from 15 to five strategic business units. One of the directors raises semi-spurious reasons for retaining one business unit even though the balance of evidence is clearly against remaining in it. The debate gets messier and messier, with less and less agreement and more and more frustration. The director coils his arms and legs and slumps into defensive nonverbal behaviour. He has not, and will not, reveal his underlying personal agenda, which is to save the embarrassment of going back to the managers who have put their very trust in him to defend their case and their jobs.

The second example is of a retail company undertaking a scenario development project. One manager invited because of his technical knowledge becomes more and more grumpy. He is moody because the subject matter is too broad to help him on his own very specific, functional issues. The rest of the team confront him with the problem, and one says: 'If you really don't see this as adding value to you personally, feel free to leave'. He did, and the team then began to make progress again.

The two examples above illustrate the profound effect of behaviour on the evaluation of strategic projects. One might indeed characterize the first example as one of 'managers behaving badly', except that would be too normative. Certainly the word 'dysfunctional' seems applicable to the first example and partially also to the second example.

Whilst strategy formulation is clearly of some emotional and territorial sensitivity, this is likely to be greatly magnified during strategy implementation. During strategic action, strategy creates turbulence in the everyday fabric of the organization. Frequently, the main vehicle for that action is the strategic project, and it is precisely here that much behavioural turbulence is felt.

For research at British Telecom (BT), the strategic behaviour of a senior team within BT – whose remit was to understand the market and technological implications of major changes in BT's external and internal environment – was explored (Grundy 1998). This key department was charged with defining strategic projects which would then form a central plank of BT's technological migration. As these projects had a multibusiness impact they were frequently fraught with complexity – not merely at a territorial level but also at an organizational one.

Although strategic project management tries to address the fit of the project with both external and internal strategic breakthroughs and strategic vision, it still does not address the deeper, more behavioural issues – see Figure 7.1, which emphasizes:

- strategic thinking needs to be founded on strategic analysis;

- strategic analysis is insufficient unless accompanied by both a 'so-what?' analysis and some creative option generation
- strategic vision should be founded on strategic options and decisions rather than primarily playing its own driving role, otherwise strategic decisions will be forced to fit the vision;
- all of these cognitive aspects of strategic thinking need to be fully aligned and also precede actual strategic behaviour and action.

Exploring strategic behaviour

It has already been shown how important stakeholders are in managing strategic projects. Stakeholders play a decisive role in determining whether projects live or die or are condemned to limbo, neither moving forwards nor backwards.

Indeed, it is often the interaction of key individuals and larger groups which dictates the trajectory of the project. But most courses and books on project management tend to focus on creating an effective team whilst neglecting some of the more subtle and indeed complex patterns of personal interaction.

The key variables which underpin the interactions of teams as the project develops will now be discussed. These variables were uncovered principally during research on senior teams working on strategy development projects at BT.

FIGURE 7.1: The SPM iceberg

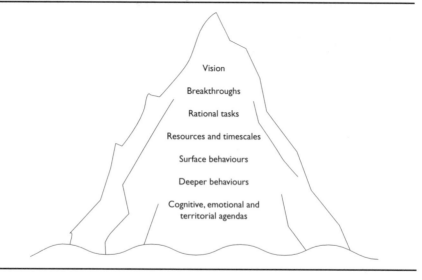

Vision

Breakthroughs

Rational tasks

Resources and timescales

Surface behaviours

Deeper behaviours

Cognitive, emotional and territorial agendas

Strategic projects and strategic behaviour

Whilst much of the strategic management literature is devoted to understanding strategic decision-making, relatively little of it is concerned with the behavioural interactions of senior managers. Suspecting that there were some important and new insights to be gleaned by studying this behaviour in real time, one of the authors was able to be unobtrusively observe a strategy department at BT.

The department contained a number of project teams and the management team, which met to evaluate and prioritize strategic projects having a major impact on BT's technology strategy. The author's research involved a number of interviews with BT managers both before and after strategic workshops. It also entailed observation of some of those workshops, and the researcher actually facilitated one.

All of the interactions of the workshops and the interviews were tape-recorded and subjected to microscopic analysis and interpretation. The results were fed back to the BT managers, generating further illuminating data. The control output of the research is shown in Figure 7.2, which explores the strategic behaviour associated with strategic projects.

Figure 7.2 presents this behaviour as a system. This is based on the premise that unless all of the parts of a system are aligned well, dysfunctional behaviour is likely to occur. For instance, if the strategic tasks of the project are not appropriately defined, then the project is unlikely to exhibit harmonious behaviours. Managers will be prone to argument and frustration, spreading their energies and efforts too thinly and in sometimes opposing directions.

Equally, if the team lack analytical processes and techniques of the kind described in this book, then they are likely to struggle in moving

FIGURE 7.2: The system of strategic behaviour

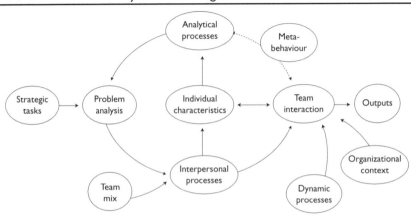

problems forward. Even if analytical processes are well aligned, unless managers' interpersonal processes are running smoothly, there is likely to be significant, if not severe, disruption to behaviour.

If it is unbalanced or not fitting to the task, the team mix will also hamper project success. Many teams are assembled based on either who is available or on the basis of technical skills. It is therefore largely by accident that the team will be able to get on with each other well enough to achieve project goals. To help diagnose consistency of team roles, it is a very good idea to get project members to reflect on their preferred team styles, for example using the Belbin typology. Belbin differentiates between team styles such as the plant, shaper, resource investigator, team-worker, chairman and finisher – see the next section.)

Organizational context is another key source of behavioural harmony. An organization where certain key team members are nervous for their jobs or anxious about pending promotion will provide a rocky environment for an effective team. Also, if the organization is extremely complex, political or divided up into disparate and opposing sets, cultures will find it hard to host effective projects.

Besides these key variables, one should also pay attention to the key outputs of the project. Where these are poorly targeted, there are likely to be more disruptive behaviours emerging. Without clear strategic goals, personal agendas will tend to distort interactions, producing knock-on effects. Other stakeholders then dig in or begin to play clandestine games to achieve their goals.

EXERCISE: EXPLORING STRATEGIC BEHAVIOUR

1   For one project which went well in the past, how was alignment created behaviourally? Use Figure 7.2 as a diagnostic technique.
2   For another project which did not go so well in the past, how was misalignment created, and how were the effects then amplified in the system of strategic behaviour?

The culmination of misalignment of this system of strategic behaviour may result in what could be characterized, to paraphrase a very successful UK TV comedy show, as 'managers behaving badly'.

Before examining the role which strategic behaviour plays in project management in greater depth, it is necessary to take a look at a complex project which a management consultant experienced some years ago. This illustrated some of the dysfunctional effects of strategic behaviour on projects all too well.

CASE STUDY: ZEBRA BANKING CORPORATION

Some time ago, one of the authors worked for a large strategy consultancy firm, which will be called Vulture Consultancy Group (which was not, incidentally, KPMG). Zebra Banking Corporation was a major client of Vulture. Vulture was commissioned to do a major project to study Zebra's competitive advantage through its technology infrastructure.

The management consultant was a newly qualified MBA who had joined Vulture Consultancy to broaden his experience of consulting projects in both a service and technology environment.

The project team consisted of:

- the consultant (as senior consultant, full-time),
- a technology consultant (full-time),
- the project lead (a consultancy manager, part-time),
- the consultancy director (occasional),
- a senior manager of the client (part-time).

The senior manager of the client was a very experienced IT manager who coincidentally was available because he had just returned to work after recovering from a mild heart attack.

The senior consultant was new to Vulture Consultancy and to its culture and processes, although he did have four years' consulting experience and some senior line experience. The technology consultant was more junior but nevertheless bright. He was actively contemplating leaving Vulture to do an MBA and was slightly cynical about Vulture's way of operating.

The part-time project leader was a very experienced consultant who probably had limited chances of making director level, after having worked for 15 years in the organization. Of high nervous energy, this high visibility project appeared to worry him more than a little. By nature an operator, and without an MBA or other significant formal training in strategic thinking, he seemed at times ill at ease with the nature of this challenge.

The consultancy director, a smooth operator, seemed at least as interested in the newly joined consultant's old accounting firm as he was in the Zebra project. Questions like, 'How much did they pay, and what was it really like working with Bean-Counter Consultants?' seemed to be high on his agenda.

The consultancy budget was set (at current prices) at around £300,000. The project's goals were to identify Zebra's total relative competitive position (*vis-à-vis* IT) across all of its product/market range. As a major and diversified bank, this was no mean feat.

The proposal for the consultancy project had been put together by a team of five consultancy directors and managers drawn from across Vulture's consultancy units. Only one of those individuals – the consultancy director – was to be involved in the project itself. The other members of the project team had no previous sighting of the project's scope, its methodology, its outputs, nor of its time inputs and time constraints.

A formal presentation of the project outputs was scheduled as part of the Zebra Banking's annual IT conference with 700 staff at a hotel near Heathrow. The conference was to be hosted by Zebra's IT director and its chief executive.

Questions for the reader

- What do you make of this project's current chances of success based on this limited information?
- How well do you think the team will get on, especially as the project nears its deadline, given the individuals disparate skills, experience, agendas, culture?

Behavioural difficulties

Not surprisingly, the project exhibited some pronounced behavioural wobbles:

- Three subcultures rapidly developed: the senior and the more junior consultant (the 'survival' culture); the consultancy director and project director (a 'please-the-client-at-all-costs' culture); and the representative from the client ('do I have a future here', panic culture).
- Even with the best intentions and by working off-the-clock, a cost overrun of 50 per cent became apparent by the fifth week. Fortunately, the consultancy firm was able to pass on the majority of these extra costs to Zebra, due to the sympathy and largesse of its IT director.
- The project director began to become more and more hyperactive, ceasing to involve himself part-time and becoming almost full-time. His manner gave rise to concerns about his nervous disposition.
- The senior consultant, stressed one night after working on this intensive project, misjudged a bend while driving and, to save a major accident, ploughed his car into a nearby field. The car was nearly a write-off but the consultant escaped with a minor blow to the head.

- The client's own representative on the project began to have unpleasant premonitions of the end of the project, and after a meeting with one of the MDs of Zebra's business units, suddenly asked if he had been here before (as a déja vû experience).

As time drew nearer to the project presentation the consultancy director took over the reins from his more nervous adjutant. Neither core member of the consultancy team was to attend the presentation (maybe so no awkward questions could be asked?). The director set about writing a 90-page overhead presentation for his one-hour slot. A crude calculation of the frequency of these overheads was one every 40 seconds – leaving obviously very little time for questions.

Everything was in place for a set-piece presentation but something highly unexpected was about to happen as the core consultancy team put the final touches to the consultancy director's overhead bullets. The conference had been cancelled due to a salmonella outbreak at the hotel where it was to be held, and an alternative site couldn't be found on such short notice. The relief – and at the same time the disappointment – was palpable.

The consultancy presentation was subsequently given by the consultancy director and the project director to a small number of senior Zebra Banking Corporation managers. The presentation went well, and some of the insights were partially taken on board by the bank.

EXERCISE: BEHAVIOUR

Based on a reading of the case study and using Figure 7.2, what would you say were the behavioural variables which caused major dysfunction within the project team? Consider especially:
- The definition of the task,
- Its outcomes,
- Team mix,
- Metabehaviour (especially its absence),
- Team dynamics.

Behavioural lessons

Whilst being an apparently extreme situation, the above case study may be representative of at least a number of complex strategic projects which have not been well thought through, especially in terms of their likely behavioural implications.

A number of key behavioural lessons now crystallize from the case study:

- The strategic tasks were not sufficiently well defined, focused or owned by the key team members.
- The team mix was highly unsuited to the job, and members exhibited conflicting personal agendas.
- There was an absence of preagreed analytical and behavioural processes for the team.
- Team members had widely unequal and varying status.
- There was an apparent lack of metabehaviour to steer the team.
- The outcomes of the project were not particularly well defined.
- The organizational contexts both in the client and in the consultancy group were not conducive to smooth team-working (an atmosphere of tension and fear existed).

Diagnosing team roles

In this section we examine the mechanics of team roles. We have chosen the Belbin team-roles typology because this is not only well known but also easy to use and robust.

Belbin team roles can be used by a team:

- help the individual identify his/her professed team styles, and thus aid in developing their personal effectiveness;
- encourage specific individuals to try out and develop their skills in other team-role styles;
- diagnose overall strengths and weaknesses of the entire team;
- help manage team dynamics more effectively;
- help plan future moves into or out of the team, and also for team formation.

Invariably, the use of Belbin team roles sparks a shift in self-awareness, and thus in effectiveness, within the team. It was certainly found essential in the British Telecom strategy discussed earlier.

The key Belbin team roles are as follows:

- plant,
- shaper,
- implementer ('company worker'),
- co-ordinator ('chairman'),
- monitor-evaluator,

- completer-finisher,
- team worker,
- resource investigator.

Plant

Plants are innovators and can be highly creative, providing ideas for major developments. They may prefer to work by themselves at some distance from the team, using their imagination and often working in an innovative way. They may tend to be introverted and are inclined to react to criticism and to praise. Their ideas may often be off-the-wall and need shaping.

The main use of a plant is to generate new proposals and to solve complex problems. Plants are often needed in the initial stages of a project or when a project is failing to progress. Plants have usually made their mark as founders of companies or as originators of new products.

The plant was so named when it was found that one of the best ways to improve the performance of an ineffective and uninspired team was to plant one of this team type in it. But you can also think of the plant as the team member who provides the basic ideas for growth.

The tendency with the plant is that he will devote too much of his creative energy to ideas which may appeal to him but do not contribute to the team's strategic and personal objectives. He may be put off if his ideas are rejected and may withdraw from the team, at least temporarily. It can take quite a lot of careful handling and judicious flattery (usually by the co-ordinator) to get the best out of him. But for all his faults, it is the plant who provides the vital spark.

Too many plants in one team, however, may be counterproductive as they tend to spend their time reinforcing their own ideas and engaging each other in combat.

Shaper

Shapers are highly motivated with lots of energy. Usually they are extroverts and possess strong drive. Shapers encourage others to do things. In the face of barriers they will find a way round. Shapers are excellent at putting energy into a team and are useful in groups where politics would otherwise dominate. They are well suited to making necessary changes and do not mind taking less popular viewpoints. They will always try to impose some shape on the group discussion.

The shaper sees the team as an extension of his own ego. He wants action and he wants it immediately. There is a danger that people inside the team are likely to be steamrollered by the shaper.

Implementer (company worker)

Implementers have a lot of common sense and self-control. They love hard work and like to tackle problems systematically. They are usually less concerned with the pursuit of self-interest. Implementers may lack spontaneity and not easily be able to change direction.

They are useful to an organization because of their capacity for work and for their consistency. They succeed because they are efficient and because they have a sense of what is directly relevant and practicable. An implementer will do what needs to be done.

Co-ordinator (chairman)

Co-ordinators are able to help others to work towards shared goals. Mature and confident, they are very good at delegating and channelling activities in the pursuit of group objectives.

Co-ordinators are particularly useful when running a team with diverse skills and personal characteristics. Co-ordinators may well conflict with shapers due to their contrasting styles.

The co-ordinator sees most clearly which member of the team is strong or weak in each area of the team's function and focuses people on what they do best. He is conscious of the need to use the team's combined resources as effectively as possible. He is the one who defines roles and work boundaries, identifying any gaps and fill them.

Monitor-evaluator

Monitor-evaluators are very sensible team members who do not get carried away by impractical ideas. They are slow decision-makers and prefer to think things over. Monitor evaluators have well developed judgement and highly critical thinking ability.

Although the monitor-evaluator is by nature a critic rather than a creator, he does not usually criticize just for the sake of it but only if he can see a flaw in the project. He is often the least highly motivated of the team; enthusiasm and euphoria simply are not part of his agenda. This is compensated by his detachment and objectivity. He is also excellent in assimilating, interpreting and evaluating large volumes of complex data, analysing problems and assessing the judgements and contributions of others.

Completer-finisher

Completer-finishers have a huge capacity for follow-through and attention to detail. They will not start anything that they cannot finish. They tend to be anxious inside yet externally they may appear relaxed. They are typically introverted and are often not keen on delegating.

Completer-finishers are invaluable where the project requires close concentration to detail. They bring a sense of urgency to the team and are good at meeting deadlines. The completer-finisher tends not to be an assertive member of the team but generates a continuing sense of low-key urgency which keeps the team moving forward to its goals.

Team worker

Team workers help to support the team's morale. They are particularly concerned about other members of the team; they are adaptable to different situations and people, and are always diplomatic. They tend to be popular members of a group.

Team workers help to prevent interpersonal disruption within the group and thus allow all team members to contribute effectively. They will go to great lengths to avoid interpersonal clashes. As a promoter of team harmony, the team worker counterbalances the tensions which can be caused by the shaper and the plant.

Resource investigator

Resource Investigators are often enthusiastic extroverts. They are good at networking with people both inside and outside the team. They are adept at exploring new opportunities and developing contacts. They are particularly good at picking up other people's ideas and developing them. They are also skilled at finding out what is available and what can be done.

EXERCISE: WHICH BELBIN TEAM ROLE CORRESPONDS TO YOUR OWN?

1   For each team-role typology (plant, shaper, implementer, co-ordinator, monitor-evaluator, completer-finisher, team worker and resource investigator) score yourself with the following ratings: 1 = hardly applies at all; 2 = applies a little; 3 = applicable; 4 = very applicable; 5 = extremely applicable.
2   What is the 'so what?' from this analysis, particularly:
   - Which are your two most favoured role styles and what significance does this have?
   - Which are your two least favoured role styles and what significance does this have?
   - What effect does this have on how you operate in your current team?

It is useful to examine how Belbin team roles impact on the more strategic work which complex projects necessitate. The following summaries help to reveal the implications of team roles for strategic thinking and implementation:

- Plant: generates off-the-wall ideas which feed into breakthrough strategic thinking. But on its own these ideas may be half-formed, underdeveloped and may fail in practice.
- Shaper: helps to develop strategic ideas into workable strategies.
- Implementer: actually helps get the implementation done.
- Co-ordinator: brings together the ideas of different team members and reconciles them. Also establishes the key roles so people know what they are doing.
- Monitor-evaluator: helps to make the ideas into an effective business case – and monitors results.
- Completer-finisher: maintains a focus on project milestones.
- Team worker: harmonizes team interaction and its personal agendas.
- Resource investigator: ensures that interfaces with the organizational environment happen smoothly.

Managing team roles explicitly is an essential part of turning strategy into action through the medium of strategic projects.

Specific techniques for understanding strategic behaviour in projects

The techniques for understanding the strategic behaviour associated with strategic projects break into two levels, namely agenda analysis and dynamic analysis. In each case the potential problems and difficulties which might arise when implementing them are critiqued together with possible solutions.

These techniques include: agenda analysis, which is the personal and strategic agenda (PASTA factor analysis) and understanding subpersonalities, and dynamic analysis, involving behavioural scenarios and wishbone analysis, and difficulty-over-time, energy-over-time and frustration-over-time curves.

Personal and strategic agendas

Coupled with the need to influence behaviours and underlying agendas, it may be necessary to dig deeper into those agendas for specific individuals. Personal and strategic agenda analysis allows one to go much deeper.

Called the PASTA factor because of our finding at BT that both personal and strategic agendas are often inextricably intertwined almost like spaghetti, this analysis can yield some major insights. In order to get a good handle on someone else's PASTA factors, it is advisable to simulate the out-of-body experience, which entails one imagining and identifying with the feelings, thoughts, habits, everyday concerns and history of key stakeholders. PASTA factor analysis is an essential prelude to creating behavioural scenarios for your strategic project.

One resistance to using PASTA factor analysis is likely to be the discomfort which managers experience when reflecting on their own agendas. Here it is helpful for another manager(s) to tentatively suggest or hypothesize that someone might have certain X, Y and Z agendas. The awkwardness of doing this is significantly alleviated if the enquiring manager(s) explicitly say that they are having the equivalent of an out-of-body experience. This is usually taken in a humorous vein, thus enabling the strategic intervention to become fluid again.

Before we leave the topic of PASTA factors, it is also useful to see that an individual may not always have a coherent set of agendas. The very same individual may pursue one strategy one day, another strategy on another day (sometimes called stratophrenia). A useful way of getting one's mind around this is to use the notion of sub-personalities. For example, a particular stakeholder might have several mini-personalities:

- Personality A that wants to be seen as being very clever, actually, the cleverest in the team.
- Personality B seeks to protect at all cost what has worked in the past, especially where the person has put their own stamp of approval on it.
- Personality C, contrary to A and B, is actually quite helpful and supportive of change.

In doing the PASTA factor analysis you would need here to weigh up the likelihood of a particular subpersonality coming to the fore in this situation.

EXERCISE: EXPLORING SUBPERSONALITIES

Choose one person on your project team who is relatively hard to get along with.
1   Which subpersonalities can you identify in that individual?
2   Which subpersonalities do you get on best with and which do you get on least well with and why?
3   How might you adapt your behaviour to deal with this person's more difficult subpersonalities?

Behavioural scenarios and wishbone analysis

Behavioural scenarios involve semi-structured storytelling about how the future of the strategic project may develop. A first technique is to plot some key assumptions concerning the behavioural influences in the project. Figure 7.3 illustrates these, also identifying how certain behavioural assumptions which might have seemed to have been either of less importance or lesser uncertainty can quickly move into the south-east of the uncertainty grid – its danger zone.

Where one or more assumptions occur in this danger zone, it is at that point that a particular behavioural scenario can be drawn out. One scenario thus may be that the project team leader resigns and is then replaced by another team leader – who then immediately conducts an entire review of the strategic project with the result being a radical change in its direction.

Behavioural scenarios also can be refined by storytelling. For example, one can pick out transitional behavioural events. These events will lead us from the current state of the strategic project to one which is quite different. Or, one might start off with a particular future and then work backwards to define the kind of behavioural storyline which might lead up to that scenario.

A potential problem with using behavioural scenarios is that it is very possible that the scenario turns out to be completely off the mark. The very nature of scenarios makes the possibility of misjudging the future a significant risk. However, the alternatives – either of not looking into the behavioural future or extrapolating from the behavioural past – do not seem viable. If there is real doubt that one particular scenario fails to reveal the main behavioural turning points, then you might consider developing a second or even a third one.

FIGURE 7.3: A behavioural uncertainty-importance grid

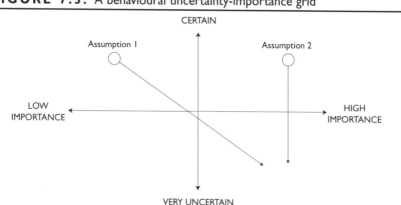

Or, one might use the metaphor model of the uncertainty tunnel from chapter 5 to help understand:

- the behavioural antecedents of the projects,
- the factors which might amplify or dampen behavioural change affecting the project,
- the first-, second- or third-order behavioural consequence of any important and sensitive event within or outside the strategic project.

Finally, you might identify one ideal behavioural state of the project or its behavioural vision and then try to map out all the behavioural factors which would need to be aligned in order to deliver that behavioural outcome. This can be drawn as a fishbone-like picture, except this time starting from the left-hand side of the page and working forward into the future. Because the goal of this picture is not to diagnose a problem but to create an opportunity, and because it deals with the future rather than the past, this technique becomes behavioural wishbone analysis.

With wishbone analysis the main area to be wary of is that however imaginative managers are they may fail to capture the one or two factors which still need to be aligned but currently are not, especially when dealing with behavioural issues. Wishbone analysis is most effective when accompanied by scenario storytelling. This ensures that all the things which need to go right do actually go right.

EXERCISE: BEHAVIOURAL SCENARIOS AND WISHBONE ANALYSIS

Choose one key project which you are currently involved in.
1   What behavioural interactions might you foresee as impacting on the project medium-term (positive or negative)?
2   What specific stories can you tell about how the various actors within the project team might deal with each other?
3   What wishbone analysis can you now construct for a scenario where all behaviours become aligned?
4   What could you now do to help bring about this positive behavioural wishbone?

Key lessons from the BT research

The BT managers themselves were frequently frustrated at the slow progress of key strategic projects. Their discussions were often too open-ended, inconclusive and diffuse to produce more focused outputs and thus action. Their interactions were swayed by a number of behavioural factors which appeared to handicap their effectiveness.

The cause-of-behaviour analysis (COBRA), which was a central part of the feedback to managers, is shown in Figure 7.4. This tailored fishbone analysis proved to be a very powerful intervention in the management team, as there was apparently unanimous agreement 'to see if we can try something better'.

In the facilitated sessions the team again ran into difficulties as old behaviours, not surprisingly, persisted. A most interesting finding was the tendency of key members of the team to focus on more microscopic issues involving them often going off at a tangent, rather than holding their attention at a more strategic level. Subsequent feedback showing the level and dynamics of discussion (see Figure 7.5) helped the team to understand the dysfunctional effects of excessive 'picking apart' behaviour. Figure 7.5 shows a typical discussion going through high, medium or low levels of generality. This technique did prove helpful in discerning who in the team had the greatest tendency to 'rabbit hole' the discussions, and is a useful mental aid for any strategic project facilitator.

FIGURE 7.4: Cause-of-behaviour analysis

FIGURE 7.5: Levels of discussion

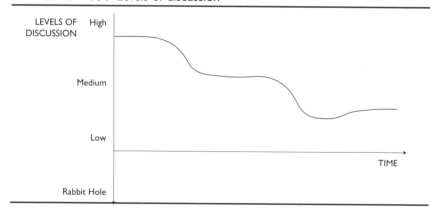

Another important finding occurred from studying later project interactions. Only when the team had gained a narrower focus of attention and when it was more able to share the cognitive maps and assumptions of its key individuals, was it able to achieve far greater momentum and harmony in its behaviours. So the greater the cognitive clarity exists within a team, the less behavioural turbulence is likely to exist.

A further finding was that certain behavioural drivers had the tendency to govern the cognitive subject matter of the managers. The main drivers of this were the personal agendas of individuals. These agendas contained a mix of emotional, territorial and cognitive elements which were all highly intermingled. So, for example, one manager held certain views about the attractiveness of a particular technology with BT's strategy. His cognitive assumptions were imbued with considerable feeling. But, at the same time, those views represented a particular 'ideas territory' which he had staked out as being 'right and appropriate for BT'.

This notion of 'ideas territory' is likely to be very helpful elsewhere, especially when a particular strategic project is complex and where a particular idea of how it will work or not work can come to dominate the wider project team's thinking. To challenge the dominant ideas territory is to make as much of a political challenge as it is to challenge the specific influence and power of an individual.

Finally, when managers were able to self-regulate their own behaviour and cognitive interplay, some very notable shifts in behaviours occurred. One particularly interesting change occurred when using the importance-influence grid. As the BT managers began to discuss what issues they had high vs low influence over, they became remarkably calmer and more fluid. Instead of operating at a predominantly low and microscopic level of debate they began to glide effortlessly up and down through the levels. In their own judgement, they delivered a good deal more (and in a shorter period of time) than in their previous sessions.

Having considered some analytical techniques for managing the interactions between managers engaged in strategic projects, let us now turn to a strategic change project, Champneys Health Farm. This illustrates not merely the behavioural and political aspects of strategic project management but also how an integrated strategic project programme can be defined and implemented. This case study is based on a documentary on BBC television and on an interview with Champneys' managing director by one of the co-authors in 1997.

CASE STUDY: CHAMPNEYS HEALTH FARM

Background and project diagnosis

Champneys Health Farm is located at Tring, Hertfordshire, UK. Champneys is a select, rural retreat for its members who reside principally in and around the Home Counties, England. Traditionally it is a most exclusive retreat, charging expensive prices for its luxurious and relatively exotic services in body and skin care generally.

By the recession of the 1990s, Champneys was suffering considerably. Falling demand meant that its cash flow had deteriorated to the point where it experienced an annual cash deficit of £1 million. Its owners decided that enough was enough, and sold out to foreign investors.

In business terms, Champneys was in the situation of a strategic turnaround. So its new, foreign investors decided that a new breath of life needed to be injected to secure Champneys' future.

In late 1995, Savoy-trained Lord Thurso was recruited to spearhead Champneys' recovery. As its new chief executive, Lord Thurso set about formulating a turnaround plan which would secure Champneys a viable future. At this time Champneys also featured on a BBC2 television production, 'Trouble at the Top'. Some of the quotes by Lord Thurso are taken from that television programme and some from an interview with the author.

Because Champneys prided itself on its exclusive customer service, this turnaround project needed to be managed with great sensitivity to people issues.

Strategic diagnosis

In the tradition of turnaround specialists, Lord Thurso set himself a tight deadline to formulate and project manage his turnaround project plan. This was just one month. In the course of that month Lord Thurso was to spend the bulk of his time listening to Champneys' various stakeholders, particularly its members and regular customers, its staff, and its current managers.

The projects undertaken for the Champneys turnaround included (with people-related projects asterisked):

- sampling Champneys treatments (by Lord Thurso),
- simplifying management processes,

- improving management reporting processes,
- management restructuring*,
- management recruitment*,
- the communication plan*,
- the strategic vision*,
- developing a business strategy*,
- customer database,
- maintaining organizational morale*,
- culture change*,
- getting rid of Health-for-Life,
- premises strategy,
- the business case and its approval.

To begin with, when Lord Thurso took over Champneys he weighed 16 stones. As a parallel agenda, Lord Thurso undertook to reduce this weight, coincidentally in parallel with what became Champneys' own corporate slimming exercise. Most important in those early days for Lord Thurso was to sample Champneys' exotic, health-generating treatments, being his first project to help turn-around the business..

Lord Thurso's early diagnosis within the turnaround project indicated that Champneys suffered from a number of underlying problems (see Figure 7.6 which portrays a fishbone or root-cause analysis of its malaise). These included:

- a legacy of underinvestment and decay,
- a decline in standards generally,
- an overzealous attempt to market Champneys' time shares to customers outside Champneys' core customer base,
- promises made to members which could not be kept,
- a top-heavy management structure,

FIGURE 7.6: Fishbone – Champneys

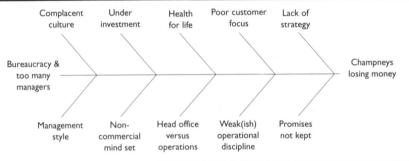

- relatively poor or inappropriate management and financial controls,
- a lack of sense of strategic direction generally.

Lord Thurso, on his first inspection of the property after taking over, commented:

> It is clearly very tired. These rooms would have been considered five-star when they were built but, clearly the expectations of five-star [have] changed. It is bland, it is grey, it is a very dead, dull room, it has no colour, and it has zero on the excitement scale.
>
> *BBC2*

Champneys strategic positioning itself also seemed to be unclear:

> I have asked the question of everybody, 'What are we selling?' and I get a lot of long-winded answers. The real answer is that no-one has thought about it.
>
> *BBC2*

Lord Thurso also reflected:

> ... What had been created in the past was the infrastructure for a £100 million company even though it was only a £10 million company.
>
> It had all these people here who were called brand managers. And none of them understood what a brand was. And that was the extraordinary thing. None of them understood the elementary concept of a brand being a promise made to customers that has values and a character. If you said to them, 'What does Champneys mean?' the answer was, they hadn't thought it through.
>
> *Interview*

Many of these issues must have been apparent almost as soon as Lord Thurso drove up Champneys' drive. As soon as he arrived he found a mass of memos from his managers:

> There are piles and piles of paper. It is a fairly classic thing. There are too many managers sending memos to each other. And I am suspicious of any company that is capable of generating so much paper when they are told they are expecting a new chief executive.
>
> *BBC2*

The following reveals Lord Thurso's quite different management style:

> I tend to communicate by getting up and sitting in someone's office. I loathe memos. In my last company I banned them completely

for two months. I said, 'The next person who writes a memo will be fired'. It was amazing, we didn't have a single memo written for two months. It was brilliant, people actually started talking to one another.

Interview

Two significant projects were clearly identified – simplifying management processes and improving management reporting processes.

At the same time, management lacked the fundamental information that it required:

We do not have good financial information. In fact, not only is it not good, it is actually awful. The management accounts that I have seen are mathematically correct, but they are not informative.

BBC2

So, besides simplifying the management process, a further project would need to be improving management reporting processes. Lord Thurso commented:

There was a management structure which didn't work. The management reports were gibberish. I asked simple questions, 'Do you know what your cash flow is?' and the guy couldn't tell me... They didn't produce balance sheets. They produced huge, thick reports, full of graphs, trend analysis. But the one thing that they didn't do was to produce reports where you could find profit, where you could find cash flow. I said we will really have to start from scratch.

I remember sitting on the lawn on holiday... trying to read through two years of drivel, the management accounts... I can usually work things out, and I just couldn't make it work.

Interview

Instead of rolling out a turnaround plan straight away, Lord Thurso spent precious time soliciting the views of all its key stakeholders, especially of its disgruntled customers. This enabled him not only to be absolutely sure that his chosen path was the right one but also, in behavioural terms, was owned.

This period of listening was primarily so Lord Thurso could establish a rapport with his new staff and thus to provide a platform for influencing them effectively:

To be honest, I had already made up my mind before I arrived here what I would do. I had actually decided before the day that I started that I was going to take a million pounds out of the costs...

I wanted them to have thought that I had thought it through. They wouldn't have understood that I was capable of thinking it through very quickly, and that it was really clear what had to be done. It was really a very simple problem, and it needed some pretty straight-forward solutions.

After I arrived, I said 'I will have a month, and I will take no decisions until the end of the month'. It was a good thing. I did fractionally amend certain decisions but 90 per cent of it was exactly what I had thought previously.

Interview

The above highlights how the leader of any strategic project needs to be a quick thinker but at the same time recognize and accept the pace of the organization. This does not come easily to some senior managers who are particularly bright.

Lord Thurso realized intuitively that Champneys was the kind of situation which could so easily fail if a number of stakeholders decided, rightly or wrongly, that he was the wrong man for the job. Quite quickly Lord Thurso concluded from his own personal course of treatments that his operational staff were a real asset – to be retained, nurtured and developed. He said:

The closer I get to the front line the better I find the troops are. And that is very pleasing, because if you have good officers and lousy soldiers you have got a lot of work to do, but if you have good soldiers and lousy officers, then you have to work to train or change the officers.

BBC2

In some contrast, Lord Thurso found the management which he inherited, although up to the task of managing in a more steady state environment, not really up to a turnaround. The top-heavy management structure was not only an expense that the business could not afford, it also impeded the recovery plan, inviting two further interrelated projects – management restructuring and management recruitment.

The change process

This knowledge posed a major dilemma for Lord Thurso if he were to move very fast and introduce a new, slimmed down management structure. The shock might topple the organization, undermining morale at the cutting edge of customer service. In these situations there is probably no single right answer. Arguably, by leaving the Champneys' managers in suspense for one month, he prolonged the agony of uncertainty. On the other hand, by at least listening to them over this period he would have a better idea of who was and was not able to make the transition – and also how many, in simple, financial terms, he could take with him.

Once his first, crucial month was up, Lord Thurso needed to move fast to communicate and implement the first stages of his turnaround plan. This necessitated a further project – the communication plan.

Lord Thurso reflected just how serious the problems at the old head office had become:

> And there was a business over there that had been completely neglected at head office. There was a flipchart in every office, which to me was a symptom of this very introverted style – the moment anybody had a meeting someone was on a flipchart. The whole thing was driven by the processes rather than by the objectives. If there were objectives they were tacked onto the process.'
>
> People worked hard and interacted and interfaced and essentially went around in circles. There was no questioning of, 'Why are we here?' or 'What is the meaning of the universe?'
>
> It was quite clear that I had to make a very clear... very definitive statement that there was a complete change coming. It wasn't quite as bloody as it looked, because I redeployed quite a lot of the people I had here back into the units. That refocused them on where the action was.
>
> I described it once as 'this head office was once a great black hole which sucked energy out of the units; things vanished into it never to be seen again'. Whereas my idea of head offices is that it should be a tiny, tiny star in the sky, twinkling light down, completely out of the way.
>
> *Interview*

The above highlighted a most important project – formulating a strategic vision for the company. It also emphasized the importance of tackling the key organizational obstacles to any change project.

Lord Thurso's own vision for Champneys is profoundly simple. Lord Thurso prefers the idea of vision to mission because mission statements are harder to grasp onto, particularly in terms of the behaviours which are implied by them:

> If you cannot remember a mission statement (I cannot remember our old one), if you have to refer to something, that's wrong. To me, any mission statement which is 'we will have care for our customers, be nice to our staff, be nice to grey squirrels on Sundays', you know, you have gone to sleep.

It has got to be something that encapsulated the spirit. 'Nowhere else makes you this good – yes, it is a spirit statement. That's why, NASA, 'To get a man on the moon', makes sense. At Champneys it is: 'Nowhere else makes you feel this good', and that should apply to the staff as well.

Interview

Potentially, Lord Thurso faced major resistance to his plan, especially from his senior managers who expressed their loyalty to their previous MD and to past strategy (during the television documentary). In business terms there was little alternative but to severely reduce the number of his central management team. Lord Thurso addressed the team at a management meeting:

> Please view my arrival not as something disastrous but actually as an expression of support by our shareholders.
>
> The problem in a nutshell is that we are losing money. You are all intelligent people, and therefore you will know that there will be a cost-cutting exercise. We have an expression in the fitness centre of 'no pain, no gain', but there will be pain.
>
> We are, with the cost of head office, losing as a company approximately £1 million in cash terms per year. It is my intention and target that by the end of the next year we will be cash break-even. The direction I have decided to follow is to put Champneys absolutely and without doubt at the top of the tree.

BBC2

He had decided to tell them collectively of his decision so that he delivered two clear and separate messages. The first message was that there was an impelling need to restructure and reduce the management resource. The second message was to specific individuals – that they were, or were not, to be members of the future team. Within the restructuring project there would be two sub projects – diagnosing current skills and defining the future skills needed to deliver the strategy. Indeed, besides developing an overall strategic vision, a further project was also required – developing a business strategy. Key subparts of this project were: a marketing strategy for current activities, a review of wider strategic options, a customer services strategy, and finally a premises strategy. This was also related to a further project: to enhance Champneys' customer database.

An alternative would have been to speak to individuals separately, both to communicate the need for the change and whether or not they still had a job. This alternative approach would have had the merit of removing the period of uncertainty during which his managers would have been concerned about their job security. But equally it would have meant that whilst Lord Thurso was interviewing his managers some would have heard about the organizational change sooner than the others.

These simple logistics highlight the behavioural implications of making a strategic change in an organization. For whichever way Lord Thurso played it, the effect on individuals' feelings, perhaps of hurt and fear, might have ramifications in their future and also that of the remaining team.

The impact of these redundancies was obviously severe on the managers. Champneys' property manager, Willie Serplis, attempted to put a brave face on as he came smiling to the television interview following his meeting with Lord Thurso. His smile quickly faded as he told:

> Do you want to ask the question then... 'How are you?' Not very happy. I just lost my job, which is better knowing – but what can I do? You want to be angry with someone or something, but it doesn't make sense. You can dress it up in all the esoteric bullshit you know – downsizing, redundancy – but the reality is, for no fault of my own, I have just been fired.
>
> *BBC2*

Lord Thurso himself looked emotionally strained when he was asked how he felt about this part of the process:
I would find it hard to sleep if I felt that anything I was doing was wrong in any way. I dislike doing it, but it is a necessary operation that has to be done on the company. All that one can do is to do it as humanely and professionally as one can.

> Most of them have been angry because at the end of the day we all like to think that we have a value in an organization and, effectively, when you are made redundant someone is saying that you don't have a value in the organization. When I say that it isn't to do with your performance it is to entirely do with the financial structure of the company, it actually doesn't help them very much.
>
> *BBC2*

One can imagine the atmosphere within the management block at Champneys as the reality sank in that it was the end of an era. Also, those staying realized that they would be expected to achieve a quantum shift in the level of effectiveness if the business were to come back into profit.

The above account highlights a further, short-term project: maintaining organizational morale.

It was then Lord Thurso's turn to address his operational staff. Lord Thurso appeared to be in a lighter mood as he informed his staff not merely about the severity of the situation but also of the fact that he was planning other job cuts:

> The last part of the strategy and the bit that does concern all of you is that new court and the concept of a headquarters is going to be quite radically scaled down. There are 22 people sitting here and we have probably half that for the number of places that I actually have available. You are intelligent and you will have worked this out. And therefore some people are going to have to be redundant... And I do recognize the pain that this will cause you. I am sorry that some of you will be going, but please understand that it is nothing to do with you and your capability. It is simply about how this business has been run over the past few years and the requirement to put it on a proper cash footing.
>
> Finally, I would like to give you a little thought. All my life I have been involved in giving first-class service to people and I believe it is a wonderful thing to do. Be always ready to say 'yes' whenever a client or guest comes to see you and asks for something and you are tempted to say 'no'. Stop, think, and that will help us to create a level of service unheard of in this country.
>
> *BBC2*

Lord Thurso's own larger-than-life character was a crucial ingredient in signalling that the changes necessary were very, very real. He reflects on the progress of his customer service project, which is also closely linked to the ongoing project of culture change:

> But the key at the top should have a kind of evangelical fanaticism about what the strategy is. Unless you have this, you are not going to manage to convince people. For example, last year I called our plans 'Going from Good to Great'. And we didn't go from good to great, we got better. So I said, 'This is "Good to Great Part Two"'. We could be back here next year doing part three or even part four. But one day we will get there and I ain't leaving here until we do.
>
> I believe that all human beings are capable of change for the better. This may be an optimistic view. But I therefore start from the premise that it is better to work with people rather than change them. I find that the grass on the other side of the fence is not often greener.

When you are sorting out a business and getting the headcount right, yes you have to cut to get it right. But some people would go in and say, 'I can't work with that general manager and fire them and get another one. And then after six months you get another one. Personally, I prefer to say, 'Why is this not working? Let us look at it and actually help this person'. I find that you then get staff who are more loyal.

Interview

But this involves recognizing that staff's agendas may not be nicely aligned with the vision. Lord Thurso tells us about the practicalities of achieving the necessary culture change – another project – to radically shift old behaviour patterns:

If I am honest with you, I am only a small part the way through. All the things, these wonderful things that managers do, that is all part of our game. But the guy at the bottom says 'Sod you, I only have 40 hours to do my job'. What he is saying to you is 'if you want me to do this, give me a reason'.

And that guy at the bottom isn't going to say, 'Wow, that guy at the top, he is a zing. Now I will suddenly smile at customers'. There has got to be something in it for him. And part of it is being controlled, led, cajoled, pushed into it. And a part of it is being rewarded, feeling nice, all of the rest of it. It is a huge culture change that virtually every company in this country needs to actually genuinely understand what a customer-orientated organization is. I have grave difficulty in thinking of a truly customer-orientated organization in the United Kingdom. I mean, there must be one somewhere. Mine isn't yet. It is a tremendous culture change.

Interview

Besides dealing with internal stakeholders, Lord Thurso had to manage the expectations of the Champneys' members whose business was needed to secure a successful future. These members had been disappointed in the past by its prior management who had, perhaps, set up expectations about improvements in standards that had not, or could not have, been delivered. Lord Thurso then decided to end the previous management's scheme for time sharing not only to those sales activities but also to buying back the time share. Getting out of this business area proved to be one of the most difficult projects.

Lord Thurso was quick to realize that the Health-for-Life time-sharing scheme needed to be halted: 'From what I have seen the constant push-push-push on Health-for-Life has given the wrong impression in the marketplace. I think maybe we should cut that right back' (BBC2).

He also determined that the physical facilities and amenities at Champneys did not provide a sustainable foundation for its future marketing strategy which was aimed at repositioning Champneys as an exclusive resort: 'What a great architect friend of mine once described as the "wow" factor. What we have got here is the "er" factor. What we need is a "wow" factor' (BBC2).

So, besides the organizational changes which Lord Thurso instigated, he also set about developing an ambitious project to revitalize the physical fabric of Champneys. This included a major uplift in the entrance and facade to the central building and the driveway, and conversion of the management block to produce 20 additional treatment rooms, which was hoped would provide the spur to expand Champneys' customer base.

These renovations would provide a further benefit, signalling to the employees that Champneys was genuinely going to be set on the road to a prosperous future.

The turnaround projects and their strategies

But to achieve these plans, Lord Thurso needed to build the confidence of his investors who might well have thought that a turn-around was possible without major investment of this order. To achieve this he needed to produce a robust business case which, yet again, became a key project. Lord Thurso realized that to provide the basis for this confidence he would need to achieve a number of things:

- the restructuring of management had to be implemented successfully;
- better financial planning and control needed to be stabilized with the help of its new finance director whom Lord Thurso had brought in;
- Lord Thurso's restructuring would need to have delivered the required cost savings;
- although a gap still remained to break even with these cost savings, it would need to be closed by expanding revenues;
- to achieve this, the quality of service and standards generally had to improve considerably to the point where members felt a real difference and new members were brought in.

Although cost savings of £500 million per annum were achieved relatively quickly, it proved much slower to improve sales through improving customer confidence. But within one year Champneys managed to break even. So, Lord Thurso was able to then put into effect his plan to obtain enough investment to reposition Champneys as an outstanding health resort.

The overseas investors were able to give Lord Thurso the vote of confidence he needed in order to move into stage two of the turnaround – a major upgrading programme – whose implementation became a further strategic project. So, at last, all the planks of Lord Thurso's future strategy were in place.

We have now told the story of Champneys' strategic turnaround mainly from the point of view of the business. But if we look at this situation from a more behavioural point of view, we find that this dimension has perhaps even more importance than more tangible areas of change.

Implementing the strategic change programme

If we now look at the key forces enabling and constraining the Champneys change programme (Figure 7.7), the most important forces are more behavioural in nature.

This picture makes use of force-field analysis, which again depicts the length of each force as an enabling or constraining arrow. Each arrow is drawn, as always, in proportion to its perceived strength. The balance of these forces gives an indication of the

FIGURE 7.7: Force-field analysis – Champneys

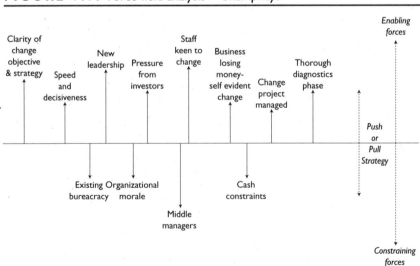

degree of difficulty involved. In this case, Lord Thurso's turn-around strategy makes what might have been a Mission Impossible project into one of moderate difficulty.

Lord Thurso said:

> You do have to have a strategy. You can fight battles without a strategy and have success, but it is a pretty haphazard thing. You have got to have a clear idea of where you are going, but equally you have to recognize that the achievement of the strategy will be a series of tactical steps.

Interview

It is also necessary to look at how implementation difficulty changes over time. Figure 7.8 gives an approximate view of the difficulty-over-time curve associated with the overall project. Initially, Lord Thurso's turnaround project faced severe difficulties. But once the new structure was put in place, and one Lord Thurso's new vision for the organization had been unveiled, this difficulty would be mitigated.

However, as time progressed, this difficulty might well have increased as the organization found a new stability and sought to resist further changes. In turn, this difficulty might then begin to reduce once Lord Thurso's programmes to improve customer service and shift attitudes begin to take hold.

Next, Figure 7.9 plots the approximate position of some of the key stakeholders who had an influence on this strategic change. This highlights that before Lord Thurso unveiled his turnaround project the balance of influence in the organization was against him; but by introducing new stakeholders, exiting some old ones, and by appealing directly to the staff, the balance of influence was reversed in Lord Thurso's favour.

FIGURE 7.8: Difficulty-over-time curve – Champneys

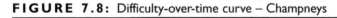
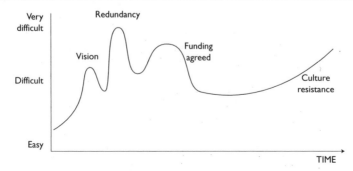

Obviously, this picture is drawn at a relatively high level. If we were to go down to a deeper level to that of the agendas of individual stakeholders, we would clearly find difference in the attitudes of individuals within these groupings. Also, the position of stakeholders would vary project by project.

To understand the influence patterns of these stakeholders we must also bear in mind some additional factors:

- The agendas of stakeholders are not fixed but will change over time vis-à-vis the various projects as new issues arise and as perceptions change within the organization.
- At any point in time agendas may be fluid and ambiguous, particularly at the start of the turnaround. Key stakeholders, particularly middle managers, may not have any clear attitude at all. Although they may have some case agendas (such as, 'I want to hang onto my job') these might be very limited. And even here, core agendas might be conditional on Champneys being seen as a congenial atmosphere to work in, given its new leadership. Never assume that attitudes and underlying agendas of stakeholders are always given.
- Individuals within one group will influence the agendas of others within the group. Through the informal network opinion leaders will signal their approval or disapproval of particular actions.
- You may need to break down the project into a number of sub-projects – as stakeholder positions will vary according to what is being implemented. For instance, a stakeholder may approve of Lord Thurso's plans to renovate the buildings and his plans to end the Health-for-Life promotion but be violently against running a smaller department.

FIGURE 7.9: Stakeholder analysis – Champneys

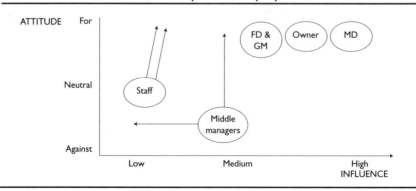

Besides Lord Thurso's management of the key stakeholders, it is also worthwhile pausing to reflect for a moment on the impact of team roles.

Lord Thurso's own role comes over very strongly as being that of co-ordinator (chairman). He also combines both plant and shaper characteristics in his visionary skills. He exudes personal charisma and was able to carry a considerable number of stakeholders with him. His new general manager comes over (from the TV programme) as a shaper and completer-finisher. His new finance director appears to be a very strong monitor-evaluator, and his existing marketing manager an implementer and team worker. So, from even a small team base, most of the roles appear well covered.

A summary of Champneys' projects

Listing Champneys' strategic change projects now according to the categories of strategic, operational and organizational they run as follows, (with the relevant figures illustrating their interdependencies:

Strategic projects (Figure 7.10)
- Strategic vision
- Business strategy
- Marketing strategy – involving market research and brand strategy

FIGURE 7.10: Champneys' strategic projects

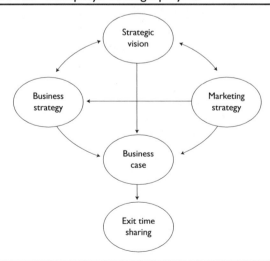

- Business case
- Exit time-sharing

Operational and systems projects (Figure 7.11)
- Sampling of services
- Customer-service improvement
- Premises upgrade
- Management process simplification
- Management reporting
- Customer database enhancement

Organizational projects (Figure 7.12)
- Management restructuring
- Management recruitment
- Maintaining staff morale
- Culture change
- Communication plan
- Organizational skills diagnosis

Not only do the above strategic programmes gain in attractiveness through being part of a strategic project set, they also gain through reduced implementation difficulty. Notice, too, how closely interrelated these are – both within the four clusters of strategic, operational, organizational and systems headings, and also between clusters.

Figure 7.13 plots the approximate sequence of those projects over time. Notice how, by staggering projects, they become more feasible. Also, notice that some projects are ongoing, such as culture change.

FIGURE 7.11: Champneys' operational and systems projects

Key lessons from Champneys

In summary, the key pointers for managing strategic projects, especially those that impact on people and behaviour specifically, are:

- Stakeholder management is absolutely central to managing the various projects effectively. Accordingly, ample time should be devoted to analysing the current and potentially future positions of stakeholders – and their driving agendas.
- Leadership is crucial in a situation where stakeholders are likely to actively resist implementation efforts. This leadership requires a degree of evangelical enthusiasm, a very explicit

FIGURE 7.12: Champneys' organizational projects

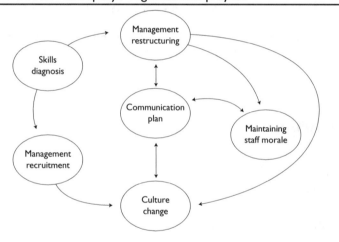

FIGURE 7.13: Champneys' projects – activity analysis

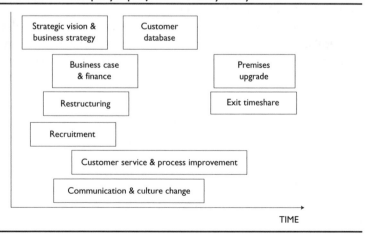

statement about the strategic vision and great practical tenacity in implementing that vision.

- Achieving headway depends on building a sufficient stakeholder platform to leverage off. At Champneys this involved key appointments of a new finance director and property manager and winning over Champneys' frontline staff.
- The difficulty over time of a particular strategic project will change. The shifts in difficulty need to be anticipated and managed rather than just coped with.

EXERCISE: REFLECTIONS ON THE CHAMPNEYS CASE

1   What parallels are there, if any, between Champneys' organization and your own?
2   What lessons are there from how Champneys' strategic change was project managed?
3   What more specific lessons are there for projects in your own organization about people and behaviour management – and especially leadership?

Conclusion

Influencing people and behaviour is a fundamental part of strategic project management. This softer area of SPM requires a combination of analytical skill, vision, leadership and imagination, and also proactive management of team roles.

The analytical tools, such as fishbone (cause of behaviour analysis) and stakeholder analysis, will be indispensable to you in managing these softer aspects of strategic projects.

It also requires interpersonal sensitivity coupled with the necessary political determination to translate your vision for the strategic project into a reality, as we saw very much was the case in the Champneys' case study.

Reference

Grundy, A.N. (1998) *Harnessing Strategic Behaviour*, Financial Times Publishing.

CHAPTER EIGHT

Managing strategic projects: checklists

Introduction

In this chapter the following areas will be discussed and detailed checklists for managing strategic projects will be provided:

- organic business development projects,
- organizational change projects,
- acquisition, alliance and joint venture projects,
- operational projects.

These checklists can be used for:

- developing your own project plans,
- appraising the project plans of others,
- as input for MBA coursework and especially for MBA projects which have a strategic focus.

Organic business development projects

Some processes for evaluating strategic projects have already appeared in chapter 5. These checklists will help to flesh out some of the richer content issues which you may well encounter. Whilst managers may feel they are well versed in these organic development projects, they may well look too myopically at the more obvious areas of inquiry.

Organic business development projects can be aimed at a number of areas including:

- new products,
- new markets by sector or by geography,

- selling more to existing customers,
- new value-creating activities,
- new distribution channels,
- new technologies.

New product projects

It is often said that nine out of ten new product ideas fail either because they are not thought through sufficiently or, and more commonly, the product concept does not quite match market need. These checklists, coupled with wishbone analysis, should help you get a better steer. Our questions now are:

- How fast is the market for this type of product growing?
- How much competitive pressure exists in its market?
- How well does the product meet its target customer needs – what are the turn-ons and turn-offs from a customer point of view?
- Which other products is it competing with and what are the relative advantages/disadvantages between each?
- How, if at all, does the product need servicing, and what are the relative competitive advantages here?
- How complex is the product, and will this level of complexity mean it is harder to launch and/or less flexible to change subsequently?
- Are there any wonderfully innovative features which add real value to the product?
- If these exist, how easily can they be imitated?
- How consistent is the organization's capability and mind-set with this product, and what implementation issues might this raise?
- What skills training is required to support this product effectively?
- Are the product's long-run unit costs likely to be sustainable long-term?
- What other changes in the organization are needed (for example to key business processes or to organizational structure)?
- Will the sales force and distribution channels accommodate the new product effectively without destruction, disruption, a dilution of sales of other products?
- To what extent might the product cannibalize on other existing products?
- To what extent will the product's innovation be project-managed well?
- How can its introduction be positioned and accelerated in the organization?

New market projects

New market development projects may overlap to some extent with new products. Nevertheless, we include some questions to supplement those on new products:

- Have you systematically prioritized which potential new markets would be most attractive to address, for example using the AID analysis, or the strategic option grid?
- How inherently attractive is this market? Consider its growth drivers and the level of competitive pressure in it.
- How difficult is it to operate within that market generally?
- Do we have the natural competencies to do well in that market?
- Is this market vastly culturally different to our current core markets?
- Is this a market especially prone to discounting, high costs of satisfying customers or distribution channels, or low margins generally?
- Have we got a genuinely cunning entry strategy or just an average one?
- What channel strategy options exist and which of these is most attractive inherently in terms of its use and value-added generally or one where we have greatest competitive advantage?
- What are the most critical uncertainties about that market and how can we minimize our exposure to these?
- Will entering this particular market foreclose options to enter other markets?
- To what extent will market conditions vary internationally, and which of these markets should we really give highest priority?

Selling more to existing customers

Selling more to our existing customers may well be a neglected strategy but, nevertheless, one which may be both highly attractive and relatively easy:

- Which of our existing customer base could we potentially sell more to?
- What could we sell them, why and how?
- What things have prevented us from selling as much as our true potential to existing customers in the past?
- What latent, existing needs could we satisfy and which we are not currently satisfying?
- What latent, future needs could we satisfy and how?
- How might selling more to our existing customers strengthen our relationship with them and gain lock-in?

- Are there other buyers within the customers' organization which we can sell to (e.g., another management function, another division, etc.)?
- What specific sales or other incentives would encourage greater penetration of our existing customer base?
- Which of our key competitors is currently active within these customers and how can we erode their share?
- How can we make it unbelievably easy to buy from us and to buy more from us?
- How can these improvements be project-managed?

New value-creating activity projects

Adding value in new ways may offer exciting project opportunities but ones which managers may find it difficult to think through:

- Are there new ways in which we can add value to the customer (value-creating activities)?
- How much additional value is likely to be created for them from their perspective?
- How will we be able to capture or share this value creation given our relative bargaining power and our long-term strategy?
- To what extent should new value-creating activities be in- or out-sourced, and why?
- How readily might new ways of adding value be imitated by competitors?
- To what extent will customers seek to do these value-creating activities themselves, assuming they are worthwhile having?
- What is our natural level of competence for adding value in these new ways?
- Can we easily pilot these new value-creating opportunities?
- How will we project-manage developing these new value-creating activities?

New distribution channel projects

Opening up new distribution channels avoids the difficulties of new product and/or market innovation and may well be cheap. But in order to avoid diluting our strategy and shareholder value, we will need to be relatively selective:

- How much margin are we likely to obtain from a new distribution channel?
- How difficult is it likely to be to deal with?

- What are the key alternatives to dealing with this particular channel (for example by the Internet, sales force, an alliance, etc)?
- Will this particular channel lead to conflict with any other distribution channels? If so, how will we manage it?
- Are we likely to get a high level of returns or other quality problems through this channel?
- Will the channel actually understand our product sufficiently well?
- How much support will this channel put behind our product relative to that of other products?
- Does this distribution channel have something that fits our natural competencies and our culture?
- How competitive is this particular channel relative to other pathways to market?
- If we do not use this channel, what, if anything, is the biggest downside?
- How would we project manage new entry to that channel?

New technologies

New technologies may be a turn-on to middle managers but a turn-off to top managers whose main focus is to extract short- and medium-term values out of the business. We may therefore need some testing questions in order to screen innovative technology projects:

- Does the technology actually fit with our present or emerging definition of what business(es) we are in?
- Do we really understand the technology?
- What other things, other than technology, all have to line up to deliver real value? Use a wishbone analysis.
- Are we doing the project mainly because of its sheer technological edge and because it is inherently exciting, or because it will generate real value, and value that we can actually harvest?
- What key value and cost drivers are impacted on by the new technology?
- What new skills do we need to fully exploit any new technology?
- To what extent do we have to change our mind-set in order to get the very best out of the new technology?
- Where the technology relies heavily on the Internet, how easy is our business model copied or imitated?
- How quickly will the new technology spread, and where there are customer turn-offs in its use, how can these be mitigated or removed?
- How rapidly might the technology be superceded by further technologies, and how vulnerable does this therefore make our strategy?

- What substitute technologies are available which are in many respects better right now?
- How should we project-manage the introduction of the new technology?

Looking at new technologies, for instance, one of the authors had written a large number of articles and books prior to 2000. From January 2000 onwards there was a sudden rush of demand for knowledge management in strategy with him writing:

- two digests on strategy and acquisitions for accountants,
- a software learning package for strategic thinking,
- a distance learning MBA module on strategy for a US business school,
- a module on strategic finance for an Internet-based MBA programme.

From a base of zero, in the first nine months of 2000 this became 15 per cent of his revenue. This illustrates how organic business development projects can seem to spring from nowhere as emergent strategies, but soon, of course, becoming deliberate ones.

Organizational change projects

The checklists in this section are designed to provide managers with a lasting guide to helping them manage change on a day-to-day basis. This applies at the organizational level, at the level of more specific areas of change and also with managers' individual roles. These checklists are structured in four parts:

- understanding the macro context;
- project-managing the change process, including project definition, strategy, planning, implementation, control, learning;
- analysing content issues, externally, internally and cross-functionally;
- managing specific change applications, including for example, restructuring, quality, culture change and managing individual role transitions.

Understanding the macro context of change

- Does the proposed change directly or indirectly impact on strategy, structure, culture or on a mix of these key ingredients of strategic change?
- Do we propose to manage it as if all three, or two, of the above elements are affected by macro-level change or in relative isolation – and if the latter, then why?

- Does the pace and degree of internal change genuinely match the pace of change in the external business environment where this is a key driver of internal change?
- Is there appropriate leadership to steer the change through?
- Does one's mission adequately reflect a realistic strategy for the business in enabling it to compete and the underlying values implicit in corporate culture?
- Does the proposed change fit with the organizational paradigm or seek to achieve a paradigm shift?
- Is any change intervention of sufficient critical mass and well focused enough to achieve a quantum shift in the paradigm?
- How well is this change intervention positioned in the organization and what ongoing attention, both symbolic and real, is top management prepared to give it?

Project managing the change process

The key phases of project managing the change process are:

- diagnosis and the definition of the project,
- strategy and planning,
- implementation,
- control and learning.

Typically, most change projects focus principally upon their implementation with the other phases being given less attention to diagnosis and also to the change strategy.

Definition of the project

- Have we identified the real nature of the change problem or opportunity?
- Have we diagnosed our current position?
- Is the objective of the change project clearly specified in terms of where we want to be and with what tangible benefits and by when?
- How wide is the gap between where we are now and where we need to be for the change project? How does this stack up against preconceived ideas of how long and difficult the change process will be?
- What are the key enabling and constraining forces within both the change project and its context which will influence progress towards meeting the change objectives?
- Have these key change forces picked up both tangible and less tangible factors as they now are (i.e., not in terms of an ideal) in the change process, for example leadership, communication, skills, key

stakeholders, readiness for change, culture and style, systems, adequacy of resources, timescales and clarity of change plans?

- Do any of these forces identify possible stoppers?
- What is the overall balance of forces – do these show the change project as being manageable, very difficult or as Mission Impossible?
- Has the strategy for the change project now been reshaped in the light of the force field analysis?
- Has a stakeholder analysis been performed in order to ensure the force-field analysis is complete, and to evolve influencing strategies to help mobilize commitment to change?

Strategy and planning

A particularly important activity is developing an effect strategy for the change project before detailed change plans are laid down:

- Has the overall change objective per the definition phase been refined into a small number of more detailed and specific change objectives?
- What are the key strategic options for how the change project will be implemented and how are these positioned on the AID grid?
- Are these objectives supported by key change milestones which specify phases of the change process, clear outputs and outcomes of each phase, and who is responsible for achieving these milestones?
- Has a network of appropriately resourced activities been drawn up to support the achievement of these milestones?
- Has the change project been thoroughly evaluated in terms of tangible and less tangible benefits and costs and who are these owned by in the organization?
- What key risks and uncertainties have been identified? Does this include interdependencies with other areas of change and possible changes in management intent?
- Have the initial force-field analysis and stakeholder analysis been updated for further changes since the diagnosis phase?
- Has an appropriate and competent leader of the change project been appointed and does he have a change project team with adequate skills and an appropriate style to ensure smooth implementation?
- Has the change project been suitably communicated in a skillfully targeted and timed way to all those playing a central role in the change and those indirectly affected by the change?
- Do business plans adequately reflect any unavoidable drop in performance due to the inherent problems of managing a particularly difficult transition?
- Is there an explicit business case for any major change?

Implementation

The implementation of any change project can be very frustrating as the project fails to mobilize or suffers multiple setbacks. This calls for a number of questions:

- Where key milestones are not being met does this suggest that the 'problem' has not been properly defined in the first place? The constraints are more severe than expected or new and unforeseen constraints surface? The communication strategy did not work? There is a problem of leadership or skills, or both? The capability to digest change is less than was previously thought? The change process requires more resource than first thought, or has been delayed or starved of resource? New (antagonistic) stakeholders have emerged or support from once favourable stakeholders has ebbed away?
- Does the above suggest that the overall change strategy needs to be revisited?
- How can action plans now be tailored to accelerate progress or remove bottlenecks?
- What new contingencies and risks have emerged and how might action plans be strengthened to deal with these?

Control and learning

Besides difficulties in implementation, we may also need to address the extent to which the project has been effectively controlled and also what learning has come out of it:

- Are the milestones of the change project being met in terms of tangible benefits? Less tangible benefits? Tangible costs? Less tangible costs? Timings?
- How effectively has the change process been implemented relative to past experience within the business area? Past experience of business areas elsewhere in the organization? Other organizations undertaking similar change?
- Have change project management processes been applied consistently throughout the change project, including monitoring of enablers for and constraints to change and regular stakeholder analysis and project management systems for planning, control and feedback?
- Did the change project actually meet its key objectives, and if not, why not?
- What should we now do, therefore, to secure the intended benefits of the change?
- How might we influence key stakeholders to commit to any further necessary or appropriate change?

- What lessons can now be drawn about how we diagnose, plan, implement and control change generally and our overall capacity for and capability to implement change?
- How can we disseminate these learning lessons in an open way, and without embarrassment?

Analysis of content issues

Besides the above process issues we may need to do a health check on some of content issues of the project:

- Does the change project involve several departments across the organization, and if so, how does this impact how change is managed?
- To what extent does it involve external parties and stakeholders, including customers, suppliers, regulatory authorities, etc.? Have they been brought on board with the change?
- Is the change project seen as a quick fix (less than six months), a medium-term campaign (between six and 18 months) or a long campaign (between 18 months and five years)? Is this timescale realistic?
- Is this change resource-intensive in terms of internal technical skills, external skills or management time, and will this be forthcoming?
- What is the critically perceived degree of difficulty of the change management technically and politically? Is this fully reflected in the change's project strategy?
- Does the change involve cross-border management and linguistic and cultural differences and, if so, how will these be managed?
- Is the change project amenable to benchmarking? If not, how is it proposed to keep an objective track of benefits yielded and the effectiveness of the change process?
- Has an analysis of key change issues showing key interrelationships between these issues been completed?
- Have all the relevant content issues been surfaced, for example using force-field analysis, stakeholder analysis and analysing the systems of change (strategy, structure, culture and style, people and skills, systems)?
- Have the soft and less tangible issues been given sufficient emphasis in analysing the change or does it feel as if managers want to shortcut, and thereby short circuit, the steps of change required?

Specific change applications

Before moving on from organizational change projects, certain types of projects warrant special attention. A number of common applications now come up regularly as key problems facing managers:

- strategic and financial planning,
- restructuring,
- change affecting specific roles and management style,
- quality management,
- culture change,
- information systems,
- performance management/rewards systems,
- management development,
- role transitions,
- management buy-outs.

These are now dealt with individually in some depth.

Projects involving strategic and financial planning

A strategic and financial plan is a complex activity which involves a number of outputs and a variety of stakeholders with different involvement. This is an area for project management par excellence and yet one which is only peripherally touched on by most strategy text books. It is also an area frequently not well managed within organizations generally.

- Does the strategic plan genuinely take into account the impact of external change?
- Does it involve the specific measurement of competitive advantage or disadvantage in terms of value added, and at what cost, to target customers vis-à-vis key competitors?
- Is it consistent with the mission, and is this mission credible given the risk and uncertainties in achieving strategic goals?
- Is financial appraisal used to evaluate the economic value of business strategies (i.e., in cash flow terms and not just reported earnings projections) or are these strategies left untested in terms of shareholder value?
- Is the strategy feasible given current financial constraints, and do these constraints need testing themselves?
- Does the strategic plan reflect the organizational and operational capability (strengths and weaknesses) of the business – can we excel in what we propose?
- Are there clear strategic and financial milestones for success which link to quarterly or biannual business performance assessment?
- Is the strategic plan communicated in appropriate detail to sufficient relevant levels of management and staff responsible for implementation?
- Is there adequate scope for emergent strategies to develop within the overall strategic and financial framework (i.e., in-built provision for innovation and exploitation of hard-to-foresee opportunity)?

- Are adequate change project mechanisms set in place to implement the strategy (for example, change project teams, off-site review work-shops, rewards for actions to implement change, etc.)?

Restructuring projects

Restructuring projects are now undertaken on an almost routine basis by most larger organizations. Restructuring is often managed in relative isolation from other projects and is also positioned as geared towards delivering more short-term benefits. Restructuring, if managed as a strategic project, can be handled much more effectively than this, especially if the following questions are addressed:

- Is the rationale for the restructuring fully thought through, and does this reflect not merely current needs but anticipate pending changes in the business?
- Is there a history of frequent restructuring which has resulted in a permanent and unnecessary state of instability in the organization? If so, how can this be managed more strategically in the future?
- Has the restructuring put managers into artificial positions without genuine business benefits which are patently transparent and which will aggravate organizational ambiguity?
- Are new appointees genuinely capable of being effective in their roles given their skills, their style, and also the degree of team-working within the organization?
- Has the restructuring been communicated in such a way to lay bare the business-led reasons for the restructuring?
- What is the timing of the announcement of restructuring? Has it been deliberately timed to prevent reflection and debate and thereby result in simmering resentment?
- How does the restructuring complement other projects or initiatives in the business, and how should it be managed alongside these?

Change projects affecting specific roles and management style
- Has the way in which the future organization will be affected been thoroughly thought through in terms of tangible benefits and costs, less tangible benefits and costs, and risks to the business?
- Have all the knock-on effects of the change project been thought through, for instance on the bosses and subordinates of those whose roles have changed, not only in terms of the content of responsibilities but also in terms of style?
- By what method have staff been chosen to be appointed or reap-pointed to positions, for example have they gone through a thorough and recent assessment of their competences?

Quality management projects

Whilst not perhaps quite as popular as they were in the late 1980s and early 1990s, quality management projects (or their more modern equivalents) need to be project-managed:

- How does the quality management project link in with the organization's underlying paradigm, especially in its controls, routines, rituals and overall culture?
- Is the organization, and particularly senior management, prepared for a long haul on quality?
- Is the focus of the quality management project mainly internal or is it inextricably linked with competitive strategy?
- Does this focus flow through to external benchmarking of external value delivered to customers and also to benchmarking of key internal processes?
- Have expectations of managers been set appropriately from the outset during all communications to prevent early cynicism?
- Are top management prepared to mirror quality in their own behaviour and style?
- Which specific senior managers are least likely to behave in ways which show an active enthusiasm for quality?
- Is quality management made equally applicable to major management processes (e.g., strategic planning, performance review and individual appraisals) as well as to more specific operational issues?
- Has it been generally accepted in the organization that quality management involves a major and strategic change or is it seen merely as a good initiative to be doing?
- Is there a balance between the measurement and control of performance (which quality management may imply) vs trust and empowerment at the individual and team level as part of a quality culture?
- Is the emphasis on quality in danger of becoming a new ritual without regard for which aspects of quality are of greatest strategic value?
- Is there an appropriate balance of effort between efforts to rectify quality disadvantage vs efforts to achieve a distinctive advantage through quality?

Culture change projects

Many major organizations in the 1990s went through culture change initiatives which were project-managed with varying success. The need to reorientate organizational mind-sets is unlikely to go away, and the following questions are therefore as applicable as ever:

- What is the fundamental reason for launching an attempt to manage a culture change project. Is it to get rid of bureaucracy? To reduce complexity and cost? To focus on the customer? To remedy competitive disadvantage? To amplify the power base of a new leader?
- Is this initiative linked to tangible areas of change projects such as restructuring, role redefinition, bringing in new blood, physical relocation to a new site, or to a change in ownership or status of the business? If not, how is it proposed to make the change happen without making changes of a more tangible nature?
- Has the scope of the change project been fully addressed? For instance, does it cover head office, business units, international businesses? Does it also penetrate a number of levels of management and operational staff?
- How central is the culture change project positioned in the organization with visible and ongoing backing of top management?
- How will the culture change project's effects, both positive and negative, be monitored?
- How will management track the value of the culture change project through tangible and less tangible impact on actual business performance?
- How sustainable will efforts to change the culture be – for one, three, four or more years, and at what cost?
- How will new stories within the emerging paradigm be identified and broadcast?
- Will the culture change project have tangible bite – will we be prepared to remove or sideline major antagonists?
- How will we address the problem of decoy behaviour (or behaviour which merely pays lip-service to change)?

Information systems projects

Life in today's organizations is almost unrecognisable with the expansion of office technology and communications. Information systems projects are demanding at a business, technical, cultural, and especially political level. Therefore, consider the following:

- Are all projects aimed at changing information systems part of an overall information strategy which is, in turn, linked to both business strategy and intended organizational change?
- How have the cost/benefits of any change project been evaluated in terms of both internal and external benefits and costs, including customer value, access to markets, customer lock-in, improving responsiveness, operational efficiency and capacity?
- Are changes in information systems seen as primarily of a technical issue vs also generating important and more difficult people-related

and political issues? In the latter case, does the organization have the necessary tools (such as stakeholder analysis) and processes to gain maximum ownership for change?

- Who are the key stakeholders of the end outputs of information systems and as agents within the change process itself?
- Is there a risk of overrun against required timescales which might result in an expensive and disruptive crash programme or a dilution of project benefits?

Performance management/rewards systems projects

Performance management systems (including 360-degree feedback) is the modern way towards running flatter organizations where managers have more autonomy but also more accountability:

- How are performance management systems linked to strategic plans, budgets, reward systems and employee recognition?
- How complete in scope are these systems? Where the project scope involves those only covering part of the organization, are there plans to roll this out ultimately, and are these plans well communicated?
- Have proposed changes in reward systems (for example, amending company car schemes) been fully thought through in terms of their symbolic importance in the organization?
- Is there an appropriate balance between rewards systems vs recognition efforts to provide genuine and sustainable increases in motivation?
- Are staff punished for making mistakes or is this seen positively as part of a learning process within limits which the business can tolerate?
- To what extent are staff rewarded and recognized for being proactive in moving change projects forward?
- Does the converse apply if they have been negative or lethargic in managing change projects?

Management development projects

Increasingly, management competence is seen as an important source of hard-to-imitate competitive advantage. Many projects to develop management skills are poorly focused or fail to provide for adequate follow-up and reinforcement to ensure their full value is delivered. This invites a number of questions:

- Are management development projects seen as being outside the scope of projects aimed at implementing strategic change, or merely peripheral to this? Or are they seen as being central to the change management process?
- Where management development projects are targeted as catalysts for change in the organization, have they been centrally positioned and

actively championed by top management? Do development project programmes help managers to understand the external and internal needs for change and translate this into concrete learning through work on live, strategic change issues? Is there a channel to enable learning outputs to be fed back into the live decision-making and change process? Does this provide a sufficient critical mass, in terms of complete coverage of specific business unit teams, to achieve sustainable shift in perspectives and behaviour? Do these programmes deal also with the individual's own role issues in managing change and also his style as change agent?

- Are management development projects aligned with strategic planning and budgetary timetables to provide both input and output to live decision processes? Quality management, culture change and customer care initiatives? Underlying plans to develop both individual and also organizational capability?

Project managing individual role transitions

- To what extent is any new role, which you or others have, clearly defined or is this, in many respects, ambiguous?
- In the latter case, do you see this as an opportunity to reshape your new role or are you in danger of freezing due to uncertainty?
- Does your new job involve a quantum change in scope or a major shift in style and therefore a project to make this happen? If so, it is likely that you will experience a significant drop in both performance and self-esteem during the transition.
- Are there any friendly sources of support which you can draw upon during the most difficult period of transition both within and outside the business?
- Have you quickly identified and prioritized the key issues which need resolving during the first few months of your activity and also those which demand longer-term attention, and are you programming these?
- Based on the analysis of the previous question, what are the critical success factors which will help you through the transition period?
- How will you project-manage a process to improve the cohesion of your own team and increase their loyal support? This may entail, for instance, a two-way dialogue on what they need and what you need from the situation, and how both of these needs can be met.

Management buy-out projects

Management buy-outs may rank as one of the most difficult projects which you may ever choose to contemplate undertaking. To help avoid this becoming Mission Impossible, consider the following:

- What are the main objectives of the buy-out project, and to what extent are these shared by key management stakeholders, for instance, freedom from head office diktat, the possibility of making a significant capital gain, protection of job security, challenge of developing the business into new areas, and opportunity to renew the management team?
- Has the proposed management team the ability and balance to produce a quantum improvement in business performance or does it smack of more of the same?
- What tangible changes will be made to support the symbolic event of the buy-out, for example changing the company name, relocating premises, throwing out all the old stationery, reorganising managers' old office layout, removing unnecessary status symbols? How will these be project-managed?
- Is there a robust strategy for improving the competitive position of the business or are the buy-out plans mainly aimed at producing the right set of numbers to please venture capitalists? How will this strategy be project-managed?
- Does the buy-out team have clear milestones for progress which are achievable but stretching?
- How will the issue of an exit route to sell the business on (where this is applicable) be managed by the management team throughout the lifetime of the buy-out? Are we managing the buy-out result effectively?

Acquisitions, alliance and joint venture projects

Acquisitions

Acquisitions are notoriously difficult projects to manage, before, during and after the deal. They combine a multiplicity of management processes and perspectives, including ones from:

- strategic management,
- financial management,
- operations management,
- organization and people management,
- specialist disciplines like taxation and legal.

Besides complexity of content, acquisitions are also equally complex in terms of process. They involve multidisciplinary team-working, often to tight deadlines. There is considerable uncertainty within the process, as acquisitions involve negotiation between at least two key parties – the vendor and the acquirer – and also their professional advisers, who will be multiple.

There are also likely to be other stakeholders, including the group head office, besides the acquiring business unit itself. Our earlier brief case study of the acquisition by BMW of Rover Group underlines the risks of managers getting it wrong, not only at one stage of the process but at several.

Acquisitions need to be managed through a number of key stages:

- setting strategy and objectives,
- acquisition evaluation,
- negotiating the deal,
- integration,
- post-review and learning.

Setting strategy and objectives

Many acquisitions lack a robust strategy. To avoid this, ask the following:

- What is our own strategic position (i.e., of the acquirer), and is it strong, average or weak?
- What strategic options generally for corporate development, alongside and including acquisition, do we have, including organic development, alliance, or buying in the relevant skills directly?
- Do we have the natural capabilities to screen and evaluate acquisitions (without getting carried away with the thrill of the chase) and also to negotiate a favourable deal and to integrate it effectively?
- Is this a good time for us to be thinking about acquisitions, for example in terms of the economic cycle, competitive conditions and those of financial markets generally?
- More specifically, what are our most important objectives for an acquisition project, and are these good or bad? Good reasons for making an acquisition might include increasing our own shareholder value so we can add tangible value to the acquired business; to acquire scarce capabilities (for example management or technical skills) that we can apply elsewhere; and to build our own competitive advantage. Bad reasons for an acquisition project might include to grow the business (as an end in itself); to enhance our own personal careers; because we feel threatened by increase competition; and because others are doing it, and we might get left behind.
- How will this phase be project managed?

Acquisition evaluation

Acquisition due diligence is often biased towards internal appraisal. To counter this, ask the following questions:

- How inherently attractive are the markets which our target is on? Consider its growth drivers and the level of competitive pressure.
- What is our target's underlying competitive position, and is it OK, average or weak?
- What is the basis of its competitive advantage, and is this likely to be sustainable given anticipated market and competitive change?
- How does it add distinctive value to its customers, if at all? If so, how does it capture this in the form of financial, and thus shareholder, value?
- How competitive is its cost base (against existing players, new entrants and/or distribution channels)?
- Are any of its products or markets moving into maturity or decline (life-cycle effects)?
- What is the strength of its management?
- How vulnerable is it likely to be to key staff leaving?
- Given our integration plans, how difficult and uncertain is integration likely to be?
- Where does the business currently make the most/least money, and where does it destroy shareholder value at the present time?
- Where is the business likely to make the most/least money in the future?
- What can we genuinely bring to the party in the way of value-added to the acquisition?
- How will this phase be project-managed?

Negotiating the deal

The deal is the most important phase of the project – and one which may be poorly handled by the inexperience. Consider the following:

- Do we have a strong and experienced acquisition team – especially in terms of due diligence skills and negotiation skills?
- Will the team work well with each other and avoid getting carried away with the thrill of the chase?
- What competition might exist for the deal, and is this likely to push up the price to a level at which we become indifferent as to whether to go ahead or not with the deal?
- What is the relative balance in the bargaining power between buyer and seller? What is the relative pressure to buy or sell, and who has the most options?
- How skilled is the vendor's team in negotiating, and where are their likely vulnerabilities and weaknesses?

- Are we absolutely clear as to what we are bringing to the party vs what value is already inherent in the acquisition – so to avoid, in effect, paying twice?
- Are there in-built checkpoints within the deal-making process for whether we carry on or not?
- Who will have the ultimate say over what we are prepared to offer?

Integration

Integration is an activity which will pay off in a very big way. If it is not project-managed then acquisition value will almost invariably be destroyed. Consider the following:

- What key synergies are anticipated to be harvested through the acquisition?
- What changes are required in order to achieve these synergies – to products, services, operations, systems and processes, structures and people?
- Who are the key people who are essential both to protect and develop the business?
- How can they be convinced that it is worth backing the organization following this period of pronounced uncertainty associated with the acquisition, for example through selling the benefits of the acquisition in terms of future opportunity for their own development and reward? Providing them with a clear role in integration and further development? Spelling out openly the criteria for success and failure? Protecting their self-respect through active incorporation of core best practices into a new paradigm? Having a clear and well communicated strategy for steering change?
- Is it planned to announce changes in leadership and structure quickly as opposed to playing a wait-and-see game with the result of mounting uncertainty?
- Will changes in systems and control routines be handled with delicacy, sensitivity and sensible timescales set to make changes? Where systems and control changes are required from day one are there arrangements to support this externally?
- How will the issue of any culture change be handled, especially where it is intended to integrate a large part of operations? Does this reflect any preacquisition diagnosis of the key differences in culture between both organizations?
- How will learning about the acquisition be secured in terms of both what we have got for our money (internal and eternal capability) and also on the effectiveness of integration process?
- How will the phase of integration be project managed as a whole?

Post review and learning

- Given our original strategic objectives were these fully, partially or not achieved at all? In each case, why? Use fishbone analysis.
- To what extent were we able to add value to the acquisition, and was this value deliberate (as intended originally) or emergent?
- How effective was the integration process?
- Given the three questions above, what are the lessons for future acquisitions and for our management of them?

Alliances and joint ventures

Whilst acquisitions capture the headlines in the financial press, many organizations move their corporate strategy forward in a slightly more stealthily fashion through alliances (otherwise known as joint ventures). A strategic alliance can now be defined as a longer-term strategic partnership between two or more organizations where there is investment in the venture by all of those partners, sharing both reward and risk.

Alliances may be thought of as being less risky than acquisitions. It is true that often the exposure of an alliance partner may be less (due to sharing of risk and the fact that the commitment, although longer term, is usually not quite so permanent). However, the riskiness of an alliance (sometimes known as a joint venture) can be higher due to:

- the very looseness of the arrangements;
- the need for a good deal of co-operation and openness;
- the fact that alliance partners may often have different aspirations (and possibly ones in tension or conflict), or different levels of bargaining power;
- the strategies of partners may change over time (and alongside that the personal agendas of key players in top management);
- the alliance itself will evolve and change as will its competitive environment.

Having said the above, alliances can be extremely profitable, for example witness Securicor's alliance with British Telecom to form the mobile telecommunications company Cellnet. Cellnet became so successful that Securicor's total shareholder value as a group was substantially increased, independently of performance in Securicor's traditional businesses.

Some key questions to reflect upon for any alliance, split up into the phases of formation and development, are:

Formation

- What is the fundamental purpose of the alliance? What distinctive value does it add?

- Why is it likely to be better than other possible alliances?
- What are the different options for structuring and resourcing the alliance?
- To what extent is the alliance well timed?
- How are the various needs and competencies of the alliance partners genuinely complementary?
- To what extent are these needs and competencies in tension or in potential conflict?
- To what extent is the alliance genuinely, therefore, a positive sum game or an arrangement where all parties are significantly better off through participating in the alliance?
- What is the potential for the alliance leading on into a full acquisition, long-term?
- Culturally, are the alliance partners likely to get on with each other – well, satisfactorily or, perhaps, badly?
- Have all partners got sufficient interest and commitment in the alliance to make it genuinely effective?
- Will an alliance with another partner(s) only give a temporary advantage – as it will trigger other alliances in the industry?
- What are the potential risks and downsides to sustaining our core competencies by depending upon the alliance?
- Can we learn about how our partners do things really well and apply them elsewhere in our business without our partners becoming antagonistic?
- How long, realistically, is the alliance likely to last?
- Who, if anyone, is likely to become the more dominant partner in the alliance, and if this is not likely to be us, what is the potential value of us being in the alliance?
- Do any arrangements for potential divorce adequately safeguard our interests?
- How will the formation of the alliance be project-managed?

Development
- What investment is the alliance likely to require over time, and are alliance partners both able and willing to commit to this when the time arrives?
- What senior management and other scarce skills are the alliance likely to need, and who will support this requirement?
- How will alliance partners conduct any reviews of performance and steer the strategy forward?
- In the event that the alliance takes off even more successfully than anticipated, how will it cope with this, particularly with regard to people, structures and financial resources?

- What processes for change of partners be managed, including new ones coming in, old ones leaving or changes in partner stakes?
- How will alliance development be project-managed, for example what will its key milestones be?

Operational projects

Besides the more purely strategic projects including organic development, acquisitions and alliances, there may also be some major operational projects. These can be grouped under two main headings: operations expansion, and cost management and efficiency.

Operations expansion

- Based on the checklists dealing with selling more to existing customers/ selling to new customers, etc. from the section on organic development, what is the potential for relatively easy-to-do expansion?
- To what extent can capacity be increased by physical expansion? Without physical expansion (and by the cunning plan)? By appropriate outsourcing?
- What productivity targets, by each and every incremental resource, need to be established?
- How will expansion be project-managed?

Cost management and efficiency

- How cost-competitive are we against our existing competitors (now)?
- How cost-competitive are we against any new entrants (now)?
- How cost competitive are we likely to be on current plans vis-à-vis existing competitors and potential entrants?
- What are the key cost drivers within our current operational set-up and how can these be incrementally improved and radically challenged, for example with zero-based approaches (i.e., working up from a situation of nil resources)?
- What are the key value drivers of the business and how can incremental value be added and harvested from a lower, equivalent, or, preferably, a changed cost base?
- How can key business processes be reengineered and simplified to make operations more efficient?
- Which other companies should we benchmark and learn from, either from inside or outside the industry, to become more efficient?

- By customer benchmarking are there areas of activity that add little real customer value that we can reduce?
- How might cost management and efficiency initiatives be project-managed?

Conclusion

We have now provided you with extensive checklists which cover the important forms of contemporary strategic projects. These checklists will be invaluable for the increasing number of MBA projects which have a high strategic content. We have also related the checklists very closely to the SPM process.

Postscript

For a decision tree of where to start in the strategic project management process please refer to Figures 8.1, 8.2 and 8.3. For a review of how the key tools interrelate with one another, see Figure 8.4. This highlights the key linkage between the techniques covered in this book. These figures were compiled originally for Amgen, a biotech business.

Finally, when managing a strategic project the issue often arises as to how easy it might be for others to imitate one's innovative strategic ideas. To address this need we have created the importance-imitation grid (Figure 8.5) which helps trade off importance (in competing) and ease vs difficulty of competitor-imitation. A force-field analysis can be used to analyse the relative difficulty of imitation.

FIGURE 8.1: Decision tree 1

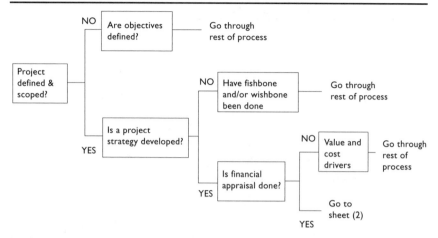

FIGURE 8.2: Decision tree 2

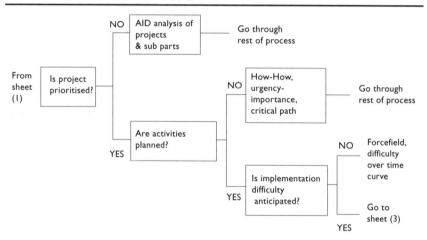

FIGURE 8.3: Decision tree 3

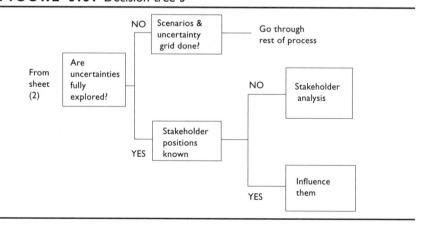

FIGURE 8.4: Independencies – implementation and project
management tools

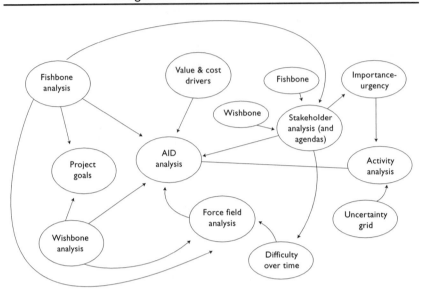

FIGURE 8.5: Importance-imitation grid

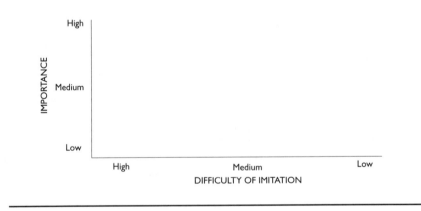

CHAPTER NINE

Everyday strategic project management

Introduction

Managing 'big picture' strategic projects captivates management attention with great ease, but it is easy to forget the more mundane or personal issues which can be managed equally well as strategic projects.

For there are many everyday-life issues which are inherently complex, uncertain and which contain an intricate network of activities. For instance, over the past 15 years or so, the following issues have been managed explicitly as projects:

- holidays (especially family),
- house moves,
- finding a new partner,
- even a divorce.

In fact the very last area, divorce, ranks as a strategic project par excellence! It combines the strategic, the financial, the political, the operational and the interpersonal in a profound way.

EXERCISE: IDENTIFYING YOUR PERSONAL STRATEGIC PROJECTS

Review your current life phase.
1   Which personal strategic projects have you got underway or are about to begin?
2   Where are these projects on the AID grid?
3   Have you thought of managing them through a project management process, either formally or informally?

Personal strategic projects are often complex, challenging and, at the same time, emotionally difficult. An excellent example of a strategic project in everyday life requiring a project management focus was a manager whom one of the authors met recently. He worked for a US investment bank, Morgan Stanley, in London's Docklands. His problem was that he wanted to buy a flat 'somewhere in London', but there were a number of reasons why this was proving difficult.

First of all, he really wanted a two-bedroom flat but probably could not afford one except, perhaps, in a very grotty area. Secondly, he did not really know that much about the ins and outs of the buying process. Also, there was the little problem of London's housing market which, in 1999, was going through another cyclical boom. And was buying a flat so urgent anyway? The thought of spending time looking around London, setting your heart on something special only to find it snatched away from you by a gazumper seemed pointless. And, he did not know London anyway.

The very starting point for this young manager was to see this activity as a strategic project. What was its scope, and did it really need to loom that large? What was he trying to achieve in his life, in his career, and in his time outside work? How long would he perhaps be working for that company in the UK? Morgan Stanley might no doubt conspire to move him to Hong Kong, New York, or wherever, as soon as the removal men arrived to move him in.

One of the authors suggested to him (from her own experiences of moving to London 23 years previously) that a strategy of looking north or south in London might help a little at least to narrow down the scope of his search.

Figure 9.1 shows how the problem which the manager faced was first diagnosed. The main symptom of the problem was, 'Buying a flat is very difficult', but the root causes of the problem not only covered the state of the housing market and the problem of the buying process, but also issues associated with the manager's own personal intent. His fishbone analysis in Figure 9.1 then paved the way for his wishbone

FIGURE 9.1: Fishbone analysis of buying a flat

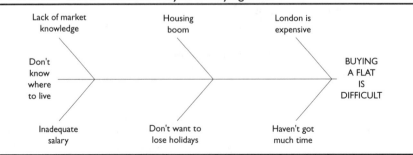

analysis in Figure 9.2. Here, not only is the manager's intent clarified, but also the whole matter is given more priority. In addition, he also seeks advice from other peers about the best/most cost-effective and convenient areas to live in, and pitfalls of the flat-buying process and how to get around them. Notably, and this is quite outside the original fishbone analysis, he decides that he needed a project plan. Once again this highlights the need to have an imaginative input to the project's wishbone.

Note also that Figure 9.2 contains other things which also have to be aligned to achieve the manager's vision. This includes getting a good pay rise at the end of 1999, and the housing market not rising more than 7 per cent in the remainder of the year. Whilst the first factor might be partially under the manager's control, the second factor is not at all. In fact, the housing market did rise by around that amount.

Lastly, Figure 9.3 shows the final network of activities which he would now have to schedule in, including the first phase, mobilization:

- reviewing his career strategy,
- setting a budget,
- determining a property strategy (price range, etc.),
- defining specific acquisition criteria,
- understanding buying process – pitfalls,
- project planning,
- book holiday for property search.

Phase 2 of the project now would be property search and sourcing a mortgage. Phase 2 would overlap Phase 3: negotiation of the deal. Phase 4 would then be moving in, possibly followed by Phase 5: property improvement. And if there is any time left over, the manager might also consider a moving-in party (as Phase 4b).

Now this analysis highlights just how complex an apparently innocuous activity like buying a flat as a first-time buyer is. Notice we have not even added to this the normal second project that needs to be managed in parallel – selling another property.

FIGURE 9.2: Wishbone analysis of buying a flat

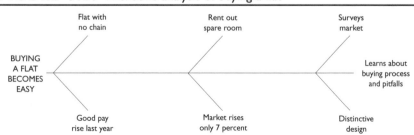

But what if extraneous events conspired to mess up the manager's now well crafted plan? For example, we could throw in a number of wobblies, such as:

- the London property market overheats, pushing prices of anything other than a grotty flat beyond his reach (this is precisely what happened subsequently);
- his company suffers a major financial setback – and wage rises are frozen at 2 per cent at the end of the year;
- another project takes precedence: he falls in love and spends the holiday time planned for flat search on a week in Paris;
- the first flat of his dreams gets gazumped;
- the second flat of his dreams turns out to have major structural flaws;
- in the third flat of his dreams the property chain falls through;
- and so on, maybe ad infinitum.

This list leads one to think that if he thought it would take three months to consummate the project, more likely it would be six, possibly nine and maybe even 12 with a run of really, really bad luck.

The above project thus highlights beautifully how crucial it is to see many everyday-life issues as strategic projects. Just as an organization as a whole can be usefully viewed as a cluster of projects, so too can everyday-life projects. Technically speaking, even having a child is very much like a project – even if this amounts to a number of project phases of variable enjoyment.

One of the major advantages of considering everyday issues to be projects is that it helps one to be much clearer about purpose. Going back to our unusual example of having a child, for instance, many parents get into this project by thinking of it as being a 'really nice thing to do' or because 'I have got to do it at some stage, so why not now?' or 'Because I can have one biologically'. None of these reasons feel as if they

FIGURE 9.3: Phase I: mobilization

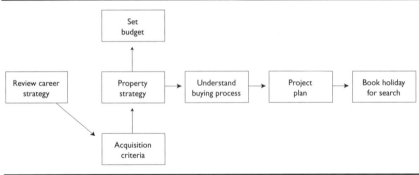

actually represent true clarity of purpose. But, potentially, one might have a child:

- to experience the fun of being a more complex family unit over and above being a couple;
- to provide a natural vehicle to the expression of one's love and care for one's partner;
- to experience the joy of seeing one's offspring develop through one's own input;
- to take pleasure in their natural achievements in life but without pushing them to achieve one's own goals and aspirations.

Although the above goals may seem self-evidently appropriate, once one actually has a family, especially during the teenager phase, one might be forgiven at times for having lost sight of one's goals, albeit temporarily.

To some the suggestion that life is a project set may come as an anathema. For example, one of the authors once made the very big mistake of saying to a lady next to him at a business school dinner that he was managing by divorce as a strategic project. She was quite appalled by this and suggested that this was a rather heartless way to look at it. But besides its legal and financial complexity, a divorce is very much an emotional project, requiring adequate time and reflection and support activities to move from the old to the new.

Having given you a flavour of how strategic project management can be relevant to everyday and personal issues, let us now examine how some of our earlier tools can help more specifically.

Tools and techniques for everyday SPM

We have already taken a look at a few of the more obvious techniques of everyday SPM. These consisted of:

- fishbone analysis for project diagnosis;
- wishbone analysis for creating a project strategy and vision;
- activity analysis for identifying the network of key project activities.

In addition, other tools of SPM are equally relevant, especially:

- AID analysis for prioritization;
- FT analysis for fleshing out the project's strategy;
- uncertainty grid for identifying those assumptions which are both very important and very uncertain;
- value and cost drivers for understanding the attractiveness of the project in greater depth;

- force-field analysis for examining its underlying difficulty;
- stakeholder and agenda analysis for reconciling the interests of key players in the project.

EXERCISE: PROJECT DIAGNOSIS

Choose one personal strategic project you are currently managing.

1   What do two of the above tools suggest to you are the really key issues?
2   What strategic project options now arise from this analysis?

To add some real colour to these tools, let us now take a close look at three interrelated projects which have affected one of the author's lives. These involved the search for a new partner (acquisition), moving in (the integration process), buying a house together (the development).

CASE STUDY: PHASE 1 – PROJECT: MARKET RESEARCH AND ACQUISITION

Whilst to some the notion that one can, and should, apply management techniques to issues in your life may seem odd, what better place to demonstrate their effectiveness? From the reader's point of view this will further reinforce the learning from the book, especially as you will be invited to apply the tools to a project of your choice in your life later on.

In 1997 my marriage came to a final, sad end, and I resolved to create a new and more exciting life for myself. After leaving a breathing space of a couple of months, during which I bought myself a very nice country property just north of Cambridge, I resolved to search for a new partner. I reasoned – I think wisely – that to begin my search based in a semi-squalid, top-floor, two-bedroom flat in the north of the town might be a turn-off to whoever I met.

So, with the infrastructure for the project now established I went back to my original definition of strategy in chapter 1: What do I really, really want?

Coincidentally, at the time I was just about to run my acquisition course at Cranfield for the MBA students. As is well known, acquisitions are often made by companies with relatively loose criteria. So how could I convey, in a novel and fresh way this year, the importance of setting clear acquisition criteria?

To set acquisition criteria for my search for a new partner appeared to kill two birds with a single stone. First, I would become a lot clearer about what I really, really want, both with and from a new partner in life. Second, I could illustrate the need to set acquisition criteria for my MBA students. So I sat down one day and wrote down my acquisition criteria.

I listed 15 criteria which I really, really wanted, including:

- age: 30–40,
- attractive,
- lively and energetic,
- no existing ties,
- professional,
- intelligent, etc.

My next challenge was to check out my personal competitive advantage for being able to attract such a target myself. Whilst having dismally failed to build up a middle-aged spread, I would not have said that my physique as it was then was strong. Having overdosed academically, well into my career – my cranial development had been at the expense of my physical development.

So an urgent and important project was to develop my physical build and strength. After sneaking into the gym hesitatingly for a few times I decided to really go for it, and over the next few months gained a more respectable physique.

More important was the need to define the scope and focus of the project. My key strategic questions were, now I had identified who I would like to have as a partner – at least generically:

- Where am I likely to find them?
- How can I meet them?

Initially, I decided to search in the Cambridge/East Anglia area. After a number of rather disappointing encounters I rapidly came to the conclusion that it was highly unlikely that someone I really, really wanted to be with was going to turn up at least on the right side of the millennium. Local possibilities looked at best of medium attractiveness and very difficult on the AID grid.

So, I switched my line of enquiry to London. Market scanning revealed not only:

- a very large population indeed,
- with a large number of eligible professional possibilities, but also
- a most favourable oversupply of the opposite sex relative to my own.

It would appear that London was reasonably awash with professional, career-minded ladies precisely of age group 30–40 who had put all into their careers but had never got round to getting married or having children. Alongside this was an equally large segment of similar individuals who were on the secondary market, following divorce.

Deciding to abandon all sense of shyness, I elected to try out the various distribution channels, including the singles party circuit and matching (dating) agencies.

In terms of cost, the singles party circuit was by far the most attractive. I found this experience, after the initial discomfort, quite entertaining. Even if I did not meet anyone particularly riveting, it was socially a lot of fun. On two consecutive evenings alone I identified no less than three possible acquisition targets, but in each case, although they were medium to high attractive, they were also very difficult. One, with whom I got on very well, unfortunately seemed to be still besotted with an ex-partner who had dumped her. He seemed to be involved in dubious spying activities – so my mind started racing, creating scenarios of him suddenly reappearing on the scene to cause untold disruption.

As with all business projects, a golden rule of this kind of project, as I have now learned, is that things are never as they seem initially on the surface.

The one occasion when I did compromise on my acquisition criteria (which, to be fair, were at that time still relatively loose), I did meet someone very nice. I went out with her for two months until she mysteriously lost interest. She was apparently doing what in project management terms is called 'managing parallel activities' – that is, whilst she was going out with me she was simultaneously exploring potentially better and more attractive offers.

Fortunately, it was when that particular relationship expired that I determined to refocus my project strategy. So it was at that point that the initial 15 criteria were defined.

I also elected during that midproject phase review, that I would invest in a matching agency, however expensive this was.

In terms of value and cost drivers I reasoned that I could get a potentially better, more effective, route to acquisition through a matching agency (see Table 9.1).

The advantages/disadvantages of both routes were thus marginal, to say the least. Cost was a significant factor. I eventually ended up paying £800 to join a dating agency and had to trek all the way to Wembley to be interviewed.

Ironically the very day I signed up at the expensive dating agency a friend had invited me to a party near Covent Garden, Central London. After doing some evening teaching in the City I travelled across to Covent Garden.

TABLE 9.1: Comparisons of distribution channels

	Value drivers	Cost drivers
Singles parties	You meet the acquisition candidate	Some evenings there were absolutely no eligible targets
	You get to meet a lot simultaneously	You could not easily explore aspects of personal background first
	The evenings could be fun	But evenings could be frustrating
Matching agency	You gained access to even larger numbers	You could not judge personalities
	You could get more complete background data first	Meetings were one-off and could be wasteful
	Photographs were provided	It was very costly

It was 9.15pm when my new partner walked downstairs into the basement. I caught sight of her reddish/brown hair through the crowd and – as one does – went straight over to her. At that time Madonna's song with lyrics of 'Do I know you from somewhere?' was ringing in my ears.

Although I was technically £800 worse off after that evening, I felt that this had been a pretty good project strategy – at least until that point.

Interestingly, out of my 15 acquisition criteria, 13 were met. Of the other two not immediately met, one was resolved during the next stage of the project, integration. During the third phase of the project, buying a house together, we were to try to minimize the final one – that she lived a mere 78 miles away from me (my criteria had been within 60 miles), but I decided to relax my criteria about six-and-a-half minutes into our first conversation.

Having said that, most of the difficulties which we did experience during our first two years together were down to these two criteria not being fully met.

Some key lessons on managing personal strategic projects from this phase are:

- With any personal strategic project you need to think very carefully about its scope and focus.
- Precisely why you are really doing it, and what you hope to get out of it? Do not be fuzzy about this.
- Do not compromise – decide what you really, really want, and do not accept the average.

- Think deeply about options for getting to your goals and their relative attractiveness and implementation difficulty
- Set your decision criteria carefully, and if you do compromise then be fully aware of the possible consequences of this.
- At each and every stage, tell scenario stories to yourself about where any particular path will lead.
- Weigh up carefully the value and cost drivers of different routes forward.
- Be prepared to look for unexpected strategies for overcoming obstacles (remembering when I abandoned the dating agency as a sunk cost because I had found potential success through simply going to a friend's party).

Phase 2 – Project: the integration process

Some time after I met my new partner she asked me if I would like to live with her. This seemed a most attractive project, the only apparent snag being that she lived 78 miles from my own home north of Cambridge, bought only seven months previously, .

Most business projects tend to focus on the tangible rather than on the less tangible. In the same way, a major mistake was made in focusing on the logistics of my moving in and her lodger moving out rather than on the integration project plan.

Whilst being a very attractive project, it did have its costs. I needed to travel once or twice a week to Cambridge to see my family, and I also had to offset the extra cost of compensating my partner in part for the loss of rent from a previous tenant. We effectively split the difference. And whilst I gained the value of living with my partner (and being closer to London and the majority

FIGURE 9.4: Value drivers of living with partner

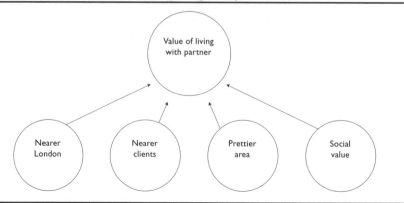

FIGURE 9.5: Cost drivers of living with partner

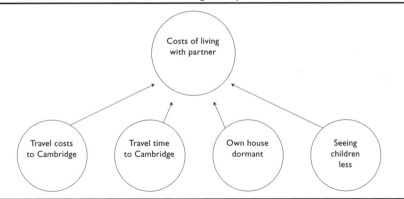

of my clients), there was some value lost in respect of my own house and of seeing my children a little less. The value and cost drivers are shown in Figure 9.4 and Figure 9.5.

During the first few months, as most partners do without any real difficulties, we really enjoyed living together. At this stage the project was absolutely top left of the AID grid. We probably spent slightly too much time with each other. Things became generally more difficult, especially as we had not sorted out creating a few boundary issues. This project shifted slightly eastward from the north-west segment of the AID grid.

After six to nine months we put a lot of effort into establishing better boundaries, joint routines and more structure to our shared and overlapping activities. This was another case of having to discover a project strategy after the project plan, and even after its implementation.

Table 9.2 shows the FT analysis to reflect the key shifts in our *modus vivendi* in living with each other. This proved to be a very effective strategy in stabilizing our relationship together.

TABLE 9.2: FT analysis of integration strategy

From	To
Spending as much time as possible with each other	Tolerating and even encouraging a couple of days apart occasionally
Unstructured evenings and weekends	More structuring, planning and co-ordination of activities
Not always respecting mutual boundaries	More realistic boundaries around these demands
Narrowly based leisure and social activities	Broader and more varied joint activities
Implicit communication and feedback	Explicit review of how things are going

Besides the FT analysis, there were a number of assumptions which were made at the start of this integration project:

- we would not get satiated with being with each other, because we got on so very well;
- there would not be any significant boundary issues;
- I would not find the to-ing and fro-ing between Cambridge and my partner's home, west of London, too difficult and tiring;
- my children would accept the fact that I would not always be around in Cambridge (as I did not see them everyday anyway) without giving me a really hard time.

These assumptions shifted significantly over time. The first assumption (see Figure 9.6) moved from north-east to east (we wouldn't get satiated with each other, however much time we spent together). The second assumption moved from the centre of the grid to due south. The third one (the logistics would be okay) shifted very, very slightly from the north-west. The fourth (my children would be happy to accept this change) shifted from the very centre of the grid to the south-east, with both of them in their different ways being less than happy.

Figure 9.7 gives an overview of the force-field analysis for this critical phase of Integration. Key enablers were: our desire to be with each other; the fact that we normally get on really well; my flexibility in respecting my partner's ways of doing things; I had my own dedicated office space; we planned and spent several weekends and short holidays away.

FIGURE 9.6: Uncertainty grid – living with partner

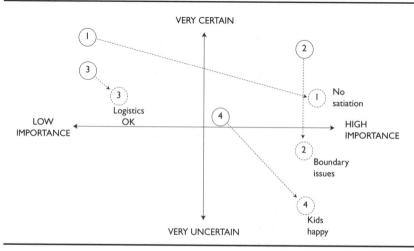

FIGURE 9.7: Integration phase force-field analysis of moving in

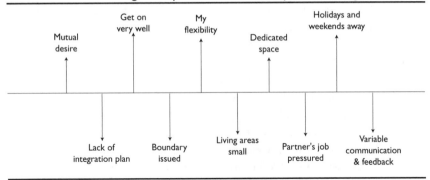

The key constraining forces were: our lack of an integration plan; lack of boundaries to limit our demands of each other; my partner's main living areas were quite small; and sometimes variable communication and feedback.

Clearly the shape of the force-field analysis in Figure 9.7 implies that integration had become more difficult, even though for the most part we were very much enjoying living together.

By analysing the project as explicitly as this I was able to discover that the core of our difficulties was not really that we had not bought a joint property. Whilst buying a house together from scratch would have mitigated these difficulties, it did look as though we needed to sort out a more structured process of living together first. This required the shifts already seen in the FT analysis described in Table 9.2 earlier.

Next, Figure 9.8 represents the stakeholder analysis for our integration project. Both my partner and myself were obviously highly influential and very much in favour of the project. Difficulties

FIGURE 9.8: Integration phase stakeholder analysis of moving in

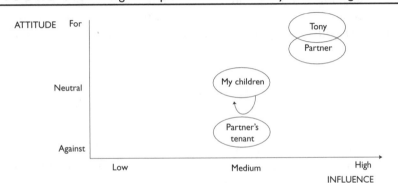

over months four to six did put something of a check on our enthusiasm, but this was temporary, however. My partner's existing tenant was very much against the project but basically was taken out of play when he became an ex-tenant. My children began by being in neutral to being moderately against, this position hardening to covert opposition because they felt that I was benefiting but at their expense. This had wider ramifications with my other big project – my divorce (which I often thought of as a personal demerger project), as one can imagine.

This analysis thus provided a helpful, if retrospective, overview of the key issues involved in managing this everyday strategic project. Ideally, if we had used these frameworks (whether implicitly or explicitly) we might have provided a smoother transition in living with each other than that which we actually experienced.

So, once again, some of the key lessons from the second phase of the project, integration, for managing personal strategic projects generally are:

- once you are into the implementation phase, keep a careful track of progress towards your goals, especially using FT analysis;
- wherever possible, make your implicit assumptions explicit and use the uncertainty-importance grid to monitor these and any new ones that come up over time;
- manage the most critical enablers and constraints of any project directly, especially emotional ones;
- keep a continual track of where the project and its subparts are on the AID grid – how many relationships start in the north-west of the grid and either nose dive or gently slide or drift towards the south-east of the AID grid?

Phase 3 – Project: future development

Moving house is never an easy personal strategic project. This particular house move seemed to head further and further east on the AID grid as the project progressed. The tangible parameters of the project were:

- to sell my four-bedroomed house near Cambridge;
- to sell my partner's four-bedroomed house west of London;
- to buy a house together, preferably 'somewhere in the middle' geographically.

We were then living together in my new partner's house as it was nearer to London, so it was ideal to sell my house first and hers last, other things being equal.

Project criteria and constraints

This house move was however subject to two overriding criteria which were relatively constraining:

- the house itself, including its location, position, external appearance and internal features all had to be no worse than what either of us had. In totality the package had to be collectively better;
- it had to be within 15 minutes drive of a very good gym.

As both of us were in favourable positions financially one would not have thought that the above challenge would have presented any apparently insuperable difficulties, but it did.

Key project options

- To await offers on both our houses and then to buy
- To get an offer on my house and be prepared to move out, and then search for another property
- To get an offer on my partner's house, and she would move in with me, then search for another property.

The first option, to buy one house and to sell two as a single chain, did not look very hopeful. The second was certainly viable as this simplified the project into two separate ones – one without a chain and one with one. Assuming my partner got near to her asking price, the third option was just about feasible, although less attractive and more difficult (AID analysis).

The initial mobilization

I put my house on the market in autumn 1999 with an allegedly crack firm of estate agents who were actually clients of mine.

I received not a single visit to my property in six weeks. Alright, it was a quiet time of the year, but it did not help not having a 'For Sale' sign up outside my house, due, apparently, to incompetence on the part of one of their subcontractors.

A second problem also arose around this juncture. Whilst I had put my own house on the market proactively my partner seemed unable to be able to actually give the go-ahead to her estate agent to publicize her house.

Although I began to become slightly frustrated with the apparent inaction, my political antennae and some use of the out-of-body technique with stakeholder agendas revealed she was not quite ready to go ahead with her sale yet. After some sensitive questioning she revealed:

- she also really, really liked her house and found it difficult to begin to let go of her deep attachment to it;

- she did not relish having people around looking at her house;
- but, even more crucially, her job was now looking less secure by the minute, and she was thinking of potential job moves entailing relocation which might dictate where we would live.

A strategy of delay

Coming back now to our present options, whilst accelerating a project is always an option, so too is project delay. In fact, I then decided to delay sale of my own property. Hopefully, once my partner became clearer about her career future we could revisit the issue.

By taking my house off the market (in December 1999), I was also able to avoid the impression that it was getting stale and would be discounted in price. Also, there were still some newly built properties 200 yards away which, although subjectively less nice than my own, were a good £10,000 cheaper. Hopefully, once they were sold I would then have a clearer run in the new year, making it both more attractive and easier to sell my house.

In April 2000 two things happened. First, my partner left her job to start her own business. This meant that we could more or less live anywhere in the south-east. Second, the other competing houses in the same area as my house had been sold. So, not only did I put my house on the market, but also, within a further three weeks, my partner did so too.

Since autumn 1999 the UK property had surged forward. When my new, and far more sensible, estate agent gave me a new valuation I was knocked backwards by what he thought it was worth. My partner's house had also surged forward in value too, as of course had the houses which we were trying to buy. I therefore put my house on the market at a price £20,000 higher than just five months previously. Initially people poured in at two to three visits a week, but no one put in an offer.

The stakeholder dimension

So far we have primarily looked at this project from a more tangible point of view, save for my partner's agenda. As we seemed to be getting to the point where a sale seemed imminent, I turned my attention to the less tangible and softer aspects of managing the project.

Whilst attending to the agendas of the other members of my family (especially my children) had not been quite so urgent to deal with up to this point – although I was always aware of how important these were – they were now getting pressing. I had not wanted to discuss my sale in detail with them until we got closer to a deal. To have done so would have both undermined the current enjoyment of my house and would have proved disruptive in the event that a sale failed to materialize. But as the uncertainty over the sale seemed to dissolve I decided to talk to them about my future arrangements for seeing my children, during alternate weekends, as my plan was to no longer have a home near theirs.

I now had five key stakeholders to consider. I have noted their likely attitude to my selling my house and no longer therefore having a local home to entertain my children in once a month:

- my 16-year-old daughter (neutral or against),
- my 14-year-old son (against),
- my ex-wife (probably against),
- my partner (who was for),
- myself (who was for).

Previously, I had intended to replace my house with a rented flat that I could get out of in two to three years time. This would have released the capital I needed to get a nicer house with my partner. This was not a very cost effective solution (and very much second best to having the run of a four-bedroomed house for two weekends a month), and my partner was quite naturally not in favour of it. Objectively speaking, this seemed an expensive and inefficient solution to the problem.

Project strategy and objectives

What had I been trying to accomplish by having a home in Cambridge rather than one nearer to my major clients? As every good strategic project manager does, I asked myself five key questions:

- What were my objectives, anyway, in retaining a presence in Cambridge?
- How well would these be likely to be fulfilled by retaining a smallish, rented flat?
- What were the other options for meeting my wider objectives?
- What were on the agendas of all the stakeholders in the project, separately and for each one of the project options?
- What was the best process for involving them in the debate?

These questions, which with hindsight seem highly logical and structured, took quite a lot of reflection and emotional self-searching to arrive at.

In regard to the first question, going back to my objectives, I reflected on the goals of my original house-buying project:

- to be physically close to my children,
- to have a really nice place for myself,
- to help attract the right kind of partner,
- to invest my capital in,
- to have good times with my children (following the separation),
- to be able to give my ex-wife a break twice a month.

The project of buying my house originally had satisfied the first four objectives but not actually the fifth one (having good times with my children). Quite naturally, they resented the disruption of the separation, and I typically found having them for the weekend in a home I then visited twice a month highly stressful. Also, as I was hardly there at all, the second objective was irrelevant. As I had already found my new partner, then the third was irrelevant too. I could now fulfil the fourth by investing my capital elsewhere. The only difficulty in selling up was to be able to give my ex-wife a break from my children twice a month (the sixth objective).

So then I focused on the two key questions:

- How could I have good times with my children without a Cambridge property?
- How could I still give my ex-wife a break from both children twice a month?

From this line of thought came the strategy of:

- moving house to be within an hour's drive of Cambridge, so I could easily visit in the day, or even in the evening without staying overnight;
- being able to cover for my ex-wife overnight up to twice a month either by staying in a good hotel locally with my son twice a month, or by staying locally in a bed-and-breakfast;
- by seeing my daughter either by taking her out for a meal twice a month or by having her to stay with us once a month, or a mixture of the two;
- trying to do more things with my children that they wanted to do and I could enjoy too, rather than just going through the mind-set of having them around (which meant them scrapping over my satellite TV stations). This takes me back to the fifth objective – having good times with my children.

The latter two points were arrived at by working backwards from my children's agendas and having had full out-of-body experiences. Incidentally, my son would not have been able to stay with me and my partner because he was addicted to an early morning weekend paper round. Also, his obsession with satellite TV, especially Worldwide Wrestling and Formula One might have driven my partner mad after a couple of weekends.

Testing out the stakeholders
I have gone into this in detail just to emphasize not only how complex some personal strategic projects are but also how they become riddled with constraints. And it is precisely these constraints that are in most need of challenge, especially those associated with stakeholders. This brings us to my earlier questions four and five.

In June 2000 I decided to bite the bullet and put my proposal (that I and my son stay in a local hotel) to him, who being younger than my daughter had a lot longer to go in terms of his weekends with me. He was probably also the most difficult to manage of the five stakeholders.

He was initially not very pleased at my proposition of staying in a really nice hotel, but I then explained to him carefully that:

- to keep the situation as it was would cost the equivalent of £350 per night (my monthly house costs apportioned over two nights a month);
- my son and I could still have plenty of fun in the new arrangement, and perhaps could do more as I would not need to spend several hours doing housework;
- he could still watch satellite TV to his heart's content.

Although he still regarded the loss of space as a negative he did say 'OK'.

I reasoned that my daughter would be less negative as she had a serious boyfriend and it was actually down time for her to be with me. This was, however, an assumption, and as decision time drew nearer this assumption headed south-east on the uncertainty-importance grid. Many people complain about something because it has taken away something they were attached to, whilst deep down they actually enjoy what has replaced it. Also, the loss of something previously taken for granted highlights its true value – and this case was no exception.

My ex-wife's concern, based purely on my out-of-body experience, was that she wanted to be able to escape for the weekend and perhaps to have a child-free house whilst she was there. I felt I could probably put a good case to her for it being unreasonable to maintain two homes indefinitely and that she would see that logic. These assumptions remain untested. (In June 2000, when her new partner left her, this actually eased these negative agendas.)

For myself, doing my own stakeholder analysis made me realize that hitherto I had been in danger of putting everyone else first and myself second. I decided that my degree of influence in the stakeholder grid needed to rise from medium to high, and that I needed to go more directly for what I really, really wanted (the Spice Girl approach to strategy).

Acquisition projects and the thrill of the chase

Following this review I felt very satisfied at my progress and genuinely thought that I had the whole project nearly cracked. In June 2000 I also reached a point where the ball seemed to be squarely in the net. I found what seemed to be a beautifully renovated barn halfway between my partner's house and my home in Cambridge and also within 12-and-a-half minutes drive of a top-class gym – with pool, and cross-trainer machines. As I fell in love with the property I found myself thinking that it was a real pity that we can't just buy this outright and sell both of our properties later on – and separately – especially as someone else is coming around for a viewing in ten minutes time and no doubt will then go on to put in an offer for it.

As we have already seen in project management, time is a key source of competitive advantage. Also, strategy is about the cunning plan.

Remembering that John Towers's consortium Phoenix was able to save Rover (see the end of chapter 5), the thought ran through my head that if John Towers can raise a couple of hundred million pounds to buy Rover I should be able to borrow several hundred thousand pounds to buy this wonderful, renovated barn.

So, having telephoned my partner – who had seen the details and did like the property very much, even though she had not seen it in person – I put in an offer immediately to buy the property. Half an hour later the next viewers also put in a similar offer.

I would now like my reader to ask him/herself at this stage, 'What really big assumption have I now made that might conceivably not be fulfilled with the passage of time?'

Having checked out the very next day that indeed I could borrow that amount, I discussed with my partner possibly increasing our offer slightly, to make a preemptive strike. She seemed concerned about this and suggested that we take a quick drive over there the same evening so that she could check it out for herself. So we did.

We arrived at the house, which we could not incidentally look inside as the owners were not there, and wandered around outside in the vast grounds. She was very, very quiet for about ten minutes.

I thought, 'Here we go again,' as I began to have my out-of-body experience of where she was likely to be coming from. It did seem that there were a few things that she did not like. Teasing her concerns out of her it transpired that:

- Although the house was lovely outside, the land (two-and-a-half acres) was huge and more of a field than a real garden. She did not really want to sit out in a field like a sheep.
- Whilst in a beautiful rural setting, you could, with a slight wind, hear the busy main road a mile away, and the single-track country lane, which ran right past the main bedroom window, was still noisy when the odd Range Rover tore past on the school run or afterwards to the pub.

So, our offer was speedily withdrawn. I had to agree with my partner that it was not as quiet and idyllic as on the previous Sunday morning. The key assumption that I had made – which I had felt was very important and virtually certain – that she would really like the house a lot when she saw it had not been met.

Examining the other options and broadening the project scope

Sadly, the only other property I had come up with was a fantastic modern house with an exterior just like my partner's house (a distinct turn-on for her). Unfortunately on enquiry we discovered that Railtrack were about to dig a massive open tunnel at the very end of the back garden which would facilitate the passage of 40 fast trains an hour during rush hour. So we were all back at square one.

Sadly, whilst the property market cooled off there were very few properties that met our ever-tightening criteria. By this stage I had widened the geographic scope of our project beyond Welywn/Stevenage area to a number of areas to the north and north-west of London: Cuffley/Goffs Oak, Hadley Wood, Berkhamsted and even to where she was currently living, although that area failed to get me nearer to my children. This would also have made it as difficult as ever to do a day trip to Cambridge, and therefore weakened my argument for selling my property but not renting a flat.

Rediagnosing and redefining the project

By now the project began to feel horribly iterative, as many strategic projects are, as I went back to first principles to ask the questions:

- Why was the project so very, very difficult? I therefore did a fishbone analysis for it in my head.
- What would happen if we just delayed the project?

The fishbone analysis was very revealing. Apart from the most obvious reasons for difficulty, including the project's complexity, the disparate stakeholders, and property market constraints, two very important additional root causes, which were within one's own influence, were my own impatience and pressures on space in my partner's house.

Going back to strategic options

So, going back to project options again, I considered the implications of a new 'be patient' option which entailed taking a more relaxed and detached stance to the whole project – just waiting for its wishbone to naturally line up given the passing of time. This option appeared relatively attractive as we could then ensure that a) we found absolutely the right property; b) we bought it for sustainable reasons; c) we would not have to discount our own properties significantly; and d) I could continue to enjoy my Cambridge house for a while longer and at least until my daughter reached 17.

Also, by clearing out some redundant materials in my small office at my partner's house I was able to buy another six months of time before I would begin to asphyxiate again.

Other options were:

- to retain my house as an investment property, perhaps reserving a couple of rooms for myself and my children;
- keeping my house as an investment property (fully rented) and borrowing for a stake in our new joint house;
- simply doing nothing.

This turn of events highlights once more the need to look further afield than investment options to simple operational improvements when looking at project options. It also highlights that delay is often a very real project option.

Interestingly, having looked at other geographical locations available midway between our houses I was beginning to find myself beginning to go off them as none of them represented a true improvement relative to staying where we were. This also led me to some strategic thoughts, which had perhaps previously got lost – about where we wanted to live longer term. Here we were moving house nearer to my children for perhaps three or four years when possibly/presumably that move might commit us to an area for probably at least ten years or maybe indefinitely. This had become a case of the tail wagging the strategic dog.

Some key lessons, generally, for personal strategic projects from this case study are that:

- personal strategic projects do – even with considerable prior thought – have a tendency to become horribly messy and ambiguous;
- they therefore require continual reclarification, opening up new options – and simplification;
- whilst Gantt charts and critical path analysis might give us some clues of how to proceed in the more stable phase of the project, they are frequently spoiled by interdependencies and uncertainties;
- the analytical project analysis techniques like fishbone analysis, wishbone analysis, AID analysis, the option grid, and stakeholder analysis help a lot in restoring this clarity;
- stakeholder analysis, in particular, needs to be done continually, and is especially valuable when it incorporates yourself and your own agendas, too;
- just as you seem to have reached a solution you are likely to find yourself frustrated by some new twist of events. Always expect the unexpected;
- you may then have to look for the real solution in unlikely places – even those close to your original starting point;
- where the project has become truly intractable then it is always helpful to go back and ask why it has become so difficult, and then do a fishbone analysis;
- above all, these projects require a continual return to your vision and sheer tenacity.

Now try the following exercise.

EXERCISE: MANAGING YOUR OWN PERSONAL STRATEGIC PROJECT

Think carefully about the range of the personal strategic projects which are implicit in your life. These could be:

Career
- A new job inside the organization
- A job outside the organization
- A new career entirely
- A training course (for example an MBA)

Home
- Buying and/or selling a house
- A major home improvement
- Acquiring a major consumer durable

Leisure

- Joining a gymnasium
- A holiday
- Starting a hobby

Social and family

- Finding a new set of friends
- Finding a new partner
- Just going out with someone
- A dependant relative
- Births, marriages, funerals
- Other major social events
- A party or dinner party
- Changing one's image

Health

- Recovering from a major illness
- Getting fit
- Changing diet
- Getting rid of a back problem

Other

- Writing a book
- Creating a work of art
- Buying a computer and actually getting onto the Internet from scratch (which can be a major project)

Now, having identified your project:

- What does a fishbone analysis tell you about any problems which give rise to the project in the first place?
- What is the project's overall vision?
- What are the key strategic options (strategic option grid) and how relatively attractive are these?
- For one (attractive) strategic option, what things would have to line up to deliver it to its full potential (wishbone analysis)?
- For the same project, what are its value and cost drivers, and why is it really worthwhile doing?
- What are the key uncertainties and how do these map on the uncertainty-importance grid?
- What are the project's key enablers and constraints (force-field analysis) and how can it be made easier to implement?
- Who are the key stakeholders and where do they appear on the stakeholder analysis grid given their likely agendas?
- How can they be influenced to become more in favour of the project, if possible?

Conclusion

In this book we have sought to demonstrate that project management is a truly all-embracing, visionary discipline. Whilst it does contain some essential programming techniques, it is very much also about synthesis, vision, imagination and innovation. This is the very heartland of strategic thinking.

But it is also absolutely practical and is grounded in taking day-to-day issues – whether these be of a business, an organizational or even of a personal nature – and subjecting them to the process of SPM. Besides its use in turning business strategy into implementation (and thus a reality), and on management courses, do not forget to make it a way of life.

To demonstrate that this is not just our own personal view, let us end with a quote from *How Not To Stay Single* by Nita Tucker (1996):

> There's a difference between 'making something a project' and 'hoping it will turn out'. The difference is in your level of commitment and your responsibility for reaching your goal.
>
> When you undertake a project, you assume there will be a tangible end result and that you will reach it. When you set out to buy a house, you expect to end up with a house. When you enrol in school to become a real estate agent, you expect to get your licence. When you decide to open a branch office, you know one will open. The question about a project isn't whether something will happen at the end, but how and when it will happen.
>
> You understand that this approach is effective in other fields of endeavour, but you think finding a relationship is different. It's not. You need to adopt the same attitude toward finding a relationship that you would toward any other important undertaking.
>
> I can hear you whining: 'That's so manipulative. How can something spontaneous happen when it's all part of a plan?' I have travelled all over the world and not once did a pair of tickets to India show up in my mailbox when I least expected it. It took making it a project – planning the dates, saving the money, deciding where I would go. I'm sure there are plenty of examples in your own life where you took the time to arrange to have something important happen. You didn't consider that manipulative. Why have a double standard when it comes to relationships?
>
> ... My success came when I stopped thinking of a relationship as something that was in the hands of fate and began thinking of it as a project that was under my control.

Personal strategic projects are therefore a feature of our everyday lives, but we perhaps rarely apply the same techniques and discipline to these projects that we do (hopefully) to business projects. Whilst some of the insights one might gain in managing these projects intuitively and spontaneously, they frequently defy mere intuition and demand a more analytical approach.

Perhaps a good proportion of the insights about one of the author's personal strategic project of new partner acquisition, integration and then buying a property jointly could have been arrived at intuitively. But this would have been woefully inadequate in dealing effectively with the complexity of those situations.

We both hope that you have discovered much by applying SPM techniques to a personal strategic project in your lives in the last longer exercise. We hope that you continue to use these techniques not only in your business lives but also apply them to a variety of other personal strategic projects as they come up.

Postscript

In autumn 2000 the house move was finally consummated as a strategic project. The joint authors moved to Goffs Oak, within 200 yards of where Posh Spice of the Spice Girls allegedly once lived. David and Victoria Beckham have both been spotted in the vicinity. We have our own two-a-side football pitch at the side of the house, and integration proceeds apace. Which only goes to underline the importance, when managing strategic projects, of holding out for what it is that you 'really, really, really want…' in managing strategic projects.

Reference

Tucker, N. (1999) *How Not to Stay Single*, Vermilion.

Appendix –
strategic project management,
some key terms

Activity	A discrete area of action that leads towards project goals. An activity normally has an expected duration, an expected cost, and expected resource requirement. Activities are often subdivided into tasks.
Control	The process of comparing actual performance with planned performance, analysing variances, evaluating possible alternatives, and taking appropriate corrective action as needed.
Cost	The direct and indirect cost of achieving the project result.
Critical activity	Any activity on a critical path. Most commonly determined by using critical path analysis method.
Critical path	The sequence through the network activities of a project that determines the project completion time (i.e. the sequence that takes the longest to complete). The critical path will generally change from time to time as activities are completed ahead of or behind schedule.
Critical path analysis	A network analysis technique used to predict project duration by analysing which sequence of activities (path) has the least amount of scheduling flexibility (the least amount of float).
Deliverables	The specific benefits of a project (or phase of a project). In particular, any measurable, tangible, verifiable outcome, result or item that must be produced to complete the project or part of the project.
Float	Time planned into the project or project stage/phase that allows for possible overrun elsewhere.
Gantt Chart	A graphic bar chart display of schedule-related information. In a typical Gantt chart, activities or other project elements are listed down the left side of the chart, dates are shown across the top, and activity durations are shown as date-placed horizontal bars.

Milestones	The time by which a particular deliverable has to be achieved.
Network	The interdependent activities which all have to be completed – and in a particular sequence – for the project's result to be delivered.
Objectives plan	The overarching goals of the project (more general than specific deliverables). The detailed programme of activities that will deliver the project on time.
Programme	A group of related projects managed in a co-ordinated way.
Project	A complex set of activities that have the intention of delivering a specific result at a pre-targeted time and cost. Projects are temporary endeavours undertaken to create a unique product or service.
Project life-cycle	A collection of generally sequential project stages / phases whose name and number are determined by the control needs of the organization or organizations involved in the project.
Project network diagram	Any display of the logical relationships of project activities. Always drawn from left to right to reflect project chronology.
Project schedule	The planned dates for performing activities and the planned dates for meeting milestones.
Result	The collective deliverables of the project (both in terms of quantity and quality).
Scope	The size, duration and scale of impact of a project.
Stakeholder	Those individuals (or groups of individuals) who might either (a) give the project a 'go-ahead', (b) be influential on that decision, (c) implement / manage the project, (d) be affected, (e) be affected by it otherwise (as users of, even as 'victims').
Strategy	The 'cunning' plan that will guide the project to a successful conclusion – and with competitive advantage.
Time	The total duration, not merely to complete the project activities but also realize its deliverables.
Work breakdown structure (WBS) or how-how method	A grouping of project elements that organizes and breaks down the total scope of the project. Each descending level represents an increasingly detailed definition of a project component.

General references

Ansoff, I. (1965) *Corporate Strategy*, New York: McGraw-Hill

Braybrook, D. and Lindblom, E. (1963) *A Strategy of Decision*, New York: Free Press

Goldratt, E.M. (1990) *Theory of Constraints*, Massachusetts: North River Press

Grundy, A.N. (1993) *Implementing Strategic Change*, Kogan Page

Grundy, A.N. (1995) *Breakthrough Strategies for Growth*, FT Pitman Publishing

Grundy, A.N. (1998) *Exploring Strategic Financial Management*, Prentice Hall

Grundy, A.N. (1998) *Strategic Behaviour*, FT Pitman Publishing

Lewin, K.A. (1935) *Dynamic Theory of Personality*, McGraw Book Company

March, J.E. and Simon, H.A. (1958) *Organizations*, New York: John Wiley

Mintzberg, H. (1994) *The Rise and Fall of Strategic Planning*, Prentice Hall

Mitroff, I. and Linstone, H.A. (1993) *The Unbounded Mind*, Oxford University Press

Peters, T. and Waterman, R.H. (1982) *In Search of Excellence*, New York: Harper & Row

Piercey, N.P. (1989) 'Diagnosing and Solving Implementation Problems in Strategic Planning', *Journal of General Management*, 15(1) Autumn: 19–38

Porter, E.M. (1980) *Competitive Strategy*, The Free Press, Macmillan

Porter, E.M. (1985) *Competitive Advantage*, The Free Press, Macmillan

Quinn, J.B. (1980) *Strategies for Change: Logical Incrementalism*, Homewood, Irwin

Stalk, E. (1990) *Competing Against Time*, The Free Press, Macmillan

Sun Tzu (1991) *The Art of War*, London and Boston: Shambhala

Tucker, N. (1999) *How Not to Stay Single*, Vermilion

Index